THE VIEW FROM A
MIDWEST FERRIS WHEEL

Joanne!
Enjoy your
trip to the frash

Lolita Ditzler

The View from a Midwest Ferris Wheel

A memoir
by
LOLITA DITZLER

Adelaide Books
New York / Lisbon
2020

THE VIEW FROM A MIDWEST FERRIS WHEEL
A memoir
By Lolita Ditzler

Published by Adelaide Books, New York / Lisbon adelaidebooks.org
Editor-in-Chief
Stevan V. Nikolic

For any information, please address Adelaide Books
at info@adelaidebooks.org or write to:
Adelaide Books
244 Fifth Ave. Suite D27
New York, NY, 10001

ISBN-13: 978-1-954351-27-1
Printed in the United States of America

To my mother whose daily jottings in her diary made it possible for me to write the story.

Contents

"I see nothing in space as promising as the view
from a Ferris wheel."

—E.B. White

Chapter 1

The Love Story Began

Kenny and I were locked in each other's arms wishing our last Saturday night date didn't have to end. The following Monday, 26 July 1954, he'd begin a four-year hitch in the navy. We sat in his folks' forest green '51 Nash Ambassador in front of my family's rural home. Earlier we'd seen the movie *Seven Brides for Seven Brothers* in Rockford. During the drive home, I scooted across the sleek, dark green seat covers to snuggle close beside him. After parking, he'd pushed the bench seat back as far as it would go to give us more room behind the steering wheel.

It was a warm, moonlit evening and both front windows were rolled down. A faint odor of cigarettes lingered, a reminder the car belonged to a family of smokers. The radio was set to WGN in Chicago. Perry Como crooned "Little Things Mean a Lot."

Kenny kissed me and murmured in my ear, "I love you, Honey."

I was stunned. It was the first time he'd said that. It took me a few seconds to respond, "I love you, too, and I'll wait for you." A couple of tears slid down my cheeks.

"Good. I won't ask you to, but I'm glad you said you would."

I think, subconsciously, we were reenacting the many World War II movies we'd seen–the boy leaving home to answer Uncle Sam's call and his girlfriend promising to be faithful while he's gone.

A loud bong emitted from the radio followed by the deejay intoning, "It's the witching hour."

I said, "It's midnight. I've got to go in or Mom'll be turning on the spotlight."

My mother didn't wait up for me, but she was a light sleeper. She heard Kenny's car tires scrunch on our gravel driveway when he brought me home from a date. If I sat in the car talking, necking and listening to the radio longer than she thought I should, she'd turn on the fixture attached above the door to the screened-in porch. That spotlight, aimed toward the end of the sidewalk where Kenny always parked, glared in our faces.

My steady wrapped his right arm around my waist as we walked along the concrete sidewalk toward the house. With every other step, his right knee clad in synthetic, black dress slacks brushed against my left leg wrapped in a floral-print, cotton, gathered skirt. When we reached the wooden steps leading to the porch, he gave me a lingering goodnight kiss followed by, "See you early Monday morning."

Kenny headed back to the car and I went inside. We each faced four years of loneliness.

He was off on a new adventure to see the world. I remained on the farm and continued high school.

All the next day, the popular love songs playing on the radio seemed meant just for us, especially Nat 'King' Cole's "Too Young." I was positive time would prove that at sixteen and eighteen we were not too young to be in love.

Monday I was out of the house before Dad and Mom arose to milk the cows. I wore the same marble print, sleeveless, cotton dress that I'd bought for Kenny's farewell party the previous Friday night. The turquoise color matched my eyes.

The morning was warm and bright at four-forty-five when Kenny and his family picked me up to see him off at the Rockford railroad station. My boyfriend and his buddy, Billy, who enlisted together, would ride the train about a hundred-twenty-five miles to Great Lakes Naval Base north of Chicago.

Butterflies square-danced in my stomach as Kenny and I climbed into the Ambassador's back seat with his mother, Hazel. His father, Rolland, drove and his younger brother, Tommy, rode shotgun. We arrived at the depot a half-hour later. As we exited the sedan, Hazel murmured to her son, "Be sure and kiss Lolita last. She's the most important."

Billy and his fiancée, Marilyn, who was also my fifteen-year-old cousin, arrived with his uncle and aunt, 'Tip' and Lilas. When his widowed mother died four months ago, he moved in with her brother and his wife, who were childless. He told Kenny his relatives were welcoming, but he felt like a boarder. With no real home, I understood Billy's desire to be engaged before he left. I thought it was a mistake for Marilyn to make such a serious commitment when she faced two more years of high school.

We all gathered outside the small, flat-roofed, wooden depot. The boys dressed in jeans, polo shirts, white socks and brown loafers went inside, purchased tickets and returned. No one else appeared to be riding the early morning train.

We made small talk for a few minutes until the conductor shouted, "All aboard."

Kenny shook hands with his brother and his father, pecked his mother on the cheek and then gave me a brief, friendly kiss on the lips. I blushed.

My family didn't openly display affection. We demonstrated love for one another by the things we did. For example, at meal time most parents gave their children two choices eat it or go without. Whenever I didn't like the food Mom prepared, I was allowed to heat a red and white can of Campbell's tomato soup. I ate a lot of tomato soup.

The two young men adopted a John Wayne swagger to the train, climbed the steel steps and entered the passenger car. They were empty handed. The only memento each guy could take to boot camp was the taste of his girlfriend's kiss lingering on his lips.

With a blast of the horn, the sleek, brown and orange diesel locomotive pulled the attached cars away from the station. The guys waved out the window and we returned their gestures until they were out of sight.

Hazel and I were part of the age-old custom that decreed men went off to serve their country while women waited at home. At least, the world was at peace. President Eisenhower ended the three-year, Korean conflict with an armistice signed twelve months ago, 27 July 1953.

On the way back to my house, Hazel talked about her garden. "I have small green, tomatoes on my three plants. The short row of yellow beans has finished. I don't have nearly as big a garden as I used to, but I do still plant a few flowers, too. The boys always hated having to weed the gladiolas before they could go play with their friends."

I replied, "Mom doesn't have a garden. She's too busy working outside with Dad.

Saturday, we finished baling the first crop of alfalfa hay."

I entered our kitchen in time to join my parents for breakfast. They faced one another across the oil-cloth covered, round oak table with one edge pushed against the wall. Dad was finishing a bowl of corn flakes and Mom took a bite out of her second slice of toast. Large, white coffee cups sat in front of each of them. The aluminum percolator stayed hot sitting on a black, coil burner atop the white, electric stove.

Wainscoting covered the bottom third of the walls with paper featuring red and green farm scenes on the upper portion. I walked across the maroon linoleum and pulled out the empty wooden chair that sat between the two adults. My stomach was still in knots, but I managed to eat a piece of toast and drink a glass of water.

Billy didn't pass the physical exam and returned home the next day. When an infection cleared up, the navy accepted him a few months later. The two buddies never crossed paths during their four-year enlistments.

I was glad Ken remained at boot camp. The sooner he started, the sooner he'd be finished.

Thursday and Friday, I received letters bursting with details of my sailor's making new friends, doing calisthenics and running the obstacle course at Great Lakes. He signed each sheet, *All my love, Ken*. He left his boyhood nickname, 'Kenny', at home. If his mother said, "Kenneth," he knew he was in trouble.

Saturday evening, my folks and I attended the annual summer festival sponsored by the Town & Country organization in Davis, Illinois, the village where our post office was located. Later at home in my room, my thoughts drifted back to a similar fund raiser two years ago.

The Friday night air was sticky after a day of rain and a forecast of more showers. The main street was blocked off to make

room for the free entertainment, bingo, food stands and travelling carnival. The grocery store, confectionery, drug store,
bank, barber shop and beauty parlor closed at the end of the
day. Only the two taverns on opposite sides of the street did
business. Each bartender set a case of beer to hold the front
door open hoping to catch a breeze. The din from the boisterous crowds and juke boxes inside spilled out.

At the north end of the thoroughfare, a local trucker
pulled in a flatbed semi-trailer to serve as the stage. Benches
were created by laying wooden planks on top of piles of cement
blocks provided by the area lumber yard. Red Blanchard, a
popular comedian and musician from the Chicago radio station WLS, headlined the eight o'clock show accompanied
by the Carolina Sweethearts, two pretty, young women who
sang duets. Every Saturday night, residents of the community listened to the entertainers on the "National Barn Dance,"
a country music variety show, and looked forward to seeing
them in person. Only a few vacant seats remained when my
parents and I arrived at seven thirty.

After the program, my parents moved to a wooden bench
at the bingo tent. They enjoyed the game, but I hated it. I
couldn't win if I was the only one playing. A little, white ball
with one of my numbers on it would be lost.

Luckily, I bumped into my boyfriend, Ronnie. We were
involved in a summer romance.

On a couple of Sunday afternoons in June, the chubby,
blond fellow with an infectious laugh, drove from their
farm south of Durand to ours north of town to see me. His
neighbor, Jim, who fit the stereotype tall, dark and handsome,
rode shotgun in Ronnie's decrepit, Ford pick-up. The thirties vintage truck, his father's cast-off vehicle, had survived
two older brothers. It was a faded grass green with patches of

brown rust giving it a camouflage look. The right front fender had been crumpled and straightened leaving it wrinkled like an old person's face. Baling wire, the farmer's fix-it, held the right side of the front bumper in place. During the afternoons, the three of us sat cross-legged on the grass in the shade of the big elm tree in our front yard. We talked about the coming school year–Ronnie would be a junior while Jim and I would be sophomores. The guys left about four o'clock to help their fathers with evening chores.

Ronnie and I joined hands and strolled round and round the small midway accompanied by various sounds from the stands. We heard the amplified voice of the caller intoning the lucky numbers for 'the old corn game'. The stack of wooden milk bottles housed in a tan tent crashed to the pavement from the impact of a baseball pitched by a local athlete. A balding, paunchy, middle-aged man standing beside his tall, upright scale urged folks to "fool the guesser, your weight within two pounds or your age within two years."

I loved going on the carnival rides, but they made Ronnie sick. He'd apologized for his shortcoming. I tried to be understanding, but, frankly, I was bored.

I was surprised and thrilled when a bold Kenny Ditzler stepped up to me and asked, "Would you care to ride on the Ferris wheel?"

I ignored Ronnie, gave Kenny a big smile and said, "Yeah, I would."

Kenny was with his boyhood buddy, Wayne, who'd just met a gal from Orangeville, a small town west of Davis. The petite, dark-haired girl agreed to go on the ride with him, so he urged Kenny to ask me.

The three boys and I attended the small Durand High School located in the village a few miles east of Davis. Kenny was two years ahead of me, but with a total enrollment of about a hundred students, we all knew one another.

Wayne, the Orangeville girl, Kenny, Ronnie and I meandered to the south end of the main drag where the rides were set up. Finally, I was doing something besides walking around and chatting with friends. I felt like skipping, but that would have been childish.

As we passed the food stands, the pungent smell of chopped onions for the hamburgers and hot dogs followed by the sugary sweetness of pink cotton candy tickled our noses

At the Ferris wheel ticket booth, Wayne and Kenny each laid down two quarters. The other girl and I joined them in line waiting for the current riders to finish their spins.

The operator, a skinny, scruffy, carnie guy, looked to be in his twenties. His black hair needed trimming and his five o'clock shadow was at least two days old. He wore jeans streaked with grease, shabby, high-top tennis shoes and a clean, white T-shirt with a pack of cigarettes rolled in the left sleeve. When he began emptying the seats and refilling them, Wayne and his girl walked up the ramp first. Kenny and I followed and took the next wooden bench painted white with gold trim and padded with brown leather. As we skimmed over the top, Kenny could see that Wayne's arm was around his girl. He slipped his right arm around my shoulders saying, "I hope you don't mind. I've got to keep up with Wayne."

I leaned against him. I didn't realize it at the time, but that was our beginning on a humid, Friday night, 18 July 1952. Sixty years later, Ken and I took a commemorative Ferris wheel ride in Davis.

As Kenny and I made another circle, he asked, "Did you come with Ronnie?"

"No, with my folks. I can't go out with boys yet. I'll be fifteen in September. I hope that's what my folks are waiting for. Are you dating anyone?"

"No, I was always more interested in sports than girls. Last spring, my sister insisted I take someone to our Junior Prom so I asked my classmate, June."

I suddenly hated that cute, blonde who rode the same school bus I did.

When our Ferris wheel ride ended, I told Kenny, "Thank you." We went our separate ways.

I'd expected Ronnie to leave me in the lurch, but he stood right where I'd left him. We continued walking around together. About ten o'clock, Dad found me and said, "Time to go home."

My parents considered Ronnie a nice boy. Our families belonged to the Trinity Lutheran Church in Durand. Our small congregation shared a pastor with Bethlehem Church in Brodhead, Wisconsin, which was about fifteen miles away. Ronnie and I participated in the joint youth group, Luther League. On the second Sunday night of each month, about a dozen teenagers met in the Brodhead church basement for Bible study, games, refreshments and flirting. Mr. and Mrs. Huddleston, a Brodhead High School coach and his wife who were parents of two young sons, chaperoned the organization.

On Saturday, the final evening of the three-night festival, my folks and I returned to Davis by quarter to eight to claim seats for the program. Young men from the Monroe, Wisconsin, Turn and Schwing Club performed Swiss gymnastics in front of the spectators.

When the exhibition finished, Kenny stepped out of the crowd. Again, he asked, "Do you want to ride on the Ferris wheel?"

I gave him a big grin and eagerly replied, "Yes."

After our ride, Kenny took my hand and we spent the evening together. I never saw Ronnie. I briefly wondered if he'd stayed home to nurse a broken heart.

Kenny was a town kid with beautiful blue eyes and light brown hair in a Dagwood, a very short cut with a longer fore-lock to comb back. The high school senior was a skinny guy, a little under six feet tall and less than a hundred and fifty pounds, but he attempted to prove his strength at one of the stands. He swung a huge maul three times trying to ring the bell suspended at the top of a tower, but no gong and no big, teddy bear for his efforts. As a consolation prize, the middle-aged, attendant handed him two, skinny, yellow, paper leis. They would have complemented the brown, black and white Hawaiian shirt he wore with his jeans, but he looped them over my head, dropped them around my neck and said, "These'll look better on you." I wore jeans topped with a blue, cotton, peasant blouse.

A little later, Kenny and I waited in line for the Octopus. The ride resembled the sea creature with eight arms attached to a central axis moving up and down while whirling around. The cars attached at the end of each arm also spun in small circles.

Bernice, a middle-aged, friend of Kenny's parents, stepped up to me and said, "Be careful. Don't lose your heart."

"I won't," I replied confidently.

Later while undressing in my bedroom, I pulled off the yellow leis and tossed them into my waste basket. Then second thoughts kicked in. Kenny was a nice guy and kinda cute. He sure seemed interested in me. I retrieved the paper necklaces and draped them over a screw that held the mirror to my dresser. They ended up hanging there for seven years.

For the past five years, my folks and I lived in the northwest corner of Winnebago County, Illinois, just a mile south of the Wisconsin state line. We rented the average-sized, 240-acre dairy farm on a fifty/fifty basis from Merle, and his wife, Emma, who also farmed in the neighborhood. Dad and Mom provided the machinery and labor. The milk cows and hogs belonged jointly to the landlord and tenant with income and expenses split evenly.

Every morning, my parents' alarm clock buzzed at five o'clock. They rolled out of bed, dressed and headed for the barn. After a lifetime of milking by hand, they purchased two Surge machines for the twenty-one black and white Holsteins and three Brown Swiss. They named each cow and Mom kept a written record on each one.

When they finished, Dad carried three or four filled 10-gallon milk cans half-a-dozen steps to set them in a tank of cold water in the milk house. At five in the afternoon, my folks repeated the routine. The bovines ruled our lives because they produced more milk when a regular schedule was maintained. They also gave more milk in the summer than the winter.

My parents returned to the house for breakfast about seven and I crawled out of bed to join them. Dad poured himself a bowl of corn flakes and topped it with milk, sugar and a banana. Mom made coffee and I toasted bread for the two of us.

During the fifties, 16 percent of the nationwide population farmed. Radio stations featured farm programs and newspapers employed agriculture editors. My folks were typical Midwest farmers who raised corn, oats and hay to feed their milk cows, hogs, chickens and horses. The only difference, while most wives wore frocks covered by aprons to do their household chores, my short, plump mother donned slacks and a blouse she sewed from printed, cotton feed sacks to work outdoors alongside my father. When she left the farm, she put on a dress, make-up, heels and hose. She explained "I don't want to look like an old hag."

My father was built like Mr. Average. Every day, he wore waistband overalls and a sport shirt that had seen better days. He saved an unwashed, pair of jeans for his 'town pants'.

Both of them had brown hair, blue eyes and were pushing forty. My mother tweezed unruly gray hairs. Dad, like most men, considered his distinguished.

Dad returned to the barn to finish chores and talk to Billy, the milkman, a wiry, gray-haired man, who wore a wide, black leather back brace over his blue chambray shirt and jeans. The daily morning visitor was like a modern town crier carrying the neighborhood news from one dairy farm to the next. After a brief chat, he lifted the six or eight cans cooling in the tank and boosted them inside his closed, insulated truck. After completing his route, he hauled the load to Dean Foods in Rockford, the county seat and manufacturing city with a population of more than ninety-thousand. A monthly check for the milk was our regular pay.

A week after Davis Days, Kenny phoned to ask, "Can you go to a movie with me tomorrow night?"

Hearing his voice made me shiver like an autumn chill blew through the kitchen. I thought about him every time I saw those yellow leis hanging in my bedroom.

"I'll have to ask Mom." I laid down the black receiver on the walnut desk top and dashed down the stairs to the basement where my mother was ironing Dad's long-sleeved, white, dress shirt.

The limestone-constructed basement was exposed on the south side of the house. A walk-in door at ground level opened into the former dining room with an adjoining kitchen. After we moved in, the landlord remodeled the main floor creating our modern, eat-in kitchen and a bathroom to replace the outhouse.

The two lower-level rooms were painted beige with multi-colored, linoleum covering the hardwood floors. The former dining room contained Mom's ironing board, treadle sewing machine and a wood-burning stove that heated the area. Our barn clothes hung on hooks in the southwest corner and our outdoor boots and shoes sat on the floor beneath them. The old kitchen contained wooden cupboards painted white, a porcelain sink and plain, metal, hot and cold water faucets. My mother's wringer washer and rinse tub were pushed into corners. Several cardboard, thirty-dozen egg cases sat in the middle of the floor.

I repeated Kenny's question to my mother. "No, you can't," Mom said with finality.

I knew there was no point in arguing. I climbed the stairs slowly and relayed her response to Kenny.

"Well, maybe another time," he said. "Bye."

The following Thursday night, my folks and I attended the free movie sponsored by the Durand businessmen and shown in the Center Street Park. The block-long, grassy oval, which was circled by a one-way street, separated the rows of storefronts along the east and west sides. Once a week during the summer, the man with the projector climbed a tall ladder and tied ropes to stretch a white, bed sheet between two of the big trees, near the south end of the green space.

Dad parked along the street on the north end and I weaved my way among the adults who'd brought folding chairs and their children sprawled on blankets. I joined the group of teenagers who wore jeans to sit on the grass in front of the make-shift screen. I plopped on the ground beside my friend, Corky, who was also Kenny's cousin. My classmate was slender with long brown hair. We engaged in the usual girl talk about boys. I told her about Davis Days with Kenny.

I smiled when I saw Kenny and Wayne stroll up from the south end of town. Kenny dropped down next to me with Wayne on his other side. After greetings, I said, "I'm sorry I couldn't go to the movie last weekend. It's nothing against you. Mom went to high school with your mother and approves of you. My folks just won't let me do what everybody else does."

Kenny responded, "I'm sorry you couldn't, too, but I know how that goes. Dad won't let me hang around up town like some of the guys do. He says if there's any trouble, I can't be blamed if I'm not there."

When it grew dark enough to show the black and white, Hopalong Cassidy western, Kenny slipped his arm around me. The evening air cooled so we were comfortable snuggling together. We continued to meet and cuddle every Thursday night for the rest of the summer.

On a Tuesday afternoon, a month after Davis Days, Mom and I were in the kitchen preparing supper. I was setting the table while she stood at the counter, flouring and pounding round steak. The old fashioned, black office-type phone sitting on the modern, walnut desk in the corner pealed a long and a short, our ring on the party line. Mom's hands were messy and mine were clean so I answered.

After the preliminaries, Kenny said, "Can you go to a movie Friday night on a double-date with Wayne and Corky?"

I relayed his question to my mother. Adding our two friends to the evening didn't make any difference to her. For the second time, she said a firm, "No."

I repeated her answer to Kenny. He ended the conversation with, "Maybe another time.

Bye."

After hanging up, I lamented, "I don't see why I can't, everybody else can."

Mom countered with her favorite saying, "If everybody else jumped in the river, would you, too?"

"No," I reluctantly replied. She used that phrase a lot and it was a scary thought. In the first place, I couldn't swim. Plus, I'd heard stories about the deep holes and swift currents in the stream. I definitely would never jump in the river.

On Thursday night during the following week, Corky and I sat on the grass in the park prior to the free show. I complained to my confidant about my mother's rules.

She said, "It helps to have older sisters. My folks are used to Joyce and Lois going out so they don't think anything about me dating." After a slight pause, she added, "Kenny took Nancy when we went to the movie last Friday night."

I almost swallowed my gum. I imagined Kenny pining away waiting for my folks to let me go out with him. Nancy, a pretty girl with dark hair and brown eyes, was another of his classmates. Her quick smile and friendly manner endeared her to all of us in high school.

Soon Kenny came along and sat down on the ground beside me. I breathed a big sigh of relief. We engaged in small talk until dark. The Ma and Pa Kettle movie began and we snuggled together.

On the fourth Wednesday in August, my parents and I joined thousands of rural people from miles around attending the annual Trask Bridge Picnic. The largest farm picnic in the world, named for the nearby concrete span over the Pecatonica River, was held in Andrews Grove, a shady, cow pasture that sat along the south side of Highway 70 about half-way between Durand and Rockford. The Burritt Grange, a fraternal organization that encouraged farm families to band together for their common economic and political well-being, sponsored the event. My parents weren't joiners, but we supported the fund raisers hosted by various community groups.

The one-day gathering included entertainment, a travelling carnival, food and exhibits. Housewives competed in baking, canning and fancy work contests. Their husbands looked over the latest farm machinery displayed by area implement dealers. Kids prepared for the upcoming school year by gathering pencils given away by seed corn dealers.

Teens ignored the exhibits and program to congregate in the midway set up in an open area away from the large, leafy, shade trees. I met my three girlfriends, Janice, Joyce and Willabea, beside the merry-go-round at noon as planned. The three of us meandered among the rides and games of chance. We wore sleeveless blouses, jeans rolled up three turns and white sandals. Walking through the grass turned our feet grubby. The hot, afternoon sun beating down made us sweat.

When I spotted Kenny and Wayne, I introduced the gals who were high school students at Orfordville, Wisconsin, another village about twenty miles northeast of Durand. Wayne, a short fellow with dark hair and brown eyes, was immediately smitten with Willabea. She was a pretty blonde, blue-eyed girl of Norwegian heritage who was nearly as tall as he was. Sisters Janice and Joyce saw what was happening and moved on.

The four of us formed couples holding hands, strolled around the area and rode the Ferris wheel. The boys bought Cokes and we sat down on the grass under a shade tree to drink our pop and chat about ourselves and our schools. When we heard men shouting, "Sooie," in the hog calling contest followed by women screeching their husbands' names in their competition, we knew the day was ending. The boys left. Willabea and I headed for the merry-go-round and met our parents. Chores were a little late.

My friendship with the Orfordville girls began three years earlier. I met Janice while taking accordion lessons at Voigt Music Center in Beloit, Wisconsin, a manufacturing city on the state line about twenty-five miles east of us. She and I were among the hordes of boys and girls flocking to music studios across the country during the late forties and early fifties. All of us hoped to become the next Dick Contino, a famous, young, accordionist from California.

On a Sunday night in 1947, my family was among 20 million listeners cheering in front of living room radios when the eighteen-year-old Contino won the *Horace Heidt's Talent Hunt* after several weeks of competition. The young musician's bellows-shaking "Lady of Spain" earned him the gold championship belt, five thousand dollars and the opportunity to continue performing with Heidt, a big band leader who was known as the star-maker.

Dad admired the 120-bass, piano accordion, but considered it beyond his ability as a musician. When he was a teenager, he taught himself to play a small German squeeze-box with ten treble keys for the right hand and four bass buttons for the left. At that time, he joined members of his family playing for neighbors to dance at his parents' house parties. On quiet, winter Sunday afternoons, he still pulled out his worn instrument with adhesive tape covering holes in the bellows and serenaded Mom and me with "You Are My Sunshine" and other old favorites.

In the spring of 1949, when I was eleven, Dad suggested my taking accordion lessons and I agreed. Most of my friends played the piano and I envied their abilities. Every Saturday morning, we followed Yale Bridge Road to Beloit. I hated the blacktop's namesake. The rattling of the wooden plank floor on the iron bridge when our Chevy crossed the Sugar River scared me. I could imagine falling into the water.

In the city, Dad found a place to park along the State Street curb near Voigt's second-floor music studio. I hauled the brown, leather case containing that heavy, $375 white instrument up the narrow stairway, through the swinging doors on a landing and into the high-ceilinged, waiting room at the top. Mr. Voigt's office was through a glass-paneled door at the rear. The boss was a tall, blond haired, single man about my parents' age. Studios for lessons were on opposite sides of the waiting room. Kay gave steel guitar lessons in the one on the right. I suspected the middle-aged, tall, attractive, brown-haired, woman was Mr. Voigt's girlfriend.

I went to the studio on the left for my half-hour, private session. I adored my teacher, Dallas, a slim, good-looking high school junior, with black hair and brown eyes.

Six months after I started instruction, Dallas formed his students into an accordion band to prepare for a Christmas concert. With limited space available for practice sessions, he divided the forty boys and girls into groups of ten. During our Monday night rehearsals, I met Janice and we gravitated together. Among the city kids, we were two country girls who loved riding horses.

Dad and Janice's father, George, who farmed near Orford-ville, enjoyed visiting while waiting for their budding musicians. Soon the two men brought their families together for an evening at our house. In the living room, the adults played Five Hundred, a card game that pits one pair against another couple to bid and take tricks. My parents were never partners—it was usually the men against the women. The winner was the first to achieve five-hundred points.

Janice, her sister, Joyce, and I sat cross-legged on my double bed, played rummy and talked about ourselves and our schools. Joyce was my age and Janice was two years younger but only one grade behind her sister in school. Janice, who had brown hair and blue eyes, resembled their mother, Ve. Joyce took after their dad with a dark complexion, brown eyes and black hair. Although the slim girls didn't look alike, they wore the same size clothes and often traded outfits. I thought that was neat.

During the following summer, we all went to several area county fairs together. The seven of us easily fit into George's roomy, dark blue, four-door Hudson. Joyce sat between our fathers in the front seat with Janice and me in the back with our mothers.

Friendship between our two families grew when we began meeting at the Wigwam dance hall every weekend. George and

Ve hadn't cut a rug in years, but Dad and Mom encouraged them to join us.

Saturday night always meant two things at our house–a bath and a dance. When I was little, there were no baby-sitters. I went along with my parents to various area halls. Dad and a few of his friends danced with me. With the event lasting from 9:00 P.M. to 1:00 A.M., I soon stretched out on one of the wooden benches fastened to the wall. Dad's folded jacket served as my pillow and Mom's long coat was my blanket. The band played and the crowd clapped but I slept. As I grew, I spent more of the evening dancing.

I taught Janice and Joyce the various steps. Girls as partners was a hold-over from World War II when there was a shortage of guys on the home front.

The sisters introduced me to several other Orfordville students who frequented the hall that was close to their high school. Janice's classmate, Willabea, became another of my close friends. She also came with her parents. Her mother was a short, plump, white haired woman. Her dad was fairly tall, balding man with a paunch. They were friendly people, but Dad and Mom called them Mr. and Mrs. instead of Tilman and Pearl because they were about twenty years older than my folks.

The Wigwam was located seven miles west of Beloit on Highway 81 at the intersection with County H. Unlike the other establishments in the area, it didn't have a bar, which pleased my parents, who were teetotalers. The lunch counter that stood to the right of the front door sold only soda pop, bar-b-q sandwiches and packaged snacks.

Some places didn't have ventilation and shut down during the summer, but the Wigwam operated year-round. Hinged, wooden windows as large as doors lined the east and west sides of the long building. On hot summer nights, those were raised to let the cool, night air flow through. In the winter, a furnace the size of a small bedroom heated the hall, but not the restrooms, which remained freezing cold. Nobody lingered there longer than necessary.

The small stage midway along the west side of the building held a piano waiting for a player, who often was the band leader's wife. The various five-piece groups from the area usually included a fiddler, a bass thumper, and a man who tooted a horn or two. The drummer set the beat for old time waltzes, fox trots and polkas. At least one of the musicians stood at the microphone and sang top ten songs of the day plus old favorites.

During the height of the Wigwam's popularity in the fifties, the proprietor, 'Connie' Pilz, doubled the size of the rough-hewn structure, but the smooth as ice, hardwood floor remained crowded with three generations of dancers. Besides teenagers and middle-aged couples, an older group included Kenny's great uncle, Harry, and his wife, Pearl, Durand residents who'd been married about fifty years. The small, balding man and the large, white-haired woman made an unconventional couple. When the band began the familiar strains of "Home Sweet Home," the last dance, he'd snuggle his forehead under his wife's chin while they waltzed around the floor.

Several circle-two-steps during the evening brought all ages together. The mixer began with the ladies forming a circle on the inside facing the gents on the outside. The caller directed, "Everybody join hands and circle to the right. There they are boys, everybody dance."

The men led and the women followed. Usually my partner two-stepped, fox trotted or jitterbugged and we chatted while moving together effortlessly. Occasionally, a fellow came along with his own style. Only he knew where his feet were going next. With no recognizable pattern, all I could do was try to gracefully keep my feet out of his way. If his loafer crunched one of the bare toes peeking out of my sandals, it was I who said, "Excuse me."

That would be the time the leader sawed away on his fiddle for what seemed like hours before he raised his chin and called, "Everybody promenade. Ladies reverse."

On Saturday night following the big picnic, Janice, Joyce, Willabea and I met at the Wigwam as usual. Willabea and I rehashed our Wednesday afternoon with Wayne and Kenny.

She said, "Wayne's kinda cute and he sure is a nice guy. I hope I see him again." She had a crush on my boyfriend's buddy.

The following Wednesday, a warm, sunny, third of September, school began. For my first day as a sophomore at Durand High, I wore a lavender sleeveless blouse, a pleated, cotton, print skirt that hit me mid-calf with white bobby sox and brown loafers. The only tie-shoes I bought were tennis shoes for gym class.

Half-a-dozen of us, who lived northwest of town and rode the same bus, climbed the seven concrete steps in front of the three-story, brick cube that sat on the north side of West South Street. We entered through the white, wooden double doors with clear glass inserts. The landing inside separated two flights of stairs. One went down to the girls' locker room on the right and the boys' on the left. In between, wooden, swinging, double doors with frosted glass inserts opened into the gymnasium. A passageway ran between several rows of wooden bleachers that were embedded in concrete on opposite sides.

Across the hardwood floor, a stage was draped with heavy, blue, velvet curtains.

We all ascended the stairs past the two classrooms on the middle level of the building. In between them wooden, swinging doors with frosted glass inserts led to a balcony that extended over the lower-level bleachers. Wooden benches provided seating with a view of the gym.

Up another flight of stairs, the top floor included offices for the superintendent and his secretary, a typing room, science lab, two classrooms and a smoke-filled, teachers' lounge. We entered the huge study hall that accommodated the entire student body. Windows lined the east side of the large room and library books were shelved along the west side. Daily newspapers, reference books and a long, hardwood study table with matching chairs were in the back. The daily schedule written in white chalk on a blackboard covered the front wall. Our day stretched from approximately eight forty-five in the morning until three thirty in the afternoon. The eight class periods and noon break were each a little less than forty-five minutes long.

Before classes began that morning, the study hall buzzed with adolescent voices as groups of friends compared notes on summer vacation. My sensitive nose caught a slight odor of cleaning compound used on the floor during the summer. I found my assigned place among a hundred-twenty sets of desks and seats bolted to the floor in rows. The desks had stationary tops and open backs. If books and papers weren't stored neatly, they fell out onto the floor.

I squatted down to stash the used textbooks I'd purchased at a Rockford store and my brown leather, zipper notebook with Lolita Tschabold in gold letters in the lower, right hand corner. For years, I'd been disappointed when things like barrettes that were printed with first names never had my mine. When I was in fourth grade, my parents gave me this prized possession to make up for all of those slights. Other students used cardboard covered, three-holers sold in dime stores

When I straightened up, Kenny was standing behind me. He wore jeans and brown, penny loafers with white socks. His white t-shirt showed in the V of his black and maroon, striped sport shirt with the long sleeves turned up two folds. We exchanged greetings and small talk.

When the bell rang, students scurried to classrooms or desks. Farm boys, who were the majority of the fellows, exited through the back door and clambered down the fire escape for their double-period ag classes in the white, wooden, single-story shop behind the school.

I'd enrolled in five classes instead of the usual four—Geometry, English II, Biology, Civics and Typing plus the required Physical Education. I'd skipped the double-period, girls' track of Home Economics II. Last year, I'd hated every minute of Home Ec. I with its cooking and sewing. My schedule was the same with two, free periods during the day to do my assignments. Teachers didn't require homework because most students had chores to do at home after school.

My extra-curricular activities included singing with the choruses, volunteering as a librarian, belonging to the Future Homemakers of America club and playing games with the Girls Athletic Association twice a week after school.

Kenny took four classes—English, Geometry, American History and Sociology. He was one of four seniors representing their class on the ten-member student council. For extra-curricular activities, he played sports and sang in the choruses.

I always liked school, but this year gleamed like a gold star on an A+ paper. I saw Kenny every day. We talked in the morning before classes. At noon, we joined other couples staking out a spot on the balcony benches and eating our sack lunches together. He spent the rest of the period playing softball with a group of boys when it was nice weather outside or shooting baskets in the gym on stormy or cold days. I chatted with my girlfriends.

Kenny and I began each afternoon in Geometry class together. The elective, offered only every other year, attracted seven other sophomores, juniors and seniors. I enjoyed working with the squares, triangles and circles, but he didn't. Each day when we left class, he grumbled, "I don't understand what that old biddy is talking about." Our teacher was a gray-haired, substitute, Miss Schoch. A few weeks later, Mr. Prez, a short, dark young man took over the class. After a few days Kenny said, "I don't know why he wasn't here in the beginning. He makes sense."

Thursday, 4 September, teachers' institute gave me a holiday for my 15th birthday. My gifts and cards included a wine-colored suit, a white blouse and pajamas from Dad and Mom; a card and a dollar from my paternal grandparents; and a card from Aunt Frannie, Uncle Hookie and my cousin, Sis, plus a brooch from my cousin, Doris.

Mom's parents died before she was married, but my mother's eldest sister and her husband, Frances and Roscoe Rowley, loved me like a grandchild. We celebrated holidays and special occasions with them and their two daughters.

Aunt Frannie, a chubby woman with graying, brown hair, was fourteen years older than my mother and contended with arthritis. She sewed dresses for herself, her two girls and occasionally for me. She earned a little extra money making garments and altering clothes for several other women.

Everyone called my tall, bald-headed uncle with a big nose 'Hookie' except his wife who said Ross. He was ten years her senior and a veteran of World War I. To farm their 125 acres located three miles northeast of Durand, he wore a blue chambray, work shirt under dark blue, bib overalls that he never bothered to button on the sides.

My two cousins were in their late twenties, which put them half-way between Mom's generation and mine. Both of them had light brown hair and blue eyes. Doris, who was sol-idly built, helped her dad with outside work and appealed to my tomboy side. Florence, her thin, younger sister, we called 'Sis' to avoid confusion with her namesake, their father's only sibling. She drew pictures and made crafts, which appealed to my creative side. The young women were my role models and I envied their relationship.

Spending most of my time with grown-ups made me feel like a little adult who grew to be a big adult. I measured five-foot-four and considered myself tall because these three women and Mom were shorter than I.

In the evening, my parents and I celebrated with supper in Durand at Carl's restaurant before the free show. Afterward, I met Corky in the park and she gave me a card and a small orange scarf. We sat down on the grass in the park to watch the final presentation of the season, a Gene Autry western. Kenny soon joined me and we snuggled together. When I mentioned I was celebrating, he wished me a happy birthday.

On Wednesday afternoon, 1 October, baseball's World Series began. Those of us with study hall could go downstairs to the stage and listen to the play-by-play. We sat on wooden folding chairs in a half-circle around the big, brown console radio. I joined Kenny cheering for the New York Yankees playing against the Brooklyn Dodgers. I didn't know much about the pro sport, but the teen magazines I read advised girls to learn. I listened closely to the radio and to Kenny. By the following Tuesday, when the Yanks took the title for the fourth year in a row, I was on a first name basis with their center fielder, Mickey Mantle, and catcher Yogi Berra.

A couple of weeks later on a Friday night, Kenny and I joined the other high school students in the gym for a box social sponsored by the junior class. Coach Hubbartt, the class adviser, acted as auctioneer. He stood beside the long table in the middle of the hardwood floor and picked up the decorated cartons one by one to be purchased. When he lifted my shoebox covered with brown crepe paper and orange, construction paper, jack o'lanterns, I nodded to Kenny who was sitting beside me on the bleachers. He opened the bidding with, "A dollar."

Kenny's buddy, Wayne, said, "A dollar and a quarter."

My friend, Jon, who rode the same school bus I did, added, "A buck fifty."

Those two junior boys didn't yearn to eat lunch with me. They just wanted Kenny to spend more money, which would go into their class treasury.

Kenny topped them by bidding, "Two dollars." The auctioneer declared, "Sold."

After boys bought all of the girls' boxes, Kenny and I remained on the bleachers to eat ham sandwiches, potato chips, bananas and homemade, chocolate chip cookies. We washed our food down with Cokes he bought from the red machine that sat on the balcony. We spent the rest of the evening dancing to records.

A week later, Kenny was my guest at a Future Homemakers of America party. Although I wasn't in a Home Ec. class, I continued to belong to the club to participate in the social events. It was the first time I'd been inside the new, modern, home economics facilities included in the single story, beige brick grade school, which opened this year across the street from the high school. Pale green walls enveloped the double-sized classroom. Four kitchen units were in the east end. In the west end, sewing machines were stored against the north wall beneath a row of windows. A conversation center furnished with a davenport, end tables and comfortable chairs divided the two work areas. The long, blonde-wood table with matching chairs that usually sat in the middle of the floor in the west end was pushed against the south wall to make more room for the party-goers. The teacher's desk, which sat between the two doorways on the south side of the classroom, rested against the green, chalk board that hung on the wall behind it.

To 'break the ice', we played a game, pass the orange. Kenny and I ended up on opposite sides when we counted off one, two, one, two. We formed two lines and stood boy, girl, boy, girl including the teachers and their spouses who were chaperones. No hands were allowed as the orange was held under the chin and moved from person to person. Giggles prevailed as tall people scrunched down and short ones stood on tiptoes trying to adapt to one another. Kenny's team won and each of them received a Hershey Kiss. We then danced to records and enjoyed punch and cookies the girls had made in class.

A couple weeks later, Kenny and I were sitting on a balcony bench eating lunch when he asked, "Can you go to a show on Saturday night?"

"I'll ask Mom," I said with a lilt of hope in my voice because I was now fifteen.

At home, I repeated Kenny's invitation when Mom came in from doing chores. Just like twice before, she said a firm, "No." My birthday wasn't the magic dating age that I'd hoped it would be.

When I relayed my mother's response to Kenny in study hall the next morning, I was thinking about his dates with June and Nancy. I added, "I hope you won't give up on me."

He responded, "Don't worry; I'll wait for you."

That same day, Tuesday, 4 November, Dad and Mom drove to the Laona Town Hall and voted in the presidential election. Democrat Adlai Stevenson, governor of Illinois, opposed Republican Dwight Eisenhower. During World War II, General Eisenhower commanded the greatest army in history. People in all parts of the world fondly called the tall, baldheaded man 'Ike'.

In the evening, we were invited to Jack and Helen Weaver's three-bedroom, ranch-style, country home near Beloit, Wisconsin, to play Five Hundred while listening to the election returns on the radio. Other guests included two of Jack's brothers and their wives, Gerald and Laurena and Bob and Mildred, along with his parents, Jay and Amy, who lived along the way and rode to the party with us.

Mom grew up with her neighbors, the Weaver clan. Jack, the oldest child, was Mom's age and the other four followed like stair steps. The whole family was tall. Jack, Mary and Russell were broad-faced with dark hair like their mother. Gerald and Bob favored their father, who had a thin face and light brown hair. All of them married and were regular visitors at our house. Although Mary, the only girl, was two years younger than my mother, the two women were life-long, best friends Jack, a crude fellow, sold and repaired water pumps for farmers. Helen, a big woman with prematurely gray hair, sat in a corner of the L-shaped, living room visiting with her mother-in-law who didn't play cards. Jack and his father were partners rotating along with the others sitting at two card tables. I considered their children David, eleven, Margie, seven and Nancy, five, a nuisance rather than playmates, but I joined them sitting on the single bed in David's room playing Monopoly. In my mind, I called the board game Monotony.

About midnight, everyone quit playing games and listened to Adlai Stevenson concede to Dwight D. Eisenhower. Then Jack exclaimed, "Three cheers for Ike." We all joined in with his "Hip, Hip Hooray!" We would have a Republican president after twenty years of Democrats Franklin Delano Roosevelt and Harry S. Truman in the White House. Helen served coffee and spice cake before everyone went home.

At school the next day, plans were being made for Homecoming, which was coming up with the first home basketball game of the season the night before Thanksgiving. Wayne asked me, "Do you think Willabea would go with me?"

"She can't date yet either. I'll ask her to stay all night with me so we can go together."

"Thanks. That'd be great."

Saturday night at the Wigwam, I said to Willabea, "Would you want to come to our Homecoming? Wayne wanted to ask you, but I told him you couldn't date. I said I would invite you to stay all night with me so you could attend."

She immediately asked her mother who approved.

Early Homecoming evening, my mother and I picked up Willabea at her southern Wisconsin farm home. Mom dropped off the two of us in front of the new grade school. We went in through the front, double doors, bought our student tickets, proceeded down the hall past the doorway for the visitors' section of the gym and entered the door for the home team supporters. Durand was playing their arch rival, Pecatonica, another little town a few miles south. A large crowd gathered on both sides of the hardwood floor.

It was the first game in the new gym with a regulation size court. The rollaway bleachers seated eight-hundred-forty people. It was quite a change from the old high school facility across the street that only seated two-hundred-forty people alongside a smaller than standard floor. We found seats among my schoolmates, removed our heavy coats, folded them and laid them beside us.

Soon the visiting varsity team clad in purple uniforms trimmed in gold ran out of the locker room onto the floor. Everyone stood up and clapped.

Durand's team wearing white uniforms with blue numbers and lettering then ran onto the floor accompanied by applause. Kenny, the only senior, led the group followed by six juniors including Wayne. The boys idolized Coach Hubbartt, the chunky, young Social Studies teacher with a light-brown, crew cut, who yelled at them.

Everyone remained standing while our school band played the two school songs and "The National Anthem."

Marvin, Durand's six-foot-two center, met Pec's tallest player in the middle circle for the tip-off to start the game. I kept my eyes on number 22 and Willabea's gaze followed number 23 as the boys raced up and down the floor.

Durand fans clung to the edge of their seats when Pec started out with a seven-point lead.

A couple of our boys' fathers shouted orders at their sons.

Our six cheerleaders were jumping up and down on the sidelines. They wore white, turtle-neck sweaters with royal blue, knee length, circle skirts lined in white. Their feet were clad in white bobby socks and white buck oxfords, the shoe craze started by pop singer, Pat Boone.

By the end of the first quarter, our team led 16 to 13. At half time, the score leaped to 31 to 24 and by the end of the third quarter, 46 to 31. When the game ended with a final score of Durand 57, Pecatonica 44, the gym echoed with our fans' shouts of victory.

After the game, Willabea and I faced snowflakes blowing in the cold wind when we hustled across the street to the high school for the dance. After hanging our heavy coats in the girls' locker room, we stepped into the rear area. The two of us stood in front of the rest room stalls and used the wide mirror hanging on the wall to comb our hair and reapply lipstick.

Willabea wore a black, ballerina skirt with a white, long-sleeved blouse and black flats. She was about the same height as Wayne and it was one of the unwritten rules in the fifties that a girl shouldn't be taller than her date. I felt grown-up wearing a new pair of suede pumps with Cuban heels. My shoes matched my new, black sateen, cap-sleeved dress. We checked that the seams in our stockings ran straight up the backs of our legs, stashed our combs and lipsticks in our coat pockets and exited the locker room.

Inside the dimly lit gym, we sat down on the bleachers to wait for our escorts. The orchestra seated behind their lighted music stands on the stage began playing in the style of the big bands popular during the 1940's. White, poster board letters covered with glitter and attached to the blue velvet valance hanging above them proclaimed WELCOME ALUMNI.

"What do you suppose is keeping the guys?" Willabea asked.

"I can't imagine," I replied. "It's funny all of the other basketball players are here, but not Kenny and Wayne."

Finally, fifteen minutes after the dance began, our boyfriends dressed in suits, white shirts and ties joined us. Wayne explained, "I'm sorry we're late. It's all my fault. After I took a shower, I couldn't find my white shirt. Kenny helped me look for it. The only one that was in the locker room was too big for me." He pulled down on his left shirt sleeve and the white fabric bunched up between the cuff and the edge of his medium-gray jacket. "See what I mean?" he asked. "Apparently some other guy's wearing my shirt." He tucked the surplus material back under his suit coat.

"You look fine," Willabea assured him.

The band began playing a slow dance. We formed couples and danced cheek to cheek.

At eleven, the fluorescent overhead lights were turned on for the coronation. Kenny left me sitting on the bleachers with Wayne and Willabea while he stepped to the center of the floor to join Shirley, a pretty, petite junior with light brown hair. The two were crowned Homecoming King and Queen. The royal pair followed by their attendants Don and Carole plus Paul and Millie lined up to lead the Grand March.

My former boyfriend, Ronnie, approached me and asked, "Would you march with me?" I agreed and the two of us followed Wayne and Willabea to join the line of couples.

Afterward, Kenny said, "Is Ronnie trying to get you back?" I pooh-poohed that idea.

During the rest of the evening, the boys danced the slow songs with us. Willabea and I did a few fast ones together. In between, we drank Cokes, chatted and listened to the music.

My parents attended a movie while waiting to pick up us girls. When the dance ended at 1:00 A.M., Kenny and Wayne waited in the hallway for us to get our coats. The boys then walked us to our Chevy and greeted my parents.

At home in my bedroom, Willabea and I spent a long time quietly, rehashing our evening before we settled down to sleep. Willabea said, "Wayne asked if it would be okay if he came to see me on a Sunday afternoon after the holidays. I told him it would."

"It must take a lot of guts for guys to come to our houses," I replied. "Do you think our folks will let us date in 1953?"

"I hope so. Our turning fifteen this fall didn't make any difference. Dad teases me that I'll have to be thirty," Willabea said. "At least we're in the same boat."

Early Thanksgiving morning, Mom and I drove Willabea home.

A week later on Sunday afternoon, I heard a horn honk about four o'clock. I jumped up from the black upholstered, rocking chair and hurried to look out the north, living room window.

Ditzlers' green Nash was cruising slowly by our clapboard-covered, white, two-story home. I guess Kenny was too shy to stop.

During the first week of December, all county roads were given names. At the intersection east of our farm, a green sign with ivory letters proclaimed the blacktop running past our home was Laube Road. It would take a while to drop our old designations such as: the fire's at the old Joe Waller place; the accident happened on death curve; or turn left at Burrell Kinney's corner.

On Tuesday, 23 December, after lunch, all high school students gathered on the bleachers in the gym for the Christmas party. It was a noisy group. Everyone was in a holiday mood looking forward to a ten-day vacation. The giant, decorated tree sitting on the stage gave the air a hint of pine. More than a hundred wrapped packages were piled beneath it. Miss Holt, our pretty, young, blonde music teacher, stood in front of us and led us singing classic carols. Then the ten members of the student council distributed the presents.

Two weeks earlier, we drew names for the gift exchange. Superintendent Norsworthy admonished us to keep the slip of paper pulled from his brown fedora. I'd followed the rules and bought a box of three handkerchiefs for Jane, a freshman. Kenny ignored the edict and traded for my name. He gave me a beautiful necklace, bracelet and earrings set that looked like silver, but was coated plastic inset with rhinestones.

Christmas Eve at home, my parents and I began the evening with our traditional ham supper. To me, it seemed flat with just the three of us. I missed the celebrations that included Aunt Frannie, Uncle Hookie, Doris and Sis coming for supper and presents. That get-together was dropped two years earlier.

During the summer of 1950, when my cousin, Sis, was twenty-five and creeping toward spinsterhood, she joined the Catholic Church and married Joe. Her groom was a tall, thin, dark-haired, twenty-one-year-old of Irish descent who lived a couple miles down the road. It was quite unconventional for the bride to be older than the groom.

When we received the formal wedding invitation in the mail, I was an excited twelve-year-old. "What will I wear?" I asked.

"We're not going," Mom said brusquely. I knew my parents didn't approve of Joe, who was a Catholic and a drinker. I didn't ask any more questions.

Later that summer, Mom wrote Aunt Frannie a letter ending our get together. I don't know how she worded it, but basically, my parents didn't want to invite the new son-in-law to our home on Christmas Eve.

After our meal, we moved from the kitchen to the decorated tree in the living room. I was the only one with packages to open. Dad and Mom each could spend twenty-five dollars as they pleased, but neither one bought anything yet.

My folks gave me a Royal Deluxe portable typewriter, a pair of gray, rubber, stadium boots trimmed with faux fur around the top and a car key on a chain. They would soon be teaching me to drive so I could get my license when I turned sixteen in September.

Although we no longer celebrated together, the Rowleys still gave me gifts. I received a paint set from Doris, gloves from Sis, and a sweater from Uncle Hookie and Aunt Frannie. Aunt Florence, Uncle Hookie's single sister who lived in Los Angeles, wasn't actually a relative, but she sent me a bottle of

Prince Matchabelli perfume in a crown-shaped bottle. I was thrilled with my presents.

On Christmas Day at noon, we joined a crowd of strangers at Frank & Gus's Cozy Inn family restaurant in Beloit. The brothers served a free turkey dinner with customer donations going to the Salvation Army. After the meal, we went to a show. When we returned home, I used my new typewriter to write thank you notes for my gifts.

Friday and Saturday nights, Dad drove me to town so I could watch Kenny play in Durand's first Holiday Basketball Tournament. When the opening game between Dakota and Winnebago began with the tip-off at seven thirty in the new gym, Winnebago took that game 68 to 61 and would play for the championship Saturday night. Durand then beat Pecatonica 57 to 48, pitting us against Winnebago for first place.

Saturday night in the preliminary game, Dakota captured third place by beating Pec 64 to 57. Durand and Winnebago then took the floor playing for the championship. Winnebago started out ahead ending the first quarter 15 to 10. By half time, Durand captured the lead 27 to 22. Our cheerleaders were jumping up and down and screaming encouragement to the team. Winnebago cut that lead to 39 to 37 in the third quarter. The visitors outscored our boys in the fourth quarter twenty points to twelve making the final score Winnebago 57 and Durand 51. We settled for second place. Trophies were awarded.

After the players showered and dressed, Kenny and I hurried through the cold to the old gym across the street. When he paid our thirty-five cents per couple admission to the record dance, two smiling juniors said, "Thank you."

The room was wall-to-wall teens from all four of the schools involved in the tournament.

Although the teams were rivals on the basketball court, many of the students were friends or relatives. At midnight, we ended the evening dancing cheek to cheek as Vera Lynn sang "Auf Wiederseh'n Sweetheart." When Kenny and I came out of the school, Dad was waiting for me with the Chevy running to keep warm. My boyfriend walked me to the sedan and greeted my father.

Tuesday's mail brought an Evening in Paris perfume set and hanky for me from my grandparents. We didn't observe Christmas with Dad's folks, but I exchanged gifts with them. I gave Grandma a sterling silver pin and Grandpa a pail of Plow Boy chewing tobacco plus two red, everyday hankies.

New Year's Eve, we celebrated at the Wigwam. Instead of my usual skirt and sweater, I wore the plain, black dress I'd bought for Homecoming. It was the perfect foil to show off the jewelry Kenny gave me for Christmas. At the dance, Janice, Joyce and Willabea admired my gift.

At midnight, Simpsons' Nitehawks played the traditional "Auld Lang Syne" and the huge crowd scrambled for the balloons released from large plastic bags secured in the rafters of the rough-hewn, building. The four of us stayed on the sidelines. We donned paper hats, blew our cardboard horns, shook tin noisemakers and shouted, "Happy New Year" to greet 1953.

Chapter 2

1953

January dragged by as monotonous as the cold, snowy winter weather.

The first Monday morning in February was Ground Hog's Day, but no one at school was concerned about the animal seeing his shadow. Instead of the usual chatter and laughter in study hall, clusters of kids talked in subdued tones. Some of the girls wiped tears.

On Sunday at home, I listened to a WEKZ radio newsman report that Saturday night about midnight on a Wisconsin road, a convertible driven by nineteen-year-old Ray and crammed with six more Durand young people collided with a carload of six teen-age guys from Monroe. Our English teacher, Miss Cullinan, twenty-four, and Patricia, twenty-one, who worked in the local electric shop, were taken to the St. Clare Hospital in Monroe where they died. The Durand driver and his other passengers including our math teacher, Mr. Prez, and gym teacher, Miss Elsner, were treated and released.

While Kenny and I were discussing the accident, he reminisced about the teacher directing their senior class play the previous fall. "Miss Cullinan went with a bunch of us guys to Freeport to pick up some furniture to use on the stage. The car was crowded and she ended up sitting on Fred's lap. When we all got out of the car, Fred's legs were asleep and he just crumpled right down." My boyfriend smiled at the anecdote.

All of us were in Miss Cullinan's required English classes during her two years here. We would miss the petite, young woman with fair skin, dark eyes, and dark curly hair, who always wore spike heels to appear taller.

No school Wednesday. The faculty attended Miss Cullinan's funeral in her home town of Pekin, about a three-hour drive from Durand. Thursday, Mrs. Downing, a former teacher who lived in the village, took charge of the English department.

March brought a new era. Our first date was Saturday night, the seventh. I donned the black sateen dress I'd bought last fall for Homecoming. The plain round neck showed off the necklace Kenny gave me for Christmas. My hands trembled with excitement when I snapped the matching earrings to my lobes and looped the bracelet around my left wrist.

At eight-thirty, Kenny pulled in our gravel driveway, parked and walked up the concrete to the house. I opened the front door and he entered the living room to meet my folks. A nine-by-twelve, beige, patterned rug covered most of the soft pine floor. The varnished woodwork included three feet of wainscoting overlaying the lower part of the walls below the floral paper. With a ten-foot, ceiling, the north window required a ninety-inch, white, lace curtain.

Mom sat in her beige, easy chair with a floor lamp beside it and a brown, plastic-covered, hassock sitting in front of it. Dad's chair matched the dusty rose davenport and was flanked by a smoking stand. He didn't use cigarettes, but an ash tray

THE VIEW FROM A MIDWEST FERRIS WHEEL

was provided for the men who came to visit. White crocheted antimacassars protected the backs and arms of the upholstered furniture.

I introduced Kenny to my parents and Dad stood to shake hands with my boyfriend. The three of them made small talk while I quickly put on my gold, full-length, winter coat. We bid my parents good-bye, left the house and walked down the sidewalk to the Nash. He opened the passenger door for me to slide in. While he stepped around the rear to the driver's side, I scooted across the bench seat to the middle so I'd be close to him.

A couple weeks earlier at school, Kenny and I sat on a balcony wooden bench eating lunch when he said, "Can you go to the FHA dance with me?"

My stock reply, "I'll have to ask my mother."

When I got home from school, I asked. Miracle of miracles, Mom said, "I guess you can go." She went out to do chores.

I sat down to read the paper, but I couldn't concentrate on the news. My mind kept repeating, *I can date! I can date!*

I could hardly wait to tell Kenny. The first thing the next morning when I saw him in study hall, I blurted out, "Mom said I can go to the FHA dance with you."

His face lit up with a big smile and he responded, "Great."

The Future Homemakers of America evening was similar to Homecoming. We danced the slow songs cheek to cheek, listened to the music, drank Cokes and talked. At 1 A.M., the band ended the evening with "Goodnight Irene."

At our house, Kenny walked me to the front steps and said, "I had a nice time. Goodnight."

I could see his breath in the crisp night air. I replied, "I did, too. Thank you. Goodnight."

He turned on his heel and walked back to the Ambassador.

I climbed the wooden steps, crossed the gray, painted floor of the screened-in porch and opened the kitchen door feeling like I was a balloon floating along. After I was in bed, I couldn't go to sleep. I kept replaying my first date in my mind.

A couple of weeks later, Coach Hubbartt took the seven varsity players to the Illinois High School Association basketball state finals in Champaign. During the three days Kenny wasn't at school, I missed talking with him in the mornings and having him wink at me from across study hall. At noon, all of us abandoned girlfriends formed a lonely-hearts club and ate our sack lunches sitting together on a balcony bench.

Saturday morning, I gathered the mail from the box by the side of the blacktop road. My heart jumped when I glimpsed a post card from Kenny. In the evening, when I saw Willabea at the Wigwam, she said Wayne sent her one, too. "They're thinking of us as well as basketball," my friend said. We both grinned.

Since winter began, I tried to figure out what made me itch so much. I finally decided it must be taking showers at the end of our eighth-hour gym class. I explained to Miss Elsner, "I think I'm allergic to something in the town's water. When I was little, I had eczema and my skin has continued to be sensitive. I don't want to take any more showers."

Miss Elsner replied, "Tell your mother that you need a doctor's excuse if you aren't going to take showers."

I relayed the message to Mom. She then wrote a note to my teacher: "Dear Miss Elsner, Lolita has my permission to not take showers at school. She does not need a doctor's excuse. (signed) Edith Tschabold." That took care of that.

One of the rites of passage growing up in the forties and fifties was suffering through the communicable childhood diseases—mumps, measles, chicken pox, and whooping cough. Toward the end of March, a mumps epidemic engulfed our community. Mumps caused painful swelling of the salivary glands in the cheeks and under the jaw making it difficult to chew or swallow for about a week.

'DON'T GET THE MUMPS' was ingrained in my brain. Somehow, my father, the oldest of five children, and my mother, the youngest of four, escaped this illness. My parents feared that I would bring the malady home from school. About eighteen days later, they would both be sick with no one able to do the milking. Childhood diseases were more severe in adults. Men could have mumps 'go down on them' causing painful swelling in one or both testicles.

Being a dutiful child, I didn't get the mumps, but I went to great lengths to avoid the disease. The first Saturday in April, I complained about a mild stomach ache high in my abdomen. If I'd been a chicken, I would have said the pain was just below my wishbone. Mom and I thought lying down would cure it, but it didn't. The next day was Easter Sunday, but I didn't feel like going to church. The ham dinner Mom prepared smelled good, but I didn't want anything to eat. Monday morning, I still hurt.

Mom said, "You choose where you want to go see a doctor."

"I don't feel like riding very far," I moaned. "Let's go to Brodhead. It's the closest." I took a bath and dressed. Mom got behind the wheel of our Chevy and I slumped in the passenger seat while she drove the blacktop roads north.

Fifteen minutes later, we stepped into Dr. Stovall's store front office on the west side of the main street in Brodhead, Wisconsin. Brown plastic tile covered the floor of the waiting room. On the wall opposite the doorway, his diplomas and an eight-by-ten picture of him in a naval officer's uniform were hung on the pine-paneling. We sat down in beige plastic, up-holstered chairs. A corner table held an array of farm, fishing and homemaker magazines.

Lucille, the doctor's aide who wore a turquoise uniform, came down the hallway beside the office area, greeted us and showed the way back to the examining room. I sat on the end of the table while the plump, middle-aged woman with salt and pepper hair checked my vital signs. Then I lay down and stretched out.

Dr. Stovall, a big man with graying, dark hair and glasses entered the room. It was the first time I saw the physician who poked his fingers all around my mid-section. Each time he pushed on my lower right side, I flinched. He immediately diagnosed, "You have appendicitis. Your appendix must be re-moved immediately." Turning to my mother, he sternly said, "You should have brought this young lady in to see me yesterday."

Mom wasn't easily intimidated. She responded, "It was Easter and I wasn't going to bother a doctor for what appeared to be a routine tummy ache. She'd never had a problem before and there's no family history of appendicitis."

Dr. Stovall called the St. Clare Hospital and made ar-rangements for my operation. Surgery scared me, but I wanted to be rid of the pain.

Mom and I got back in our two-door sedan and took Highway 81 to Monroe, Wisconsin, another agonizing fifteen miles away. Each joint in the concrete road jarred me.

When Mom and I entered the four-story, brick, hospital, we were greeted by a woman standing behind a counter. She admitted me and directed us to the elevator that would take us to the surgical department. We exited the elevator on the second floor. A nurse dressed in white from her cap to her shoes greeted us and escorted us to a double room. A gray-haired patient, Mrs. Swanson, welcomed me. As the nurse turned to leave, she pulled the curtain that divided the green-walled room to give me privacy to undress. I donned the hospital gown lying on the bed and Mom tied my strings in the back. I crawled between the stiff, white sheets that covered the hospital bed and inhaled the distinctive antiseptic smell that prevailed.

Dr. Ekstam, a big man with thinning brown hair, entered and introduced himself as the surgeon who would perform my operation. He poked around my abdomen and repeated Dr. Stovall's diagnosis, "You have appendicitis." He turned to Mom, "Your daughter should spend two days in the hospital, five more at home and then she'll be able to go back to school." He left to prepare for surgery.

Soon an orderly pushed a gurney next to my bed. I hitched myself onto it and he propelled me to the OR. I shifted to the operating table surrounded by staff wearing masks and gowns. A hand placed an anesthetic mask over my nose and mouth. A voice said, "Start counting backward from a hundred." I ended with 96.

I awoke in the bed in my room. I was surprised to see my father sitting beside my mother. She explained, "I called your dad from a pay phone in the waiting room to tell him your surgery was scheduled for eleven thirty. He borrowed Merle's truck to drive to the hospital. Dr. Ekstam told us your surgery went as expected."

I talked with them and dozed. At four o'clock, they left to do chores.

The next morning when Dr. Ekstam made rounds, he said I should walk in the hallway. A little later, Mom delivered my robe, slippers and toiletries and returned home.

I struggled to get out of bed, slipped my robe over my backless gown and stepped into my slippers. My right side was tender making me hunch over as I followed doctor's orders and walked along the green, plastic tile floor in the hall.

In the afternoon, my friendly roommate said good-bye and returned to her home in Janesville. I liked having the room to myself when Dad and Mom visited in the evening.

Wednesday afternoon, I felt better and sat in a chair when Dad and Mom arrived.

They left at three thirty to do chores and returned at seven in the evening. We were surprised to see Dad's Aunt Grace and Uncle Fred walk into my room. The elderly couple, who lived in Monroe, saw my name in the hospital admissions published by their daily newspaper. They visited a few minutes and left.

The following day, Mom wrote a check to the hospital $93.30 and took me home.

Saturday morning I felt well enough to walk up the gravel driveway to get the mail out of the metal box at the side of the black-top road. In the afternoon, Dad and I delivered the apple pie Mom had baked for a ham supper at the Trinity Church.

My recovery didn't continue as Dr. Ekstam predicted. By Sunday night, my right side was so sore I couldn't lie down flat in bed. I slept propped up with two fat pillows taken from the studio couch in the basement. We assumed the healing and pulling of the stitches holding my incision together caused my discomfort.

Monday morning, Mom answered a summons for jury duty at the courthouse in Rockford. The judge excused her because of my illness and she returned home in time to prepare dinner.

As soon as we'd finished eating, we left for Brodhead. It had been a week since my operation and I wanted to be rid of my painful stitches. In Dr. Stovall's office, Lucille, his aide, led Mom and me to the examining room. I couldn't stifle a moan when I stretched out on the table.

The physician entered the room and greeted us. "How are you feeling?' he asked. "Awful," I growled.

He removed the large bandage from my abdomen and turned to his aide, "Look at this."

After seeing my stomach, the compassionate woman stepped behind my head, grabbed my hands and held them tightly.

The doctor explained, "Your inflamed appendix leaked a bit during surgery and you have an infection." He removed the stitches and squeezed out more than a cupful of disgusting gunk. It reminded me of popping an immense pimple. His ministration brought tears to my eyes, but I felt immediate relief when he finished. To make sure that I healed from the inside, the doctor packed the opening with strips of medicated gauze. During the following week, I returned to Dr. Stovall's office every day including Sunday to have him pull out the old gauze and push in new. I felt like a rag doll being stuffed.

By Wednesday morning, I was feeling much better. I begged, "Mom, please take me to school during the noon hour. I want to see the kids and get some of the assignments I need to make up."

She hesitated, "I'm not sure the mumps are over."

"Please, I haven't heard of anybody else getting sick."

Reluctantly, she agreed. We arrived at the high school at twelve fifteen. I slowly climbed the stairs to the study hall where students prepared for the afternoon session.

Kenny, who weathered mumps while he was in grade school, was part of the group that greeted me like a celebrity. The bell rang for classes and I stood alone like the cheese in the children's game, "The Farmer in the Dell." I gathered my geometry, civics and biology books to obtain assignments from the teachers. I exited the building and rejoined Mom who waited in the sedan to drive me home.

On Friday a little after noon, Kenny called to give me more geometry work. Our brief conversation gave me goose bumps.

Monday I was lying on the davenport when Kenny called again during his noon hour. My right side hurt too much for me to get up and talk to him.

In the afternoon, Dr. Stovall found more infection and phoned Dr. Ekstam to discuss the problem. After the consultation, my family physician again stuffed my incision with medicated gauze and recommended applying a heating pad. This renewed treatment continued for two more days and made me feel better.

With my recovery dragging on, I began worrying about the prom. Kenny already asked me to the dance 22 May, less than a month away. Dr. Stovall assured me I'd be dancing by then, but I wasn't convinced. Before my operation, the surgeon said I'd return to school after seven days, but, so far, a month had passed and I remained at home.

A week later, our family physician gave me vitamins and said, "You can go to school on Monday."

I could have jumped for joy, but I said, "That's good news," and sedately walked out of the office.

Monday morning, rejoining my friends in study hall was as sweet as eating cotton candy at the carnival. My English class spent my absence reading William Shakespeare's play, *Julius Caesar*. Mrs. Downing said I could just skip it because I was a good student. I heard taunts of "teacher's pet" from a few of the boys who hated the assignment, but I could live with that.

My typing teacher, Mr. Baker, wasn't as agreeable, which was no surprise. We didn't call him 'old stone face' for nothing. He insisted I complete all twenty five lessons I'd missed. I was thankful for my new portable so I could work at home.

Wednesday, Mom picked me up from school for my last appointment with Dr. Stovall. After a brief check-up, he said, "You can dance at the prom, but you should wait a month before you ride your horse." I practically danced out of the doctor's office. I could hardly wait for school the next day to give Kenny my good news.

My scar should have been a thin line six inches long. Instead, a dent remained in the middle where the gauze was pushed in and out. No bikini for me.

Back home, more jubilation—my driving permit arrived in the mail. Dad and Mom needed to prepare me to pass the state test for a license when I turned sixteen in four months.

Thursday morning when I saw Kenny in study hall, I greeted him with, "Dr. Stovall said I can dance at the prom."

Kenny grinned and responded, "That's great."

Friday, all of us music students began the school day on board a bus bound for Orangeville, another small town about twenty miles west of Durand. The schools' combined choruses and bands would rehearse during the day and present a joint concert in the evening.

Kenny and I spent the morning vocalizing with the mixed chorus. He sang bass and I was an alto. At noon, we all ate our sack lunches. In the afternoon, the band practiced. Kenny and I were free until time to ride the bus back to Durand at two thirty. He asked, "Would you like to go get an ice cream cone? There must be someplace downtown that sells ice cream."

Another couple, Duane and Margie, both dark haired, brown-eyed juniors, joined us. We walked several blocks from the school located in a residential neighborhood to the village's business district. The front window of a large grocery store exhibited a big white sign with blue letters advertising ice cream. We went inside where Kenny and I ordered double-dips of butterscotch ripple. The four of us licked our cones while strolling back to the school. In front of the building, we sat down on benches to enjoy the warm, sunny weather until time for the bus to leave.

In the evening, Kenny and I boarded the bus in Durand at six thirty to ride to Orangeville for the eight o'clock concert. The boys wore white shirts, ties and dark trousers. The girls wore white, long, sleeved blouses and dark skirts.

After the performance, the two of us snuggled together on a seat in the dark vehicle traveling back to Durand. Kenny tightened his right arm around my shoulders, leaned in close and asked, "Will you wear my class ring?"

"Yes," I quietly replied and grasped the big ring that he was holding in the palm of his left hand. I felt like shouting, "We're going steady," but that would have embarrassed both of us.

The next morning, I examined Kenny's large, ring in the light. The design was yellow, white and rose gold with black enamel trim that included his initials, KD. I wrapped the band with gobs of adhesive tape that I painted with pink fingernail polish to keep the material dry and odor free. When the polish was set, I slipped the ring on the slim, third finger of my left hand. Mom saw what I was doing, but neither one of us commented.

Monday morning, the ringing bell called the 101 high school students to their desks in study hall. Superintendent Paul G. Norsworthy stepped to the front of the room. PG, as everyone called him behind his back, was a middle-aged, bald-headed man with a fringe of brown hair circling the back of his head from ear to ear. He'd been in charge since my cousin, Sis, was a senior ten years ago. His gravelly growl easily carried to the farthest corners of the large room. First, he complimented the Friday night concert; then he cited the bad behavior exhibited by a few students during the day's rehearsal. "We have four people who went downtown in Orangeville during the afternoon instead of spending their time listening to the other performers. We are sorry to have juvenile delinquents spoiling our reputation at such an event."

I stared at my desk top as my face turned a few shades lighter than my Hot Pink lipstick. No names were mentioned, but I felt like everyone knew who we were. I'd never expected to be called a juvenile delinquent.

At noon, the four of us juvenile delinquents met on the balcony to eat our sack lunches. We were no longer embarrassed. We were just plain mad. Duane said, "PG didn't have to do that in front of study hall. He could have talked to us privately instead of making it a big deal in front of all of the other kids."

"You're right," said Kenny. "We didn't deliberately set out to break the rules.

Nobody told us Friday we had to stay at the school. This is the first we've heard that we did something wrong."

When we were in Orangeville, we'd assumed we were free to leave like we were at our home school. Sometimes during our lunch break, my friend, Esther, and I walked up town to buy a dime's worth of cinnamon balls at Bliss Grocery. Every noon, several senior boys stood on the sidewalk at the corner closest to the school grounds and smoked.

The rest of the week, I day dreamed about the Friday prom. Time crawled along as slowly as a boy on his way to the principal's office.

Thursday night, I washed my shoulder-length, dishwater blonde hair and wound it into fat curls held in place by bobby pins. Before I went to bed, I tied a bandana around my head turban-style to hold everything in place while I slept. In the morning, my hair was dry. I combed out the ringlets when I got ready for school. We didn't have a dress code but on Fridays, most of the girls wore jeans. I donned a short-sleeved, light blue shirt with my pants, white socks and brown loafers

During the day, juniors slipped in and out of the gym making final preparations to host the prom that would last from 9 P.M. to 1 A.M.

In the evening at home, I waited until after supper to take a bath and dress. Last February, I bought a medium-blue formal for the girls' chorus concert. A lace jacket with a stand-up collar and cap sleeves modestly covered the strapless, lace bodice. A matching, two-inch wide, lace border finished the bottom of the top layer of the double-tiered, tulle skirt. Taffeta lined the floor-length garment.

Kenny and I were double-dating with our best friends, Wayne and Esther, who were also going steady. Esther, a short, sturdy blonde with a few freckles, recently moved to a farm five miles east of town and enrolled in our sophomore class. She and I immediately hit it off. At eight thirty, the three of them pulled in with Wayne driving his dad's dark green '50 Ford.

Kenny wearing a light gray suit with a white carnation in his buttonhole entered our living room. He greeted the three of us and held out a small, white florist's box, "This is for you."

"Thank you." My hands trembled as I opened the carton and passed the corsage of red rosebuds to my mother. She stuck the long, sharp pin through the left shoulder of my dress and the flowers.

It was a balmy evening. I didn't need a jacket. If I felt a chill later, my boyfriend would keep me warm. As we went out the door, Mom's parting words were, "Remember, you're to be home by two o'clock."

I lifted the front of my dress as we crossed the porch, descended the wooden steps and followed the sidewalk to the Ford. Ken opened the rear door and we crawled into the sedan. A cigarette smell lingered because Wayne's parents were smokers. Popular songs played on the radio set to WGN. I stayed close beside my steady and he slipped his left arm around me. In the front, Esther snuggled next to Wayne. After exiting our driveway, he draped his right arm around his girlfriend's shoulders and used his left hand to navigate the blacktop road to Durand.

We entered the high school. Wayne bought a couple's ticket from Miss Reinebach, the science teacher who sat inside the booth on the landing beside the front door. Kenny didn't have to pay because the seniors and their dates were honored guests.

The eight-piece band led by Al Grace, a Rockford appliance salesman by day, began playing the prom's plaintive theme song, "Harbor Lights." Kenny took me in his arms and we danced cheek to cheek.

The gym resembled a seashore with a replica of a silver lighthouse in one corner.

Blue and white crepe paper streamers incased the area. Small, white, poster board anchors covered with silver glitter hung from strings attached to the false ceiling. Blue bulbs formed an arch around the front of the stage and created a haze.

At ten, the bright, overhead fluorescent lights were turned on for the crowning of the king, Marvin, the dark-haired, basketball team center, and his queen, Margie, the pretty, dark-haired, juvenile delinquent, who stood just above his shoulder. The two juniors led all of us in the grand march around the floor. A group of adults who purchased spectator tickets sat on the bleachers and admired the beautiful girls in their long dresses escorted by the handsome boys wearing suits and ties.

To allow plenty of time to comply with my 2 A.M. curfew, we left the dance at midnight to eat cheeseburgers at Tuckwood's in downtown Rockford, a half-hour's drive away. Customers crammed the wood-paneled restaurant, one of the few that remained open past midnight. We waited for a booth, waited for a busy waitress to take our orders and waited for our food. We ate quickly and piled back into the sedan. Wayne's car was about the only one on Highway 70 to Durand and the blacktop to our farm. He gripped the steering wheel with both hands and pushed the Ford as fast as he dared trying to get me home on time, but it was two fifteen when the car tires crunched the gravel in our driveway. As soon as Wayne stopped the sedan at the end of the sidewalk, Kenny popped open the rear door, stepped out and extended his right hand to me to exit. I lifted the front of my dress and we scurried along the sidewalk.

Standing beside the front steps, Kenny said a brief, "Goodnight," turned on his heel and strode rapidly back to the car.

I hoped he heard my "Goodnight and thank you."

I climbed the wooden steps, crossed the porch, entered the dark kitchen and made my way to my room. My parents were in bed and all was quiet.

Monday at school, Esther and I rehashed prom night. "Did you get in trouble for being late?" she asked.

"Yeah, Mom bawled me out the next morning. No big deal."

"I saw that Kenny didn't kiss you goodnight when he walked you to the door. Hasn't he kissed you yet?"

"No, he hasn't," I replied with a sigh.

A week later, my father was outside in his shirt sleeves doing evening chores when Tuffy, our white, English bulldog, barked. I looked out the kitchen window and saw Wayne driving his dad's Ford down our gravel lane with Kenny riding shotgun.

Wayne parked beside the barn. The surrounding outbuildings included a milk house, hog pen, machine shed, corn crib, granary, hen house, brooder house for baby chicks and a one-car garage with a tool shop attached. All of the wooden structures were painted red and trimmed in white.

The boys got out of the car and Wayne reached back inside to pick up his little black and white dog, Butchie. Tuffy started jumping at Wayne trying to get at the small animal. Wayne spun around and around protecting the pet in his arms. After several attempts, Dad grabbed Tuffy's collar, dragged him into the barn and shut the bottom half of the door. After a short visit, the guys drove out without stopping at the house. I was relieved that I didn't have to face them. Tuffy had embarrassed me. The dog was my best pal who listened to all of my secrets, but at that moment I'd have gladly given him away if anyone would have taken him.

On Thursday night, 4 June, rows of wooden, folding chairs lined the high school gym floor. Mom and I sat among the friends and relatives attending the graduation ceremony. At eight o'clock, the school band began playing "Pomp and Circumstance." Everyone stood up. Kenny and twenty of his classmates wearing shiny, royal blue caps and gowns promenaded down the center aisle two by two. The boys and girls took their places in chairs waiting for them on the stage. Following speeches by the salutatorian, the valedictorian and the superintendent, the school board president gave each senior a diploma and a handshake. The graduates filed out and formed a receiving line near the exit. On our way out, Mom and I shook hands and congratulated each of the boys and girls.

The following Wednesday night, I met Kenny at the free show in the park. He'd turned into a typical working man smoking a cigarette and bragging about his job. "Monday I started at Barber Colman. I'll be making about sixty dollars a week operating a machine. I'd applied before school was out and was hired. I knew it was a good place because a lot of people from Durand were employed there. I didn't want to go to the same factory where my folks worked."

I told him about my job offer. "Frances, who used to ride our school bus, stopped last Monday. She asked me to spend the summer taking care of her baby boy while she worked in a Freeport factory. I thought it sounded like fun, a chance to be a grown-up.

Mom said no. I wasn't surprised. I heard that word a lot."

The next day, Mom supervised my driving our Chevy to Brodhead for my first appointment with Dr. Hanson, whose dental office was upstairs over the bank on the corner of the two main streets. When the young dentist opened his practice a year ago, my mother was one of first patients. She said, "He'll give Novocain shots to fill teeth. I didn't have one because I don't like having my mouth numb afterwards."

I immediately decided to go to him for my next check-up. If I needed a tooth filled, I'd take a shot.

In the past, my parents and I went to gray-haired, Dr. Frame in Durand. He and another dentist, Dr. Young, shared quarters upstairs over Tallackson's Grocery. He only used Novocain to pull teeth. For fillings, he would adjust his fat belly over the arm of the chair, growl, "This might hurt a bit," and bear down with the drill for what seemed like hours. He was right—it hurt but I never flinched.

I brushed my teeth twice a day and didn't gorge on candy, but every summer the dentist found cavities. If men chose wives like old-timers bought horses, checking their teeth to be sure they were getting a good deal, I would probably be an old maid.

Dr. Hanson x-rayed my teeth, which was never done before. A short time later, the tall, brown haired young man who wore glasses showed me the films on a light box. "You have decay under all of your fillings. They will all have to be removed and redone. Otherwise, you will lose your teeth."

It took five appointments and just over a hundred dollars for him to replace all of my old fillings. Thank heavens for the local anesthetic. After the shot, I sat in the dental chair gripping the arm rests and sweating while I waited for the pain that never came.

What a dreadful way to spend the summer.

The day after my first dental appointment, Kenny rode down our driveway astride his new wheels, a metallic green 1937 Harley Davidson model 61. Only five other young men in our community owned motorcycles.

Kenny told about trading in his first auto, a black 1940 Chevy coupe. "Oil was dripping out of the car so fast that I had to pay a hundred dollars to boot. Can you go for a ride?"

"Just a minute. I'll have to go in the house and ask Mom." I crossed my fingers, but I expected a firm no.

Mom surprised us both when she reluctantly said, "I guess it's alright."

Before my mother changed her mind, I tied a head scarf over my hair, ran out the door, climbed on behind Kenny and grabbed the rear edges of the large seat with both hands. He pulled down his black motorcycle cap with the white bill and we roared off. Whizzing along the blacktop roads with the wind blowing past was thrilling.

A few weeks later, Kenny traded the Harley for a robin's egg blue, 1947 Indian Chief. We took several rides that summer, but none was as memorable as the balmy, Thursday night in mid-August when he unexpectedly brought me home from the free show. I wore neither a headscarf nor a jacket. Goose pimples popped up on my bare arms when we passed through the cool spot where the blacktop ran between the Laona Forest Preserve and the farmer-owned woods. Tree limbs from opposite sides met overhead creating a leafy tunnel that the sun never penetrated. It felt like it was air-conditioned. A couple miles later, Kenny turned down our gravel drive, coasted to a stop at the end of the front sidewalk, switched off his machine and lowered the kick stand. I swung my right leg over the bike to get off and he followed. He walked me to the front steps and paused. He wrapped his left arm around me, lifted my chin with his right hand, softly kissed me and said, "Good night."

His lips tasted slightly smoky with an overlay of mint. He always carried a package of Wrigley's Doublemint chewing gum in one shirt pocket and his Pall Malls in the other. For the second time that evening, goose pimples popped up on my arms. I responded with, "Good night."

He turned on his heel, returned to his cycle and roared up the driveway.

I felt like a fluffy cloud floating up the wooden steps, across the porch and through the kitchen. In my bedroom, I clicked on the pin-up lamp attached to the wall above the mirror on my dresser. My wind whipped, shoulder-length hair looked like a tangled hay stack. I beamed at my reflection while carefully combing out the snarls. At last, I could tell Esther, Kenny kissed me.

On Wednesday, Friday and Saturday nights during the summer, Kenny played softball with the Merchants team. The men wore fire-engine-red uniforms with Durand in large black letters on the chest and the name of a sponsoring business in smaller black letters across the shoulders in the back. Hundreds of people turned out to watch the seven-inning games at the Legion Field, which was located south of the business district and east of Highway 70. Some fans arrived early and sat in their cars parked along the baselines. Others squeezed together along the wooden planks on the metal-framed bleachers placed behind the players' bench. A woven wire fence protected them from errant balls.

Kenny, who'd been a good high school athlete, was in awe of these fellows who were seasoned, league players and war veterans. Sports reporter Charles "Buzz" Stauffer's accolades in the Thursday, 20 August, edition of the weekly *Durand Gazette* made him feel like he belonged. Stauffer wrote, "One of the brightest spots in the local's recent victories has been the terrific fielding play of rookie Kenny Ditzler. The youngster, playing his first season with the Merchants, has amazed veteran observers with his flawless play in the infield. Equally adept at second, short or third, Ditzler promises to be one of the smoothest performers in Durand's fine array of fielding talent."

After that ego boost, Kenny took me to several games. He nosed his parents' green Nash along the third base line close to him in the field.

The Merchants ended the season with 18 wins and only 7 losses. More impressive was their 16 to 3 record against the Rockford teams.

On the last night of August, my folks and I went to the Robin Drive-in Theater at the west edge of Rockford to see *The Moon Is Blue.* I was surprised because my parents didn't usually go to an outdoor and the romantic comedy was raising eyebrows across the nation with its light treatment of seduction and illicit sex. I thought my parents might consider the movie too risqué. I was glad the car was dark so no one could see my red face from time to time.

School started the next day. I bragged to my classmates that I'd just seen *The Moon Is Blue*. As part of my brief synopsis of the show, I said, "Instead of the usual euphemisms, the men and women came right out and said words like virgin and pregnant." My friends were impressed, especially the Catholic kids because the Pope admonished his followers to boycott the film.

With the temperature soaring close to a hundred degrees, P.G. dismissed school early Tuesday, Wednesday and Thursday.

Thursday night when Dad and I drove home from the last free show of the season, we saw streaks of lightning and heard the rumble of distant thunder. After I was in bed, I could hear the much needed rain pounding the window panes. The hot spell was broken.

When I woke up Friday morning, I was sixteen, a milestone. I could obtain my driver's license. I smiled at my reflection in my dresser mirror. The phrase, sweet sixteen and never been kissed, didn't apply to me. At the breakfast table, I blew out the sixteen pink candles on the white bakery cake decorated with pink roses and the words, Happy Birthday Lolita.

My parents gave me a pair of rust-colored heels and a small purse to match. I also received a denim purse from Uncle Hookie and Aunt Frannie plus a star bracelet from Doris. Grandma and Grandpa Tschabold sent a card with a dollar inside.

In the evening, Kenny picked me up to go to his ball game. "Happy birthday," he said as he came in the front door. "I'm sorry, but you'll have to wait until tomorrow for your gift."

We found the ball diamond too wet to use. Kenny stopped at home to change out of his red uniform and we went to a movie in Beloit.

Saturday night Kenny brought me a box of candy, two hankies and a card. "I'm sorry I'm a day late," he said. "But I needed my day off to shop."

We went to a show in Rockford with Wayne and Esther. Shortly after that, they broke up. She continued to be my best friend, but she never confided what happened between them.

After Labor Day, I settled into a daily routine of school classes. I'd included Home Economics III in my schedule. The single-period, sixth-hour class taught family living, not the cooking and sewing I'd hated during my freshman year. Every afternoon, nine junior and senior girls crossed the street to the modern, home ec. room located in the beige, brick, single-story, grade school. We sat in straight chairs gathered around a blonde-wood table to discuss our future homes. One of the seniors, Mary Helen, was engaged. All of us expected to marry and become housewives.

Our instructor, Mrs. Luepkes, was the divorced mother of a nine-year-old daughter. Black, horn-rimmed glasses matched her hair and added sternness to the face of the tall, slender woman. She educated us about budgeting, buying furniture and maintaining a well-run household.

The teacher understood that we were too modest to mention our curiosity about the physical relationship between a husband and a wife. She encouraged us to write those questions on slips of paper and drop them into the box she placed in the middle of the table. Her answers during class were our only sex education.

Sex wasn't talked about much during the fifties, especially at our house. When Kenny and I started dating last March, Mom's terse words were, "Nice girls don't and you're a nice girl."

Young women were expected to set limits. In movies, the ingénue snapped, "Fresh!" and slapped the face of a young man with 'Roman hands' and "Russian fingers'. My girlfriends and I never discussed 'going all the way'.

Birth control for teens was a taboo subject, except for boys' crude jokes about 'rubbers', their slang for condoms. Doctors provided information about the rhythm method of contraception and prescriptions for diaphragms only to wives. Abortion was illegal.

Although sex wasn't a topic for conversation, it happened and often created a problem. Some people considered pregnancy the punishment for the single gal who didn't say, "No."

The common solution was a 'shotgun wedding'. Most high school classes lost at least one female to matrimony and motherhood before graduation. The young man, who was usually older than his student girlfriend, either farmed with his father or worked in a Rockford factory. He could support a family and was expected to do the right thing.

During our sophomore year, Shirley, my best friend since seventh grade, was forced to quit high school because the cute, blonde, tomboy was 'expecting'. In June, the newspaper's daily record stated Shirley, fifteen, and her farmer boyfriend, Frankie, nineteen, obtained a marriage license.

Shirley's nuptials shook me up. I'd just started dating, but she was a wife and soon-to-be mother. I made up my mind right then that I would not give my future husband the chance to say in anger, "I never would have married you if I didn't have to."

About a month after school started, that old, green-eyed monster, jealousy, invaded my life. On a Friday afternoon, I sat alone on the bottom row of bleachers waiting for the others in eighth hour p. e. I loved sports and usually enjoyed gym class, but we were playing soccer, which I called 'sock her'. I hated getting kicked in the shins.

I'd changed into tennis shoes, and the uniform we all wore—blue shorts and white, short-sleeved shirt. I'd used blue thread to embroider 'Lolita' on the breast pocket of my top.

The first girl out of the locker room was Maggie, a chatty sophomore, who plopped down beside me. "I don't know if I should tell you this," she confided, "but at lunch today I heard Kenny Ditzler's interested in my classmate, Gloria."

My stomach clenched. All I could say was, "Oh."

I'd worn Kenny's class ring since May, but our last date was the night after my birthday, a month ago. It'd been nearly two weeks since the Saturday afternoon he'd rode his motorcycle down our driveway and chatted with me for a few minutes. I was mentally dissecting Kenny's last visit when I heard Miss Elsner say my name during rollcall. I responded, "Here."

We counted off, "One, two, one, two." As we ran outside, the teacher handed all of us twos a red pinny to tie over our white shirts to distinguish the teams. We lined up on the grass and kicked off.

It was a warm, sunny, fall day, but a cloud of gloom clung to me like B.O. I traipsed up and down the field like a sheep with the flock. My thoughts of Kenny were interrupted when a girl yelled, "Lili, get it!"

Hearing my nickname jerked my mind back to the game. I looked down, spotted the black and white ball in front of me and gave it a boot with the side of my right foot.

Finally, Miss Elsner blew her whistle and called, "Showers."

We all ran inside. I didn't know which team won or if anyone bothered keeping score.

While dressing, I pondered my situation. I believed in confronting a problem head on. I needed to talk to Kenny right away, but I didn't dare phone him. In the fifties, it was a hard and fast rule that girls didn't call boys. I thought of a plan. My friend, Corky, was Kenny's cousin so the taboo didn't apply to her. I climbed the stairs to the front door and stood outside. Soon the bell rang ending our school day. Corky exited the building. I beckoned her aside, "Would you please call Kenny after he gets home from work and ask him to come and see me tonight?"

"Yeah, I can do that," she replied. "I'll call you if he can't come." She walked down the sidewalk toward her house.

I boarded my bus. During the ride home, I thought about peeling the tape off of Kenny's ring and wearing it on a chain around my neck in case he wanted it back, but I couldn't make myself do that. I hoped Maggie had heard an ugly rumor.

About four thirty, the bus dropped me off and I entered the empty house. Dad and Mom were doing chores. In anticipation of seeing Kenny later, I didn't change into my everyday jeans and shirt but continued wearing my gray straight skirt and harmonizing sweater. I turned on the radio but I didn't pay attention to the music. I listened intently for the phone NOT to ring with a call from Corky. I sat down in Mom's easy chair and read the Rockford newspaper, but I couldn't have passed a test on the articles.

Mom came in from milking, washed up and started supper. She placed a pan of water on a black coil burner atop the white electric stove to cook a package of macaroni. She then chopped an onion and opened a can of tomato soup while a pound of hamburger browned in the large, cast iron skillet sitting on the large, front burner. When the ingredients to make slumgullion were cooked, she mixed them together in the frying pan. I set the table. Dad entered the kitchen and we all sat down at the oil-cloth covered table and ate. The knot in my stomach left little room for macaroni and hamburger. After the meal, Mom washed the dishes. I dried them and put them in the cupboard. That was usually a time for intimate discussions, but I didn't want to tell Mom about my problem. All I said was, "Kenny's coming out tonight."

It was six thirty when we joined my father in the living room. Mom picked up the newspaper, turned the floor lamp brighter and sat down in her comfortable chair to read. I plopped down on the davenport beside Dad to listen to the radio. The "William Tell Overture" faded and the announcer intoned, "Return with us now to those thrilling days of yesteryear. From out of the past come the thundering hoof beats of the great horse Silver. The Lone Ranger rides again."

I watched the clock on the wall and clicked the nails on my thumb and middle finger of my left hand while impatiently waiting for time to pass. At seven, the Lone Ranger rode off with a hearty "Hi Yo Silver." Ditzlers' green Nash pulled in the driveway.

I jumped up, flipped on the outside light and stood looking out the glass in the front door. Optimism and dread alternated through my mind like petals being plucked from a daisy. When I saw Kenny walking up the sidewalk, I stepped out onto the porch to say privately, "Hi. Can we go for a ride?"

He replied, "Sure."

We entered the house and he greeted my parents while I put on my short, light-blue coat. We then walked out the sidewalk to the sedan. It was a peaceful, starry evening but my stomach churned like a tornado. Kenny opened the passenger door for me. I sat down on the end of the bench seat and stayed there instead of sliding over to the middle like I usually did. He climbed in behind the wheel, drove down to the garage to turn around, proceeded out the gravel drive and turned east on the blacktop road.

I'd said nothing. My mouth was dry. This wasn't going to be easy.

"What's up?" Kenny asked.

I breathed deeply, swallowed and blurted out, "I heard at school today that you're interested in Gloria."

He replied, "You know there's nobody for me but you. Come here."

I slid over beside him. He circled my shoulders with his right arm and pulled me closer. The tightness in my stomach began to relax. I said, "I've only seen you once since we went out for my birthday over a month ago. You can see why I was worried."

Kenny explained, "I don't like to keep asking Dad to borrow the car in case something would happen to it. He needs it to go to work every day. Tomorrow I'm going to buy my own car. Then things will be different."

After a short ride, Kenny took me home. We lingered in the Ambassador necking and listening to the radio for a few minutes. He walked me to the door, kissed me goodnight, turned on his heel and returned to the sedan. I bounded up the wooden steps and into the house. Relief bubbled inside me like an Alka-Seltzer.

Sunday afternoon, Kenny and Wayne pulled in the driveway to show off his new automobile. I exited the house to admire his car. He opened the driver's door. The floor lights inside were red instead of white and the gear shift lever was on the steering column.

Before turning off the key, Kenny goosed the gas pedal and the engine rumbled with power. The motor featured a split manifold with dual-exhausts and Royal Scot glass pack mufflers. Teenage boys required speed. "How fast will it go?" was the common question. Racing on rural roads was the popular recreation.

On Saturday, my boyfriend visited 'used car row' in Rockford and purchased a 1947 medium-blue, two-door, Plymouth convertible with a white canvass top, fender skirts, white sidewall tires and chrome, moon hubcaps. All of the chrome was stripped from the car body except for the two door handles and the grill. The rear had been lowered, the trunk leaded in and large springs installed to keep the lid closed. The red tail light lenses were centered with blue dots. Kenny said, "See you later," and left.

I expected him to come back alone to give me a ride. In the evening, I stayed home from Luther League at Bethlehem Church in Brodhead, but he never showed up. Apparently, I'd misunderstood, but I still fumed to myself. I deserved a ride.

By Wednesday afternoon, I'd cooled off when Kenny came to ask me to go to the senior class play, *We Shook the Family Tree*, on Friday night. He usually stopped by to make dates instead of phoning. At his house, the telephone sat on a stand between the kitchen and the living room. Ours was on the desk in the corner of the kitchen. Both were attached to party lines.

Saturday, my folks and I went shopping in Beloit for needed winter things. In McNeany's, an upscale department store, I fell in love with a blue, three-quarter length, all-weather surcoat with a fake fur collar. Mom refused to buy it saying, "Twenty-two dollars and ninety-five cents is too much money."

We checked several other stores, but nothing else struck my fancy. "Please, can't I have that coat I saw at McNeany's?"

Once in a while, my mother spoiled her only child. She reluctantly replied. "Well, I guess you can get it."

A week later, Kenny rode his Indian motorcycle down our gravel driveway and stopped at the end of the sidewalk. A guy I didn't recognize was hanging on behind him on the large seat. The two got off the machine and stood beside it. I grabbed a jacket and strolled out to talk with them. My heart beat a little faster as I greeted my boyfriend with a kiss. He wore a black leather jacket, jeans, black engineer boots and a black, motorcycle cap with a white bill. He looked like he stepped off a movie poster for Marlon Brando's outlaw biker film, *The Wild Ones.*

Kenny introduced his companion as Wayne's cousin, Billy, a good-looking guy with black hair, brown eyes and a slim build. He and his mother recently moved from their home in Rockford to an upstairs apartment in Durand. His father had been killed in an accident while working for the railroad.

Billy already asked my friend, Esther, to see a movie in the evening. Kenny and I made plans to double date with them.

The following week, Kenny changed hours from days to the second shift at Barber Colman working 5 P.M. to 2 A.M. Sunday through Thursday nights. The new schedule provided more money in his paycheck and fewer bosses looking over his shoulder. As an added bonus, my boyfriend could drive me home after school before he left for Rockford. Every afternoon, I sat hip to hip beside him on the bench seat in his blue convertible. He wrapped his right arm around me while he steered with his left hand.

At stop signs, we worked together to change gears without disturbing our cuddling. He handled the footwork alternating the gas pedal and brake with his right and clutching with his left. I rested my left hand on his thigh and used my right to move the gear shift on the steering column from high to low, up to second and finally back down to third.

The drafty, canvas top didn't keep out all of the cold, November weather, but the heater kept us warm in the front seat. In the back, snow leaked in around the rear window and remained a white line along the top of the maroon cloth upholstery.

On the first Saturday night in December, I was ready to step into the bathtub when I heard our long and a short ring on the party line. With nobody else in the house, I wrapped myself in a towel to go to the kitchen. When I answered the phone, it was Donna, a bubbly, senior with light brown hair, snapping brown eyes, a few freckles and a slight lisp. After the usual preliminaries, she said, "Billy and I are going to the show with you guys. What are you going to wear?"

"I'm wearing my dark green, straight skirt, ivory, short-sleeved sweater, black suede flats and nylons." I'd have to keep the seams straight that ran up the backs of my legs, but we all made extra effort when we prepared for a date. The guys wore dress slacks instead of their everyday jeans.

When the boys picked me up first, Billy was driving his '52 green and ivory Mercury. I slipped into the middle of the front bench seat and Kenny followed. On the way to Rockford, we stopped at Donna's house along Highway 70. While Billy went inside to meet the parents, Kenny and I moved from the front seat to the back. When Billy opened the front, passenger door for Donna, the dome light came on and she exchanged greetings with us before concentrating her attention on Billy, who slid in behind the wheel. We were off to Rockford to see a movie followed by cheeseburgers at Tuckwood's restaurant. On the way back to Durand, we stopped at Donna's house. With this their first date, Billy escorted her to the door, said a quick farewell and returned to the sedan. At my home, Kenny immediately walked me to the door, kissed me goodnight and returned to the Mercury. He didn't want to keep Billy waiting.

Two days before Christmas, Kenny brought presents for all of us—a gold locket for me, a Desert Flower cologne set for Mom and a necktie for Dad. I gave my boyfriend a blue, corduroy shirt.

On Christmas Eve, Mom served our ham supper by candlelight to make the evening more festive for the three of us. I was the only one with gifts under the decorated tree in the living room. My parents gave me a new Revised Standard Version Bible, an alarm clock and thirty dollars. I planned to use the money to buy a tailored, white shirt, bedroom slippers and my class ring. Dad and Mom each had thirty dollars to spend, too, but so far they hadn't bought anything.

After I'd opened my presents, we played Pitch, a fast, card game that works well three-handed. To make it more competitive, we each tossed ten cents a game and a nickel a set into a pot. I ended up the big winner with a dollar-seventy-five.

Christmas Day, we followed our new tradition, eating the free turkey dinner with a group of strangers at the Cozy Inn in Beloit, donating to the Salvation Army and seeing a movie. In the evening, we drove through Brodhead, Beloit and Rockton admiring outdoor, lighted, Christmas displays.

Tuesday morning we went to Rockford so I could finally take my driver's test. The Secretary of State's facility was located in the lower level of the Illinois National Guard Armory on North Main Street. I passed the written test and the examiner riding in our Chevy with me approved my driving. I left the concrete building as a licensed driver, but nothing changed at home. In the evening, Dad dropped me off in front of the grade school for the basketball game the same as always. He didn't want his little girl driving alone at night.

New Year's Eve, while Dad and Mom milked, I bathed and put on my white, lace blouse, black, ballerina length, taffeta, circle skirt, nylons and black suede, flats to go to the Wigwam to celebrate.

At the dance, Willabea and her parents joined us after missing several weeks. Her father suffered a heart attack, but he'd recovered. I greeted Willabea with, "It's great to see you and your folks again."

She responded, "Thanks. It was scary for a while when Dad went to the hospital, but he's doing good now."

The evening was back to normal with Willabea, Janice, Joyce and me dancing and greeting 1954 wearing paper hats and blowing cardboard horns.

Chapter 3

1954

New Year's afternoon at one o'clock, I'd just washed my hair when Kenny unexpectedly pulled in our gravel driveway. I wanted to hide in my room, but I wrapped a towel around my wet head and waited inside the front door to greet him. The bright sunshine melted the icicles hanging from the front porch roof and they dripped on the wooden steps. Kenny timed his move beneath them so the icy water didn't slide down the back of his neck. He entered the living room and asked, "Do you want to go ice skating down behind Derwents'?"

"Sure I do," I replied. I wore jeans, a sweater and loafers. I tucked my damp hair under a stocking cap before bundling up in my jacket, mittens and boots. I grabbed my white, shoe skates and an extra pair of heavy socks. Kenny and I both climbed into the blue convertible from the driver's side.

About five miles southeast of Durand on Highway 70, he wheeled into Tom Derwent's long, gravel lane. The Plymouth crept past the barn and through the snow-covered pasture to the frozen backwater of the Pecatonica River. My boyfriend parked beside Billy's Mercury. With the Plymouth's doors open, we sat on opposite ends of the bench seat to remove our shoes and boots and put on our skates. We then made our way across the snow-covered grass to the edge of the pond. It wasn't a dangerous place. If we broke through the ice, we'd only get wet feet. Wayne, Billy, his girlfriend, Donna, and her best friend, Mary Ann, skated over to greet us.

Mary Ann and I had been schoolmates since I entered the fourth grade at Putnam country school where she was a fifth grader. Her parents came from Sweden, but she didn't resemble a typical, blonde Swede. She was big boned and chubby with dark hair and a dark complexion like her dad.

Ken and I joined the others on the ice. We all skated until about four o'clock when the sun and the temperature began sinking.

Ten days later, Dad and Mom allowed me to stay home alone after dark for the first time. I was sixteen years old and a junior in high school. I stood behind a kitchen window and swelled with maturity while watching my parents' Chevy climb the gravel driveway. They were subbing at a neighbor's Five Hundred card club, which included a potluck supper.

I was queen of the realm for the next five hours, but I didn't do anything out of the ordinary. I locked the doors like we always did, although there was nothing to be afraid of on a winter night in the country. I opened my old standby, a red and white can of Campbell's tomato soup, dumped it into a white enamel saucepan, added a can of milk and heated the mixture on the white electric stove.

After eating at the kitchen table and washing my meager dishes in the sink, I settled down in Mom's comfortable chair in the living room to listen to the radio.

Dragnet's Sgt. Joe Friday intoned, "Ladies and gentlemen, the story you are about to hear is true. Only the names have been changed to protect the innocent." After the cops caught the bad guy, I laughed when Fibber McGee opened his chaotic closet. To finish my evening, I turned to WGN's Saxie Dowell, a former 'big band' leader turned disc jockey. I was in bed asleep by the time my parents returned home.

One of the biggest influences in my life was something that didn't happen–I didn't have siblings, which made me an anomaly. When I started riding a yellow school bus to seventh grade in the newly created Durand Junior High, each of my thirty-three classmates had at least one brother or sister.

I was an only child by chance, not choice. Mom noted in her Bible the death of a baby boy born prematurely 20 October 1943. I remembered staying with Aunt Frannie for several days while my mother was in the hospital. When Dad came to pick me up, he conferred briefly with his sister-in-law. He then sat down beside me on the black frieze davenport in their living room. He put his arm around me and said, "The baby died." Tears slid down his cheeks. I'd never seen my father cry before. I wept with him because I was looking forward to having a brother or sister to play with. I put on my coat and we told my aunt, "Good-bye and thank you." He picked up my suitcase and drove us home.

In the living room, Mom, dressed in pajamas, robe and slippers, sat in her beige easy chair with her feet up on the brown hassock. Although I was a big girl of six, I climbed into her lap and curled up. She wrapped her arms around me and we grieved in silence.

At that time, parents were expected to bury their nameless child without a church service or a mourning period to acknowledge their loss. They were advised to have another baby. A year later, our family suffered a similar sorrow. Mom wrote in her Bible, a baby boy born dead 17 October 1944.

The problem was the Rh factor in my parents' blood. My mother was negative and my father was positive. That rarely caused trouble in a first pregnancy, but subsequent babies could suffer illness, brain damage or death.

I knew the advantages of being an only child. I didn't have to share my things and I didn't have to compete with anyone for my parents' attention. At times, I would have liked less attention. I considered myself over-protected.

An example occurred about a month later. My parents attached a spotlight above the door to the screened-in porch that ran along the east side of the house. The fixture was aimed at the end of the front sidewalk where Kenny always parked when he brought me home from a date. If I lingered in the car talking, listening to the radio and necking longer than my mother thought I should, that light popped on to glare in our faces.

With Easter approaching, spring clothing ads dominated the newspapers, but we didn't buy new outfits to wear to church. Instead, Dad purchased a bright orange, Allis Chalmers WD 45 tractor with a mounted three-bottom plow and a John Deere green, two-row, corn planter. When it came to spending money, rural people believed the farm came before the family.

Two days later, Mom and I prepared to start the evening milking while Dad finished plowing a field using the new equipment. When we heard him pull the tractor into the machine shed, we expected to see him enter the barn at any minute. Instead we heard him holler, "I need some help out here."

The two of us ran to the open door and saw Dad faint. He dropped to the ground just outside with his head barely missing a stray, cement block lying beside the barn's limestone foundation. I stood frozen with fear. Mom dashed into the milk house, grabbed the enamel drinking cup hanging from a nail on the wall, scooped it full of cold water from the tank, rushed back to where Dad lay and threw the water in his face.

He regained consciousness sputtering, "What the hell did you do that for?"

I grabbed the towel hanging on a nail in the milk house and handed it to him so he could wipe his face.

Dad explained, "I was climbing down off the tractor when I slipped and fell. I banged my leg on the sharp edge of the plow."

Mom pulled up his torn overalls to check his right leg. "It looks to me like that cut should have some stiches."

Mom drove us to Brodhead. Dad sat in the passenger seat and held the towel against his bleeding cut. I took my usual place in the Chevy's back seat. Fortunately, Dr. Stovall remained in his office and sewed up the gash on Dad's shin.

Farmers rarely took sick time, but once in a while it was necessary. When we returned home, Dad went in the house to rest while Mom and I did chores. We finished by carrying the three cans of milk out of the barn to the tank in the milk house. She and I each grabbed one of the handles on opposite sides of each eighty-pound container and lifted with all of the strength we could muster.

The following day, I told Kenny about Dad's fall. When he brought me home the next afternoon, he accompanied me into the living room and asked my parents, "Is there anything I can do to help you tomorrow before I have to go to work?"

"Thanks for the offer," Dad replied. "But we're getting along okay."

Saturday morning, Dad was back on the new Allis-Chalmers to spread fertilizer across a plowed and disked field where he would plant corn. I followed with the old, orange tractor pulling the drag, a spring-tooth harrow that smoothed the soil over the fertilizer.

On Sunday, 25 April, at 2 A.M., Daylight Saving Time began and would continue until Sunday, 26 September, at 2 A.M. In Illinois, each community decided whether to change from slow time to fast time during the warm weather. Zones differed from one town's limits to the next. When we entered a municipality, the first thing we did was find a clock to see what time it was there.

In Rockford, a factory city, clocks were turned ahead an hour to give workers extra daylight in the afternoon. Durand remained on standard time to accommodate the area's rural residents who labored according to the sun. We were in sync with neighboring Wisconsin. America's Dairyland banned daylight time because moving the clock upset the states large number of milk cows.

Rockford's change ended Kenny's driving me home from school. His carpool with his buddy, Billy, and classmate, Dick, left Durand an hour earlier to arrive at work on time.

Monday at the end of the day, I climbed aboard the yellow bus. I wasn't used to the hilly and curvy roads the afternoon route followed and ended up with motion sickness. I missed Kenny in more ways than one.

On Thursday and Friday nights of the first week in May, after two months of practice each weeknight, my class presented the annual junior play. In March, our English teacher, Miss Mallow, a petite, young woman with light brown hair and a big nose, chose the comedy, *Just Ducky*. She conducted tryouts for the cast and selected twelve of our twenty-five class members. I was the only one who wanted to be Vester

Blayne, the lovelorn columnist for the daily newspaper. To look like a journalist on stage, I wore my maroon suit and borrowed a pair of eyeglasses. Fifteen years later, I became a reporter for a daily newspaper.

Our friends and families filled the wooden folding chairs set up in the gym. Each night when the curtains opened, we tensely listened for the crowd's first laugh to assure us the production was a success. After the final scene, the group's vigorous applause brought us back for a curtain call.

After Friday's presentation, the cast and their dates, including Kenny who was in the audience, drove to The Amberwood restaurant in South Beloit to celebrate. When we invaded the eatery, the staff pushed tables together to accommodate the nineteen teenagers. Most of us ordered a cheeseburger and a Coke.

When the waitress brought our food, Don, a tall, thin, dark haired, senior who was Carole's steady, looked at his plate, turned to his girlfriend and whispered. Our attractive classmate offered the sandwich to the other fellows saying, "Do any of you guys want this? Don meant to order a grilled cheese, but he made a mistake and said cheeseburger. Catholics can't eat meat on Friday." She easily found a taker.

The incident reminded me that I'd made up my mind a long time ago to never date a Catholic boy. It was a foregone conclusion in our community that if a Protestant woman married a Catholic man, she'd convert to his religion. As a Lutheran, I could never go along with their beliefs.

The following Friday night, Kenny and I strolled into the underwater scene of the prom with the theme "Limelight." All of us juniors spent three days covering the gym walls and creating a false ceiling with crepe paper streamers in various shades of blue and green. Round, yellow fish and long, green fish cut from construction paper and hung from strings looked like they were swimming above us. The band began to play the theme song, "Limelight," and I slipped into Kenny's arms for our first dance cheek to cheek.

I felt like a fashion model. Two months earlier, my cousin, Doris, said, "Do you want to go shopping in Chicago to get a prom dress? That way you won't walk into the dance and see somebody else wearing the same thing."

"What a great idea!"

On a chilly Monday morning in March before the sun was out of bed, Doris and I boarded a train in Rockford. By the time we arrived in the Windy City, it was daylight, but the tall buildings blocked the sun. While waiting for the stores to open at nine o'clock, we sat in a coffee shop and ate donuts for an hour-and-a-half.

I'd heard a lot about Marshall Field's department store, which covered a city block in The Loop. Before we entered, we walked around the outside looking at the displays in their large windows. After meandering through the various departments, we ate the classic Mrs. Herring's Chicken Pot Pie in their world-famous Walnut Room on the seventh floor. We moved on to the other large downtown department store, Carson

Pirie Scott's. Although the two emporiums were impressive, I saw no garment that I thought was worth the price.

In a nearby dress shop, I fell in love with a pink, strapless, taffeta lined formal with a double layered net, ballerina length skirt. A ruffle and imitation pearls edged the heart-shaped, lace bodice. Later at home, Mom sewed the matching net stole to the top of my dress so it covered my shoulders without my hanging onto it all of the time.

Dad and Mom joined us on the dance floor. They were among the junior class parents who accepted the invitation to attend as honored guests. My mother wore a new, street-length, beige and yellow print dress made of Bemberg, an imitation silk. Our escorts, who wore carnation boutonnieres, provided rosebud corsages matching our dresses. Mom took pictures using the new color film for the first time.

After the dance, our classmate, Joy, invited all juniors and their dates for refreshments at her farm home on Highway 75 southwest of town. Sandwiches made with ground baloney or tuna fish, chips, white cake with white frosting, punch, nuts and mints were arrayed on a white, lace cloth that covered the wooden, dining room table. We filled stiff, paper plates and held them in our laps after finding seats in the carpeted living room or dining room.

Joy's parents, who were quite religious, were even stricter with their daughter than mine were with me. For example, the slender, blonde couldn't enhance her pale complexion with make-up. She was allowed to date their neighbor, Jim, who had dark hair and brown eyes. The tallest girl and the tallest guy in our class made a striking couple.

The following Tuesday evening, I was one of twenty members of the Girls Athletic Association playing our final softball game of the year on the high school diamond. The club's twice a week meetings after school provided the only sports offered to females. Afterward, we served a white cake with white frosting inscribed with the words 'Good Luck Miss Elsner' in pink icing. It was a surprise farewell for our adviser, who was leaving after teaching P.E. for two years. The short, plump, active young woman who lived in shorts was my favorite. I hated to lose her.

Later in the week, Esther suggested that we cook supper Saturday night for our boyfriends. She was dating Dick, a classmate with dark curly hair and a few freckles. He wore glasses and was only a few inches taller than she was.

Early that afternoon, Mom dropped me off at my friend's farm home to help prepare the meal. We chose a basic menu: roast beef, roasted potatoes and carrots, gravy, a tossed salad, chocolate cake with chocolate frosting and glasses of ice water. I enjoyed cooking when I didn't have a teacher looking over my shoulder.

The boys arrived at five as we specified. While they sat in gray, upholstered chairs in the carpeted, living room and visited, we panicked in the kitchen. All was going well until I attempted to make gravy. I stood on the linoleum floor in front of their white, gas stove and stirred vigorously, but the gravy in the cast iron skillet continued to look like I thickened it with gravel. As a last resort, Esther added a little more milk to thin the liquid so she could pour it through a strainer sitting over a large dish standing on the counter. Bye, bye lumps.

We seated ourselves on dining room chairs with uphol-stered seats. The wooden table was covered with a white cloth and set with their good tableware. The guys complimented our cooking. We just smiled and graciously accepted the ac-colades. After we'd finished the meal and washed the dishes in the kitchen sink, the four of us went to a show in Rockford.

On a balmy Saturday night a week later, Kenny and I went to the stock car races at the Rockford Speedway with Wayne and his girlfriend, Gloria, who lived on a farm over a couple of hills south of our place. She was petite, with short, dark hair and brown eyes. Her only sibling, Ron, was in my class, and she was a year younger.

The four of us found seats on the bleachers along the backside of the asphalt track opposite the more expensive grandstand seating. We chose a weathered, wooden bench high enough to see over the woven wire fence anchored with wooden posts. The barrier kept spectators off the track and protected us if a driver roaring around the track lost control of his late model stock car.

Gloria, who was talkative, said to her boyfriend, "I'm hungry."

Wayne, who recently graduated and worked at a small Rock-ford machine shop, asked, "Does anyone else want a hot dog?"

Ken and I both said, "No, thanks."

Wayne soon returned with two sandwiches and two Cokes.

Apparently, Gloria and I shared at least one thing in common. We both liked to eat and weren't afraid to show it. A lot of girls demurely said, "I'll just have a Coke," when a dating couple stopped at a hamburger joint. I didn't go that route.

Kenny would say, "I'm going to have a cheeseburger, fries and a Coke. What do you want?"

I'd respond, "Sounds good. I'll have the same."

The autos cruised around the track. When the starter waved the green flag, the drivers gunned their motors for the initial heat. It was our first visit and we didn't know any of the drivers. Wayne and Gloria picked a Ford and we picked a Chevy to cheer for. Races continued as daylight dimmed to night and the flood lights came on. Sometimes we picked winners, but most of the time not.

After the finale, we returned to the parking lot. Some of the cars took off with a roar and squeal of tires mimicking drivers on the track. Wayne drove his recently purchased, used Ford carefully.

The following Saturday afternoon, Kenny stopped by late in the day for our usual pre-date routine. We checked the Rockford newspaper theater listings and decided to see the movie, *Dial M for Murder*. I was a big fan of Alfred Hitchcock's suspense.

After the show, we returned to my house and sat in his blue convertible talking and necking. It was a balmy night with a starry sky. Windows were open but a slight odor of cigarettes lingered. Doris Day softly warbled "Secret Love" on the radio set to WGN. Suddenly, Kenny made a life-changing announcement, "Me and Billy enlisted in the navy. We'll leave the twenty-sixth."

My stomach dropped. I gave him a half-hearted, "Good for you."

He continued, "While we've been working the five to two shift at Colman's, we'd go outside for our lunch break at ten

thirty. We'd hear people on South Main whooping and hol-
lering and having a good time. It made us wonder why we were
working there.

We didn't like the factory and we didn't know what else to
do, so we joined the navy. I've been taking a correspondence
course in diesel engineering and it's expensive. The navy will
pay for the same training. It should make a good occupation
in civilian life. Besides, it'll give me a chance to travel."

With nothing more to say on the subject, I said, "It's getting late. I'd better go in." Kenny walked me to the wooden
steps in front of the porch door, kissed me good-night, returned to his convertible and drove off.

I climbed the steps and crossed the porch to the kitchen
door. The fluorescent fixture above the sink glowed as a night
light. In my room, I turned on the pin-up lamp fastened to the
wall above the mirror on my dresser. I changed into pajamas,
washed my face and brushed my teeth. Snatches of radio news-
casts whirled through my mind. At least, the world was at
peace, but that could change at any minute.

The Cold War, a state of political and military tension between the United States and Russia, continued and so did the
draft. Every young man registered with the Selective Service
System when he turned eighteen years of age. There were two
options: [one] wait to receive "Greetings" from the government conscripting him into the Army for two years; or [two]
choose a branch of the service and enlist for a longer period of
time. The men in uniform were trained and ready to do whatever might become necessary. The threat of nuclear weapons
wafted over the globe like a mushroom cloud. The fear of god-
less communism prompted our Congress to recently add the
words "under God" to the "Pledge of Allegiance," which was
recited in schoolrooms every morning.

It took me a long time to go to sleep. I tried to imagine what my life would be like after Kenny left in six weeks. I'd waited so long to date and soon my steady boyfriend wouldn't be here.

A week later on a warm, Friday evening, Kenny and I followed our same dating routine of seeing a movie and then parking in our driveway to talk, neck and listen to the music on the radio. When I thought that we were in danger of Mom turning on the spotlight, I said, "I'd better go in."

Kenny walked me along the sidewalk to the wooden stairs in front of the house, kissed me goodnight and returned to his convertible.

I paused a moment and looked up to admire the Big Dipper spewing stars across the sky. The silence reminded me of the classic "'Twas the Night before Christmas." Even the wind slumbered.

I climbed the steps, opened the screen door and tiptoed across the painted floor. During the hot weather, Dad slept on a cot placed against the house wall of the screened-in porch that extended along the east side. Farmers followed Ben Franklin's words, "Early to bed and early to rise makes a man healthy, wealthy and wise."

The next morning, when we gathered around the oilcloth covered table for breakfast, Dad said, "Kenny's loud mufflers woke me up when he went up the drive last night. I counted seven times that his tires squealed on the curves going back to town. That boy needs to slow down."

"I'll tell him what you said."

That same morning, Kenny's parents began their annual, two-week vacation from office jobs at Globe Imperial. The three men of the family plus Tommy's best buddy, Denny, who lived across the street, left for a week-long, fishing trip. They drove eight hours to reach the cabin they rented on Lake Rooney near Spooner in northern Wisconsin.

The following Saturday night, when Kenny picked me up to go to a movie, he brought us some of the crappies he'd caught at Lake Rooney. Mom fried them for dinner the next day and they were tasty.

Sunday night, we saw another show. For me, our dates took on a doomsday feeling as we tried to cram in as much time together as we could before he left for the navy.

The following Friday night, Wayne and Gloria accompanied us for the "all you can eat fish fry" at the Butterfly. The landmark restaurant located in the country along Highway 15 on the far side of Beloit, Wisconsin, was packed. We waited almost a half-hour to be seated at a table. Their dollar special included deep-fried perch with tartar sauce, French fries and coleslaw. With our appetites, the price was a bargain.

Saturday night, Kenny and I went to a show in Rockford.

Sunday the temperature reached the high eighties, an ideal day to go with Wayne and Gloria to the beach at Lake Geneva, Wisconsin, about an hour away. Everyone in the area must have thought the same thing. Blankets carpeted the sand. We walked carefully among the people sprawled in the sun. When we finally found a bare spot to spread our blanket, we stripped off out outer clothes. We each wore a swimsuit underneath. My boyfriend and I rubbed suntan lotion on each other's bodies before lying down shoulder to shoulder. Wayne and Gloria followed suit.

I never learned to swim and, although the others knew how, they didn't abandon me. From time to time, we all cooled off by splashing around in the shallow water near the shore. It was like a crowded dance floor populated by children.

We finished off the day by stopping in Beloit at the huge Barrel shaped drive-in for cheeseburgers and root beers before seeing a movie.

On Kenny's last Friday night at home, his parents hosted a family farewell party that included me. I donned white sandals and my new sleeveless, cotton, marble print, turquoise dress that matched my eyes. My boyfriend had sold his Plymouth convertible and drove his parents' Ambassador when he picked me up at quarter to eight. He wore black slacks and a white polo shirt.

Kenny and his brother, Tommy, who was four years younger, lived with their parents in an older, two-story house on the southeast edge of Durand. When we entered Ditzlers' home through the west door of their large kitchen, we walked on multi-color linoleum. Natural-wood cupboards with a red counter-top stood on my right. To my left, a chrome-trimmed, gray Formica-topped table stood in front of a pair of windows framed by sheer, white, ruffled, tie-back curtains. The six matching chairs padded with red and gray vinyl were being used in the living room.

Seeing the houseful of people made me feel like it was Judgment Day. Meeting Kenny's extended family indicated I was a serious girlfriend.

Most of the butterflies swirling in my stomach flew away when Kenny's mother, Hazel, warmly welcomed me. The petite woman with dark hair streaked with gray and a pale complexion wore a white, cap-sleeved blouse with a summer-cotton, printed skirt and white sandals. She called to her husband, "Rolland, Lolita's here."

The bald, middle-aged version of Kenny stood in a corner of the room engaged in conversation with his son-in-law, Joe, a farmer with a sinewy build and dark, curly hair.

Rolland always wore a long-sleeved shirt to cover the steel hook prosthesis he used after losing his left hand in a die casting machine accident at Globe Imperial in 1949. The two men joined us for introductions.

Kenny led me from the kitchen through the double doorway to meet the other guests seated in the carpeted living room. Both rooms were painted hunter green with ivory woodwork.

Grandpa Eugene Ditzler, a small, wiry man with thinning white hair and glasses, was seventy five years old, but still operated the drug store in Davis. The front portion of his two-story, brick building housed the post office where Grandma Henrietta served as postmistress. The large, gray-haired woman, who was noticeably younger than her husband, was Grandpa's second wife and the mother of Robert. He resembled his half-brother, but was fifteen years younger and had hair.

Rolland's mother, Minnie, passed away when he was eleven and his sister, Irene, fourteen. Henrietta was her younger sister. Forty years ago, when a wife died, the husband often married one of her sisters.

Hazel's mother, who raised four daughters, was also in her second marriage.

Although she became Rosa Davis two years earlier, the grandkids continued calling her "Grandma Stilwell." She was a short, plump, white-haired woman with a quick laugh. She reminded me of the grandmother pictured in the Dick and Jane primers I used to learn to read in first grade. Her husband, Harley, was a white-haired man who wore thick, 'Coke bottle' glasses and loved to tell stories. The family friend was a life-long bachelor until he married his chum's widow. Kenny remembered his grandpa, Allie Stilwell, calling his tall, thin crony "Straight Arrow."

I then met Kenny's aunts with their husbands: Irma and Leland, Freda and Jay, Doris and Rod. Last of all was Kenny's sister, Lola Mae, who was three years older. She resembled her mother but was taller and her brown hair reflected a reddish tinge. She and Joe were parents of three children and lived on a farm northwest of town. I knew Kenny's cousins from school.

With family greetings finished, the two of us sat down on the dark green, upholstered davenport with Kenny's soon-to-be-navy buddy, Billy, and his fiancée, Marilyn. She was my cousin on Dad's side, but I never saw any family resemblance between us. She was fifteen, a year younger than I, but taller and bigger boned with dark hair and a dark complexion. The energetic, high-school cheerleader moved fast and talked fast.

The buzz of many simultaneous conversations and the gurgle of laughter filled the evening. White cake with white frosting, coffee and punch topped off the night.

After we'd said our good-byes, Kenny drove me home. He assured me I'd passed muster with his relatives.

The next night, was our last movie date. The following Monday morning, I kissed Kenny good-bye at the depot where he and Billy boarded the train for Great Lakes Naval Training Center. Back home, I made do with my boyfriend's class ring circling my finger, his graduation picture sitting on my dresser and the yellow, paper leis hanging on my bedroom wall.

A week after Ken left, he sent an address for me to write back to him. My sitting on the front porch watching the corn grow in the field across the driveway and our other mundane farm activities couldn't compare to his new adventures. Still, I would follow the example of the girls left behind during World II and write to my boyfriend every day. In my first letter, I told him about Dad and me driving our two, bright orange, Allis Chalmers tractors pulling wagon-loads of grain to be ground at the Davis Mill. The sun was shining when we left home for the six-mile trip along gravel roads, but storm clouds soon gathered. When we arrived in the village, Dad let me go first. I made it back home with my load of animal feed before it rained, but he got wet.

Thursday a navy scarf arrived in the mail. I could hardly wait to tie it over my hair and show it off when school started.

Four weeks after Ken joined the service, he could have visitors. Sunday morning, his parents picked me up at eight to drive to Great Lakes. I wore white sandals and the turquoise, sleeveless dress I bought for my boyfriend's farewell party. Rolland was behind the wheel of the Ambassador and Tommy rode shotgun. I joined Hazel in the back seat. During the three-hour ride, she and I chatted about the letters we'd received from Ken, her garden and my approaching senior year.

When we passed a cemetery, Rolland interrupted with, "There's a dead place, but everybody's dying to go there." Ken shared his dad's love of jokes.

We ate lunch in a diner before pulling into the naval base located near North Chicago and parking in the huge, concrete lot. Soon the company of young men marched out to the area where families waited. When Ken joined us, I saw a sailor from his white hat sitting squarely atop his buzz cut to his spit-shined, black shoes. I hesitated to kiss him for fear I would smear makeup on his white uniform that sparkled like a pail of milk.

He didn't seem concerned when he grabbed me with a bear hug. I closed my eyes for his kiss and inhaled his scent of stale cigarette smoke and freshly applied Old Spice after shave. It was an alluring combination.

We then sat down on benches under shade trees in a grassy area. After we'd all talked for a while, Rolland handed my boyfriend the car keys and pointed out where he'd parked so the two of us could sit alone in their Nash.

The sun beat down on us as we walked across the hot concrete to the Ambassador. Ken inserted the key in the lock and opened the driver's door. It felt like an oven. It must have been at least a hundred degrees inside. We cranked all of the windows down and there was a slight breeze, but that didn't make much difference inside. We slipped into the front bench. He slid it back as far as it would go.

My sailor flipped his white hat into the back seat, ran his left hand over his bristles and said, "Don't you just love my haircut?"

"To be honest, I can't say that I do."

We snuggled close together with his right arm around me. I tried to ignore the sweat trickling down my spine. I was thankful for my Veto cream deodorant. At least, I didn't smell.

My boyfriend was making friends and getting into shape with physical training.

He told me about his induction. "I was fingerprinted and examined by a dentist and a doctor, who also gave me a bunch of shots. We were then sworn in as a group."

I didn't have much to say about my monotonous life. School would soon be starting. I was looking forward to my last year.

Soon we rejoined his family so Ken could say good-bye and return to the barracks. He shook hands with his dad and brother, pecked his mother on the cheek and kissed me on the lips. Our visit seemed as short as a bee visiting a flower. Ken and I didn't know when we would see each other again.

A week later, the mail brought a throw pillow cover with 'Navy Sweetheart' printed on it. Ken's gift made me feel like a woman in love rather than a teenager with a crush.

On Saturday, September fourth, I turned seventeen. My gift from my parents was the weekly egg check enclosed in my card. The $21.90 included my weekly allowance of $6.50. We went to Beloit where I spent $8 for a bluish-gray, fall dress with three-quarter length sleeves and $7.50 for a pair of sun glasses with ornate white frames. In the evening, we enjoyed Joey Tantillo's music at the Wigwam. My friends, Janice, Joyce and Willabea, plus the guys who asked me to dance helped me forget my loneliness for a few hours.

The Labor Day weekend hot spell continued Monday. During the afternoon, Mom and I wiped away sweat while making fudge to send to Ken. We used her old-fashioned recipe, which took more effort, but tasted better than the quick and easy variety that used a jar of marshmallow fluff and a package of chocolate chips. We took turns standing at our white, electric stove to stir the boiling mixture of milk, sugar and cocoa. When a few drops formed a soft ball in cold water, I set the white enamel pan on top of ice cubes and water in a larger pan.

When the candy cooled so I could lay my hand on the bottom of the pan, we beat it with a spoon until it was thick. Before pouring the mixture onto a greased platter to set, I added a cup of chopped pecans. Later, I cut the fudge into pieces and packed it into a salvaged, white, candy box with Fannie May in gold letters across the top. I wrapped the package with brown paper cut from a large grocery bag, tied it with cord string and printed Ken's address on the top. The next morning, Dad drove me to the Durand Post Office to mail the parcel before I went to school.

I was reminded of Mom's sending homemade candy to our friend, Bob Weaver, while he was in the Army during World War II.

As Ken and I matured, I realized the war shaped our characters although I was only four and Ken was six when Japan bombed Pearl Harbor 7 December 1941.

Everyone had friends and family fighting for our country. Ken's Uncle Bob served in the Army. Dad's three sisters—Margaret, Marion and Elnora—waited at home for their soldiers, Emmett, Raymond and Buck. Movie theater newsreels, newspaper headlines, and radio programs reported the war. In my head, I still heard the distinctive voice of commentator Gabriel Heatter saying, "There's good news tonight."

All of us on the home front made sacrifices for the war effort. No new cars were available as factories converted to producing combat materials.

In the kitchen, my mother coped with rationing of meat and sugar. She bought small wooden boxes filled with dried cod fish that she creamed and served over mashed potatoes for dinner. She found cookie recipes that used honey purchased from Hank, who was married to Mom's best friend, Mary. He worked in a Rockford factory, but during his offhours, he cared for bees at their rural home near Shirland.

Gasoline was also rationed, which led to one of the few times my dad raised his voice to me. On a spring afternoon we were cruising down a hill on Highway 75 heading home from Durand. The speedometer needle on the dashboard of our '36 black, two-door Chevy crept toward 45 MPH. I was only five years old, but I knew the speed limit was 35 MPH to conserve gas. I didn't want my father breaking the law, so I reached over and turned off the ignition key.

He exploded, "Don't you ever do that again!"

I cringed in shock. Neither of us spoke another word the rest of the way home.

When I started first grade at Rockton School, I joined my classmates and all of the kids across the country doing our bit. Instead of buying candy or gum, we spent our coins for savings stamps, which we pasted into a book. The filled book could be redeemed at a bank for a war bond that cost $18.75 and seventy-five cents and would be worth $25 in ten years.

During the summers, the government asked farmers like Dad to refrain from mowing milkweeds. In September, children fought their way through patches of the head-high, pesky plants and collected the pods. A pound-and-a-half of the floss contained in the pods could be sewed inside a life preserver, which would keep a one hundred and fifty pound sailor afloat in the water for ten hours.

On 15 August 1945, when Japan surrendered, I was turning eight and Ken would soon be ten. The war was over. People across the U.S. erupted in celebration. My parents smiled, sighed with relief and continued with their farm chores.

Back at school Tuesday, Tommy told me, "We're going to see Ken again Sunday and Mom said you can go with us." He smirked and added, "It'll give you another chance to neck with my brother."

The sophomore was a typical, annoying little brother. With the sophistication of a senior, I ignored his last remark and replied, "Thank your mother for me. I'd love to go."

The weather at six Sunday morning hinted at fall. It was cool and overcast when Ditzlers picked me up to go to Great Lakes. We all wore light jackets.

At the naval base, Ken climbed into the back seat with us women and greeted me with a quick kiss. He was accompanied by his buddy, George, who slid into the front with Rolland and Tommy. The two sailors looked a lot alike in their white, long-sleeved uniforms. This was their first leave and they could go no farther than fifty miles from camp. Rolland drove north to Milwaukee, entered a park along Lake Michigan and stopped near a picnic table. Ken's dad opened the trunk. The young men grabbed the picnic basket and cooler, carried them to the wooden table and set them on the benches. Hazel spread a table cloth before setting out paper plates, silverware and food. Everyone helped themselves to ham sandwiches, potato salad and chocolate cake. We washed our meal down with bottles of Coke. When Ken scooped up a large, second helping of potato salad with his mother's tasty homemade dressing, he said, "There's a good reason our meals are called mess."

After eating and chatting, we took the sailors back to the base and said good-bye. Ken bussed my lips before leaving the car. I was disappointed that he and I didn't have any time alone. As Tommy teased, I was looking forward to necking with his brother.

The following Wednesday, which was eleven days after my birthday, the mail brought Ken's gift, an identification bracelet with a stretchy, stainless steel band. The silver top with my name engraved on it lifted up so I could put his photo inside.

On the first Thursday night in October, Hazel called while I was attending practice for our senior class play. She told Mom that Ken's graduation from boot camp would be Saturday, a week earlier than planned, and invited me to attend with them. The next night, she called again to tell me Ken phoned to say don't come for graduation because he'd be away on a work party. Anyone who thought only women couldn't make up their minds hadn't dealt with the Navy.

A week later, I took advantage of our Friday off for teachers' institute to have my graduation pictures taken. Our class had contracted with Wagner's studio in Freeport, a city about half-an-hour west of us. The night before, I washed and set my hair in big pin curls so it would be dry to comb out in the morning. For my photograph, I wore a new, medium-blue blouse.

In the evening while we were sitting at our kitchen table finishing supper, Tuffy and Rocky barked. I was surprised to see a green Nash creeping down the driveway. Ken was home on a fourteen-day furlough a day earlier than I'd expected. I ran out of the house and threw myself into his arms as he walked up the sidewalk. After a big hug and kiss, we entered the living room and my parents joined us to chat.

Although Ken was dressed in jeans and a blue polo shirt, he was a full-fledged navy man. The tattoo on his left bicep peeked below his short sleeve. The design included a blue anchor and U.S.N. The words Mom and Dad were printed on a ribbon floating across a red heart. The artist in Milwaukee cautioned my steady against putting my name on his arm. The man said a tattoo is forever, but girlfriends aren't. Seaman lingo salted Ken's conversation. The bathroom was the 'head'. Left and right were 'port' and 'starboard'. The floor was the 'deck'. After Ken visited with us for about fifteen minutes, he and I made a movie date for the next night. He then left to spend time with his family.

Saturday night on our way home from seeing the musical, *Brigadoon*, Ken turned from Highway 75 onto Weber Road just east of Durand. After passing the only farmhouse located on the mile-long, single-lane blacktop, he pulled the Ambassador off on the grass alongside and parked. The radio was set to WGN and Kitty Kallen reminded us "Little Things Mean a Lot." He slid the seat back and we cuddled together. No spotlight if we necked too long.

Still, a light bothered Ken. A little red bulb about the size of a shirt button glowed on the dash indicating that the radio was using juice from the battery. He dug around in the glove compartment until he found a notepad, tore the cardboard from the back and covered the glimmer. He relaxed.

I trusted Ken completely. I knew from remarks he'd made about other young couples having to get married he shared my resolve that it wouldn't happen to us. He never pressured me to have sex before we were married. I appreciated his self-control.

During the following week, Ken brought me home from play practice Monday night and took Dad's place as my chauffer Thursday night. I skipped a few rehearsals to go out with him. Friday evening, we ate fish fry at the Butterfly with Wayne and Gloria. Saturday, Tuesday and Thursday nights, the two of us went to shows in Rockford followed by stops on Weber Road. Spending time with Ken during his leave was like taking several deep breaths before diving under water.

Friday was only the twenty-ninth of October, but it started snowing in the afternoon. Ken drove me home from school and gave me a final good-bye kiss. His fourteen-day leave slipped by like a long weekend. The next morning, he would return to Great Lakes. From there he would fly to Norman, Oklahoma, to be trained for duty aboard an aircraft carrier. He expected to be home again for Christmas. I would count the days like I did when I waited for Santa.

The snowflakes indicated to Mom it was time to shut the chickens inside for the winter. All summer, she'd left the hen-house door open so the old girls could roam around the orchard and keep cool. On my way to the henhouse to gather eggs, I watched where I stepped because the fowls crapped anywhere and everywhere. For the past week, she and I spent every evening from sundown 'til dark trying to drive the stupid fowls inside.

Poultry can't be herded like cows. A dozen stragglers flew up and roosted on the lowest limbs of a tall pine tree that stood near the building. That night, I got them down. I leaned the six-foot, wooden step ladder against the tree trunk and climbed from the top of it onto the wet, slippery branch. I grabbed the legs of each dozing bird and handed the squawking biddy to Dad standing on the ground. He carried them to the building. When the chore was finished, I climbed down and proclaimed, "Let it snow!"

The following Friday evening, Dad and Mom attended the first performance of our annual senior play, *Teen Time*. I was named Gay, a teen-age, Southern belle, with a 'ya'all' accent.

Our director, math and science teacher Mr. Slabaugh, included all twenty-four class members in the cast. Those who didn't have speaking parts danced at the teen center that the gruff, middle-aged woman who owned the building threatened to close.

Saturday I fought a headache all day, but 'the show must go on'. I performed again that night and felt better. To celebrate afterwards, Don, one of our class nerds with a crew cut and glasses, invited all of us to his home south of town to eat chicken ala king. I rode to the party with Dick and Esther.

Inside the large, farmhouse, the dining room table was covered with a lace cloth. Each of us grabbed a napkin, a fork and a china plate from the stack before helping ourselves from the platter of baking powder biscuits. Don's mother, a large, gray-haired woman, stood at the head of the table in front of a large kettle. She topped our biscuits with scoops of the gravy swimming with pieces of chicken, mushrooms, green pepper and pimento. We each picked up a glass of punch, found a seat in the carpeted living room or dining room and ate from the plate balanced on our lap. It was the first time I'd tasted the dish. It was delicious.

Two days after Ken's birthday November eighth, I received his new address in Oklahoma and sent him a card. Mom began sending him greeting cards, too.

The following week-end, Mom helped me make fudge and divinity as a late birthday gift for Ken. Even the weather can affect the white candy, but both varieties turned out well on the sunny, wintery Saturday. Monday morning Dad drove me to the post office to mail the treat before I went to school.

A week later in the evening, Ken called from Oklahoma to thank me for the candy. Instead of romantically murmuring sweet nothings during our brief conversation, we spoke loudly to be heard long distance. I assumed Uncle Bob was 'rubbering' on our party line. One of rural people's pastimes was taking down the receiver and listening in when they heard a neighbor's ring on the party line. Dad's younger brother often teased me about phone conversations with my boyfriend that he'd overheard.

Every night when I finished addressing my letter to Ken, I wrote S.W.A.K. on the envelope flap, which meant 'sealed with a kiss'. He inscribed T.S.T.S.T.S.A. on envelopes. I blushed when he explained in a letter that it meant 'to someone too sweet to sleep alone'. We both would have been in trouble if my mother knew what those initials stood for when she picked up our mail from the metal box alongside the blacktop road.

The night before Thanksgiving, I attended Homecoming alone. At the dance, I felt like a single swan swimming on a pond after losing her mate, but I wasn't a wallflower. A few boys without dates asked me to slow dance. When the band played a fast tune, one of my girlfriends was my partner.

A month later on the sunny, Sunday afternoon before Christmas, I wrapped presents. I was surprised when the green Nash pulled in the driveway. I didn't expect Ken until the next day. Ignoring the cold, I dashed outside for a hug and kiss as soon as he stepped out of the Ambassador. We entered the house and sat down with my parents in the living room for a short visit. When he got up to leave, we made a date for later. In the evening, we saw a show in Beloit and then stopped by our old parking spot on Weber Road. It felt so good to be in his arms again. He didn't even have to keep the heater going. We kept each other warm.

During the afternoon before Christmas Eve, Ken came to exchange presents. I gave him a Ronson cigarette lighter. He gave me a black, short-sleeved, cashmere, cardigan sweater. My first thought when I opened the box was it's beautiful. Was it too intimate a gift for me to accept when we weren't engaged? One glance at the pride in my boyfriend's face convinced me I couldn't refuse it. Besides, I'd never owned an expensive, cashmere sweater. I said a heartfelt, "Thank you." I silently hoped I wouldn't be allergic to the fiber made from goat's hair like I was wool sheared from sheep.

The night after Christmas, Esther and I cooked supper at my house for our boyfriends. She was dating, Doug, a good dancer from Beloit that she'd met at the Wigwam. He was a short, dark-haired, quiet fellow in his early twenties who worked in one of that city's factories. The guys each drove in at six on the dot. When they entered the living room, I introduced them and they shook hands. They sat down facing one another with Ken in Mom's easy chair and Doug taking Dad's dusty rose chair that matched the davenport. Esther and I returned to the kitchen to finish preparations.

It was the first time we'd double-dated with one of my friends and her boyfriend, who was a stranger to Ken. Always before, we'd gone out with his friends and I was the one trying to make small talk with a person I didn't know well. I could hear the murmur of conversation. The fellows must have found a few things in common.

In the kitchen, Esther and I cooked the same plain meat-and-potatoes meal we fixed before but this time, no problems. After eating and cleaning up, the four of us went to a Sunday evening, holiday dance at Turner Hall in Monroe.

Tuesday night, Ken and I saw a show, parked on Weber Road and made plans for New Year's Eve. It would be our last date before Ken flew back to Oklahoma.

On the festive night, I wore my new black, cashmere sweater and a beige, mid-calf length, straight skirt I'd bought to go with it. Ken entered our living room at seven and greeted my parents who were sitting in their easy chairs. After eyeing me, he said, "It looks like the sweater fits fine." I blushed and wondered what my parents thought of his remark.

We spent the evening with Wayne and Gloria. First, we went to Rockford to see the Technicolor movie, *White Christmas*, at the ornate Coronado Theater. When we arrived, the only seats left were in the front row next to the orchestra pit. While sitting on the plush red velvet upholstery waiting for the show to start, I gazed around the lighted auditorium. The walls were decorated with the facades of gilded Spanish and Italian-style buildings. Several alcoves that resembled box seats were along the sides. Green, stained-glass lamps with fluted bulbs adorned the walls. Depictions of golden, Japanese dragons and glowing lanterns covered the organ screens on either side of the stage. When the lights went out and the musical began, we craned our necks back to see the big screen.

The ceiling looked like a dark blue sky filled with twinkling stars.

After the movie, we returned to Durand and joined a room full of local people dancing at the Grange hall. A few minutes before midnight, everyone donned paper hats, shook metal noise makers and blew cardboard horns to greet 1955. At 3 A.M., Vic Wall's band played *Goodnight, Sweetheart* to end the celebration.

We topped off our evening with cheeseburgers in The Hilltop restaurant, which was part of the gas station building at the mile-corner south of town. It was four o'clock when Ken walked me to the door and kissed me good-bye. In a few hours, he'd be flying back to Oklahoma. Having him home for the holidays was my best present ever.

In my bedroom, I removed my sweater to get ready for bed. I sighed with relief–no rash. I wasn't allergic to the expensive cashmere. Ken's gift proved I was made for finer things.

Chapter 4

1955

Four nights after New Year's Eve, Ken called and said, "I just wanted to let you know that my flight back to Oklahoma was fine."

To be heard long distance, I spoke loudly into our old-fashioned, black instrument sitting on the modern walnut desk in the corner of our kitchen. I knew my parents sitting in the living room could hear my every word but I didn't care. I replied, "Well, I've been in the doghouse. When I finally got up about noon New Year's Day, Mom jumped all over me for getting in at 4 A.M. She said, 'It's a good thing that sailor is going back to the navy.' I didn't think I did anything wrong. I could account for my time. After all, it was New Year's Eve and the last night I'd see you for months. You're gone so there's no punishment. I'm immune to being yelled at."

"I'm sorry you got in trouble, but I had a good time New Year's Eve. I've got to go now. See you next summer. Bye."

"I had a good time, too, and I'm glad you called. Bye."

Ken kept long distance calls within the three-minute limit that he paid for in advance by dropping a handful of coins into the payphone. He was a conscientious person who moved on to make room for the other sailors waiting in line behind him.

The next afternoon, I stood in the basement former kitchen cleaning the pail of hen fruit that I'd gathered in the morning. I wiped each white egg with a damp rag before placing it in its own section of the cardboard, thirty-dozen case. Each Friday a route man took the eggs to the Davis Hatchery. He handed Mom a check for the eggs he'd picked up the previous week.

I heard Dad muttering in the other room as he snapped his five-buckle overshoes and put on his outdoor gear. He needed to gather wood to refill our depleted bin. He hated wading through snow that topped his boots searching for fallen, dead trees in the fifty acres of timber on the other side of the blacktop road. When he was bundled up ready to face the bright, twenty degree day, he stopped at the tool shop to grab his chain saw to cut up the trunks. He mounted the old AC tractor, hooked the trailer behind and drove to the woods. Three hours later, he pulled the load of stove-sized chunks along the north side of the house and tossed them through the open cellar window into the bin.

Our furnace in the rear of the basement burned either coal or wood to heat water that circulated through metal radiators in each room on the main floor. The second story was only used for storage and wasn't heated. Most of the time, Mom utilized the free wood that Dad provided. During extremely cold nights, when the temperature dropped below zero, she got up at 2 A.M. to replenish the fire. The only time she used the costly, slower burning coal briquettes was to keep the fire going when we went away.

Ken's next letter came from ordnance school in warm, sunny Jacksonville, Florida. He was learning to handle the ammunition and bombs carried by planes based on an aircraft carrier. He didn't seem worried about his dangerous job, so I tried not to fret either.

The last Saturday night in January, Dad drove me to the FHA dance and picked me up afterward. It was a replay of Homecoming. I wanted to join my friends for fun, but I felt like Blondie without Dagwood.

At the beginning of the following week, it was clear and cold after school as I hurried along the sidewalk to the business district. At the post office on the west side, I mailed my five by seven, colored, graduation picture to Ken for Valentine's Day. I hoped the photo would keep me on his mind and in his heart.

I joined the other members of the Girls Athletic Association to bowl at the four-lane facility located near the south end of the street. The front portion of the building contained a long, coatrack with wire hangers, rest rooms and a counter where shoes were rented and snacks sold. Three rows of wooden bleachers sat behind the horseshoe-shaped, bowlers' benches next to the alleys.

Proprietors 'Dutch' and June lived upstairs with their three small children. He worked days at a Rockford factory, so she supervised our afternoon session.

I rented the required shoes and laced them up. I searched the two racks of balls located between the alley approaches and selected one of the black, sixteen-pounders that came closest to fitting my slender fingers. It was drawn to the gutters on each side of the hardwood like a teen-age boy was attracted to cheerleaders. When my first throw stayed in the middle, I usually ended up with a split. The remaining pins on opposite sides defied me to knock them all down with my second ball. My score for each of my first two games was less than a hundred. I was frustrated.

I told Miss Filmore, the tall, slender, dark-haired P.E. teacher, I'd relieve one of our volunteer pinsetters for the third game. I knew some of the gals weren't strong enough to handle that job. At the rear of the lanes, I picked up the pins that a bowler knocked down with her first ball and placed them in the rack. After pushing the ball into the return chute, I hopped up on the bench to be out of the way of the second ball. I then added the remaining pins to the rack and used my full hundred and fifteen pounds to push it to the floor and trip it to reset the pins. I repeated this action until the girls finished their ten frames.

With graduation approaching, I was thinking about what I would do next. A magazine ad from an art school in Minnesota intrigued me. I loved to draw. Aspiring artists were urged to copy the illustration of a girl's head as a test and mail it to the institution. Out of curiosity, I sent a sketch. Soon I received a letter congratulating me on passing their test. A representative would be calling on me. Salesmen didn't bother making appointments with farmers. They just showed up at mealtime.

About a week later, Mom was cooking supper in the kitchen when a chubby, balding man wearing a brown business suit and carrying a leather briefcase knocked on our front door. He introduced himself as Mr. Peterson, the art school representative. Dad invited him to come in and sit down in the living room. The two of us listened to his sales talk.

When he finished, Dad asked, "How much does it cost?"

Instead of answering Dad's question, the agent gave his spiel a second time.

Dad again asked, "How much does it cost?"

The representative started his rehearsed speech for the third time.

Mom, who was more assertive than Dad, entered the room and told the man, "I think it's time for you to leave."

The disgruntled salesman grabbed his briefcase, stomped across the porch and slammed the screen door behind him on his way to his car.

Did I miss an opportunity for a career in art? I'll never know.

Late in afternoon on the first Saturday in May, I was alone in the house when our phone pealed a long and a short. I answered and Ken said, "Hi, Honey, I'm home." My stomach flipped with excitement. "I won't be able to see you until tomorrow. Me and Paul hitchhiked from Florida. Mom and Dad picked us up in Rochelle and now we've got to take Paul home to LaCrosse, Wisconsin."

My shoulders drooped in disappointment. I reluctantly replied, "Tomorrow morning I have to catch the school bus at nine thirty for our senior trip." During the past four years, my class conducted car washes, bake sales, newspaper drives and coat checks at basketball games to raise funds toward the excursion.

"Would it be okay if I pick you up about nine and bring you to town?"

"That'd be great. I do want to see you before I leave." As usual, our conversation was short and to the point.

When I learned my boyfriend would be coming home on a fifteen-day leave in May, I considered cancelling the five-day-tour of Washington, D.C., but I didn't. It was a once-in-a-lifetime opportunity. Besides, I'd already paid the thirty dollars out of pocket cost and I didn't know if I could get my money back or not.

Sunday, Ken pulled in a little before nine on a sunny morning. When he came around the rear of his dad's green Nash and started walking up the sidewalk toward the house, I ran out to greet him. He looked so good–tanned and fit in a white, short-sleeved, knit polo shirt and jeans. I, too, wore jeans with a short-sleeved, red-plaid blouse so I'd be comfortable on the train trip to 'D.C.' Ken gathered me into his strong arms for a kiss. I wanted the moment to last for hours, but after a few seconds, we ended the embrace and entered the house. He greeted my mother and grabbed my large, heavy, powder blue suitcase. I picked up my small, navy blue, make-up kit.

After stowing my baggage in the Ambassador's trunk, Ken opened the driver's door and we both slid onto the bench seat. I sat as close to him as I could. As soon as we exited the driveway, he put his right arm around me and drove along the blacktop with his left hand. If my boyfriend was mad at me for leaving, he didn't let it show.

On our way to Durand, Ken told me about their adventure thumbing their way from Florida to Illinois. "Paul and I already had our plane tickets home, but we overslept and missed our flight. Nothing to do but put on our uniforms and hitchhike. We got a ride from Jacksonville as far as the Okefenokee Swamp in Georgia. Then we got lucky. Two young guys driving a fairly new, four-door, Chrysler New Yorker picked us up and said they were going to Terre Haute, Indiana. They both had on white pants and white shirts that looked like some sort of work uniform, but we didn't think anything of that. They told us they were low on money, so we paid for the gas each time they stopped to fill up. It had gotten dark and we were just coming into Paducah, Kentucky, when they admitted they were running away from a boys' home and had stolen the car. We immediately said, 'Drop us off.' We didn't want to get in trouble with them.

"Three girls picked us up and took us across the river into Illinois. It had started raining when they dropped us near a fuel depot where semis were pulling out. Two trucks going north stopped. I got in one, Paul got in the other. It took a few more rides to get as far as Rochelle, where I called home collect. The folks picked us up and we took Paul home."

Ken described his buddy, Paul, as a clean-cut, muscular, good-looking fellow who was fussy about his appearance. The cocky, hell-raiser sauntered through life with a don't-give-a-damn attitude. "He'd get in trouble with the navy and just laugh about it," said my steady, who was a follow-the-rules guy. In spite of their differences, their friendship endured until the end of their enlistments. Fifty years later, the two shipmates met again. Ken and his brother, Tom, flew from Illinois to visit Paul at his home near San Diego, California.

When Ken and I arrived in Durand, my boyfriend stopped behind the yellow bus parked in front of the grade school. He gave me a lingering, good-bye kiss before we exited the Nash. He then opened the trunk, grabbed my big blue suitcase while I took the small navy one. We carried my luggage aboard the vehicle and stashed it in the back. Boys who had been watching out the rear window greeted us with whistles and catcalls. My steady grinned and I blushed.

Ken exited the bus, returned to the sedan and pulled away from the curb. I wiped tears from my eyes. The time we spent together between our "Hello" and "Good-bye" kisses was much too short.

Although I hated to leave my boyfriend, I soon caught the excitement of my companions.

After a three-hour bus ride along Highway 20 through small towns and suburbs to the Union Station in downtown Chicago, we boarded our own train car for the trip to Washington, D.C. Mr. and Mrs. Slabaugh, an attractive, likeable, outgoing couple chaperoned. The tall, balding man dressed in a suit, white shirt and tie was our math and science teacher, the father of our classmate, Dick, and a farmer. His wife, a slim, gray-haired mother of five sons, wore a stylish medium-gray suit and a matching hat.

The first thing my best friend, Esther, and I did was learn to smoke cigarettes. In movies, all of the sophisticated adults smoked. Advertisements on TV, in print and on billboards bombarded us. Their catch phrases such as, "LS/MFT, Lucky Strike means fine tobacco" and "I'd walk a mile for a Camel" invaded our jargon.

June and Shirley, habitual smokers, provided instructions and cigarettes from the carton that June's mother sent along. The two girls were bosom buddies who dressed alike every day. June was a lively, petite blonde. Shirley, with similar coloring, was taller, but always seemed to quietly stand in her friend's shadow. The four of us spent a lot of time in the ladies' lounge where we indulged without being seen. Esther and I didn't inhale but, as beginning smokers, we suffered slight nausea and dizziness for a day or so. After the trip, neither of us formed the habit. My parents didn't smoke and forbid me to.

Arriving in the nation's capital that evening, we checked into the new, modern Woodner Hotel. The girls shared one huge room and the boys another.

The next morning, we all dressed in our usual school clothes–the girls in skirts and blouses and the boys in jeans and long-sleeved shirts. We were off for three days of sightseeing. Representative Leo E. Allen welcomed us to his office in the nation's capital. He'd served our district since 1933, several years before any of us were born.

We spent our second evening in D.C. at an amusement park. Ron, a tall guy with brown eyes in a thin face, topped by dark, curly hair, took me for my first ride on a roller coaster. It was every bit as thrilling as I'd always imagined.

Tuesday, we visited historic spectacles beginning with the Washington Monument. Our guide said nothing in the city could be built higher than the obelisk, which was 555 feet and 1/8 inch tall. Inside the structure, Ron and Earl, a farm boy who tried to slick back his curly, brown locks that were the envy of the girls, joined Esther and me. The four of us climbed the 897 steps interspersed with 50 landings and walked down again. Our classmates stood in lines to ride up and down. When the others finally exited the elevator on the ground floor, we greeted them with, "Hi, old fogies. What took you so long?"

In the evening, I dressed in the new outfit I'd bought for graduation—light colored, cobra skin heels and a medium blue dress with a scooped neck, short-sleeves, and a gathered, calf-length skirt. Attending a night club for supper and a floor show made me feel like one of the movie stars pictured in Mom's *Photoplay* magazines.

The next day, a somber mood prevailed. We watched the changing of the guard at the Tomb of the Unknown Soldier and viewed the statue commemorating Raising the Flag at Iwo Jima. We each remembered friends and relatives who served during World War II.

On Wednesday night, we all wore jeans when we boarded our private train car for the return trip to Chicago. The boys and girls were separated to snooze in the reclining seats. Ron, Earl, Esther and I were still too wound up to sleep. We sat on our suitcases stowed by the rear doorway and quietly talked the night away.

Early the next day, we arrived in the Windy City. It would be noon before a school bus completed its morning route and made the three-hour trip to pick us up in The Loop. To fill the time, we saw the movie *Strategic Air Command*. It was the first time I went to a theater in the morning. After a night of no sleep, I dozed off in my seat watching actor Jimmy Stewart as 'Dutch' Holland flying his B-36 bomber through the fluffy, white clouds.

Friday, I stayed home in bed instead of going to school, but Mr. Slabaugh was on the job. He called to ask my mother why I wasn't in class. She answered, "Lolita was too tired to get up and get ready for school."

By evening, I felt rested and went to a show with Ken. Following the movie, we parked on Weber Road. I missed his embraces and kisses so much.

The next night, I donned my pink formal from last year to attend my senior prom with Ken. His leave coinciding with the event was the answer to my prayers. I doubt that I would have gone alone like I did Homecoming and the FHA dance. I wouldn't have wanted to miss my last prom, but I'd have felt like a cheater dating another guy, if one asked me.

We entered the gym decorated as a garden of roses. Paper flowers hung from the red and white streamers forming the false ceiling that started from the center and fell outward in a telescope effect to the crepe paper covered walls. Dancing cheek to cheek with Ken reminded me he was the only one for me.

At eleven, King Norman and Queen Millie were crowned and led all of us in the grand march. The band then took a half-hour intermission. Ken and I went outside to sit in the Nash and talk. It felt a little chilly, but my boyfriend's arm around me kept me warm. I asked him, "Why did you change your mind and go to ordnance school instead of taking up diesel engineering as planned when you enlisted?"

He replied, "I couldn't study diesel engineering like I'd wanted to because submarine school was filled. I was freezing my ass off in Norman, Oklahoma, and ordnance school was in Jacksonville, Florida."

I could understand his reasoning.

We began the next week with Ken bringing me home from school Monday afternoon. In the evening we went to a show followed by a stop on Weber Road. The next day, he again was waiting for me when classes ended just like when I was a junior. In some ways, I'd love to turn back the clock to that time, but I was glad graduation was approaching.

Wednesday morning, I drove our Chevy to Durand instead of riding the bus. After school, I defied convention and stopped in Ditzlers' driveway to pick up Ken. While waiting for him to come out of the house, I slid over so he could take the wheel of our sedan. I was on my way to Rockford to sign up for a hair styling course at the beauty school. The six-month session would begin in June and cost $175.

When I was little, Mom went there a few times for her annual permanent. At the time, money was tight and it was cheaper than a local salon. While I waited for her, I watched the students working on customers or practicing on each other. It looked like fun.

A couple of my high school teachers encouraged me to attend college. At the end of last year, the home economics instructor, Mrs. Luepkes, wrote in my annual, "Sorry you were so bored at times, but sometimes things which seem so elementary to you are not so to others and all students have to be considered in a mixed group. I do hope that you continue your education, because there you can feel at home and interested. Best of luck for a happy home."

At the same time, the P.E. teacher, Miss Elsner, wrote, "It has been a pleasure knowing you, Lolita. I only wish that all my students had the same ability and intelligence as you. Keep up the good work next year. Hope you will go to college."

Classes were easy for me and my grades were good, but I didn't want to go to college. The few females from our rural community who went on to school became teachers or nurses. Mom tried to push me toward her dream of being a nurse, but neither of those professions appealed to me.

The next afternoon, Ken came at five to kiss me and say, "Bye. See you next year." The following morning, he and Paul would fly from Chicago back to Jacksonville, Florida, to board the aircraft carrier U.S.S. Bennington. During the remainder of his enlistment, he would have a thirty-day leave once a year.

Sunday night I attended Baccalaureate, a religious service for our graduating class, held in the high school gym. During Daylight Saving Time, events began at 8:30 P.M. instead of the usual eight o'clock to accommodate the dairymen. Two-thirds of our twenty-four students lived in the country.

The following Friday night, 27 May, the Class of '55 gathered in the boys and girls locker rooms to don shiny, royal blue caps and gowns for commencement. We came together in the vestibule and tried to ignore the heat in the airless, lowest level of the high school. When Carlyle, a junior who was an outstanding pianist, began the "Processional," we marched two by two down the middle aisle. Families and friends filled the wooden, folding chairs set up on the gym floor. Some of the adults fanned themselves with their paper programs.

We all took seats on the stage. Sweat gathered on my forehead and trickled down my spine as I listened to speeches by Joy, salutatorian, and Lorraine, valedictorian followed by guest speaker, Rev. Williams. Superintendent Norsworthy called us forward in alphabetical order to receive a diploma and a handshake from the school board president, Mr. McCullough. Each of us then flipped the tassel on our mortar board from right to left and returned to our chair. Carlyle began a "Recessional" and we marched out to the entry, formed a receiving line and greeted guests.

I sent no formal invitations for the ceremony. Mom considered my graduation routine with no fanfare needed. A few relatives and friends sent cards and gifts to me.

The next morning, I received Ken's letter describing his new life aboard the Bennington.

He called the carrier a floating city populated with twenty-eight-hundred men. The crew launched planes every day except Sundays. As an aviation ordnance man, he fused bombs and rockets and helped squadron personnel hang them on aircraft. He didn't seem concerned about working with the explosives, so I didn't worry either.

Later, during his twenty-five-year career with the Winnebago County Sheriff's Police, Ken used this training to create the first bomb squad and dismantled explosive devise built by residents.

A week after graduation, Dad came in the house for dinner and said, "Rocky growled and snapped at me this morning." Ten days earlier, the dog bit him.

"That's enough," Mom said firmly. "I won't have a mean dog." She immediately phoned our teenage neighbor, Ellwyn, who was a hunter. She offered him a dollar to come over and shoot her dog, which he did. Dad buried Rocky behind the corn crib.

I resented my mother for what she did, although I knew it was a necessary decision. A biting dog would only get worse, not better. When I walked by the empty doghouse, I remembered the cute, little, mixed-breed, male puppy Mom bought from a Brodhead farmer for five dollars in the fall of '52. Dad built a house for him and she painted it white with 'Rocky' in brown letters above the doorway. The dog was a pampered pet and spent a lot of time in our kitchen. He wasn't allowed in any other room in the house. Mom taught him to sit up by the time he was three months old. When he was ten months old, the two of them kept our bull at bay in the pasture while the man driving the rendering works truck picked up a dead cow. To celebrate his first birthday, she gave him a new red collar and a cupcake with a candle. He'd grown to be a medium sized, tan dog with white markings similar to a collie except he was short-haired. Two more years passed before a vicious streak emerged. Like people, dogs developed their own temperaments in spite of the way they were treated.

I included the incident in my daily letter to Ken. He responded with details of his encounter with Rocky. He wrote, *I was walking around the rear of the car after opening your door when the dog grabbed my leg and tore my suit pants. I was too embarrassed to tell you what happened. I said, 'I forgot my billfold and have to stop at home to get it.' Instead, I needed to change my trousers.*

Beauty school would soon start with classes running from 9 A.M. to 4:30 P.M. Monday through Saturday. I couldn't afford to drive our only vehicle to downtown Rockford six days a week. I needed to find transportation. I checked with several people from the Durand area who worked in the city and carpooled or took riders to cut expenses, but their arrangements were set. I finally found a ride for fifty cents a day with Ken's classmate, Diane, a slim girl with light brown hair and electric blue eyes. She and her older sister, Donna, worked for our family friend, Mary, at the Agricultural Stabilization and Conservation office on South Main Street from eight to four thirty Monday through Friday. I drove myself Saturdays.

On a sunny, Monday, 6 June, I needed neither a jacket nor sweater over my white, nylon uniform when Diane picked me up in Durand at 7 A.M. I climbed into the backseat of her four-door, dark green Plymouth with a white top. My first glimpse of Donna sitting in the passenger seat surprised me. I remembered her as a short, chubby teenager who belonged to 4-H Club with my cousins, Doris and Sis. I'd heard the gossip she'd left the area right after high school, but recently returned to her parents' farm with a different last name and a small son. I didn't know she'd lost a lot of weight.

After a brief, "Good morning," the vehicle was as quiet as a library. The radio was off and neither young woman spoke another word during the half-hour ride. When I exited the sedan in front of the beauty school on State Street, the two said, "See ya later."

With an hour to kill before my classes began, I walked two blocks up the North Main Street sidewalk to the Times Restaurant next door to the movie theater. When I opened the front door, the aroma of bacon frying and coffee brewing greeted me. A lively instrumental emitted from the juke box sitting on the gray tile floor next to the entrance. The diner was long and narrow. Young men who attended the nearby Rockford School of Business filled several of the white, wooden booths running down the right-hand side of the room. They ate breakfast and fed coins into the music machine that glowed with colored lights.

I chose a red, vinyl-topped, rotating stool at the gray Formica counter on the left and ordered a cup of hot chocolate with a glazed doughnut. It became my morning routine.

At five minutes to nine, I eagerly ran up the stairs to the Rockford School of Beauty Culture located above Woolworth's dime store on the north side of West State Street. Mrs. Helen DeBella, a hard woman in looks and actions, owned the business. She was middle-aged, about five-eight and slim with a large nose that had a small bump on it. Her bleached, blonde hair was cut short and permed. She was assisted by Mrs. Bodley, a tall, big-boned, friendly widow. Like many older ladies, she kept her gray hair cut short, permed and rinsed purple. Mrs. Pinney, a petite, brown-haired, thirtyish woman, joined the staff on Fridays and Saturdays when students were busy with customers and needed all work checked. She was a sweetheart and everyone's first choice when seeking a teacher's approval. The three instructors wore pastel colored uniforms and comfortable work shoes.

I started as soon as possible in case winter weather forced me to miss some days. Illinois required a thousand hours of instruction before a student could take the state board exam to become a licensed cosmetologist. The school added twenty-five hours of manicure training. Only Patty and Betty, who lived about thirty miles south of Rockford, joined me that first week. The three of us learned hand and arm massage. Our fingers itched to begin styling hair, but all we could do was watch the advanced class work on customers. Popular new 'dos that summer were the DA, a short, razor cut that looked like its namesake, a duck's ass; the poodle that resembled the dog's curly coat; and the Italian, which was a little longer and used the new brush rollers to give the hair a lift.

At the end of the day, I stood on the sidewalk in front of the school door and waited about ten minutes for Diane to pick me up at the curb. The two young women greeted me with a brief, "Hi," when I crawled into the Plymouth's backseat. Silence during the drive along Highway 70. When I left the sedan in Durand, they said, "Bye, see you in the morning." At first, I thought the sisters were probably fighting, but every trip was the same. The silence was eerie.

By the third week, there were eleven in my class. Although a diploma wasn't required, all were recent grads from various area high schools. It was a motley collection of blondes, brunettes and one redhead. Some were short; some were tall; some were plump; some were slender. Only one was male.

Basil, a tall, sturdy fellow of Italian heritage with dark curly hair and brown eyes, planned to work in his uncle's beauty shop. 'Sonny', as he preferred to be called, said he had a girlfriend. That didn't keep him from teasing the girls by stepping up behind one of his classmates and snapping her bra, which was dimly visible through the required white uniform and full slip. Mrs. DeBella tolerated his antics with a 'boys will be boys' smile.

We began the day in the classroom learning the theory of hairstyling and memorizing the muscles and nerves in the head.

We were also taught to do facials, apply make-up and perform lash and brow tints.

We moved on to the salon to practice styling techniques on each other. Most of our customers were older ladies who wanted their thinning hair waved in the back. To do that well, we spent hours and hours perfecting crown waves, a hairdo in vogue before we were born. To hold strands in place, we used gallons of gloppy wave set, which reminded me of snot.

Whenever I served as a model, I ended up feeling like my scalp was dented. It was difficult for the girls to control my thick, shoulder-length, dishwater blonde hair that was permed only on the ends. I'd resisted Mrs. DeBella's strong suggestions that each of us adopt a short style.

Our salon was a spacious, well-lit room painted white with a gray, plastic-tile floor. Large mirrors back to back split the black Formica surface of the double dressers scattered around the area. Two customers could each sit in red, plastic-upholstered, styling chair on opposite sides. Four shampoo bowls were in the southeast corner of the room. The south wall was lined with tall windows covered by Venetian blinds that we dusted regularly. Half-a-dozen upright, black hairdryers stood in front of the windows. On hot, summer days, those windows were cranked open. Two large fans on tall, metal stands circulated the air that was thick with clouds of hairspray, the odor of ammonia, and the buzz of countless conversations.

An unfinished windowless, airless, storage area located behind the classroom and salon served as our lounge. It was furnished with straight, wooden chairs and included a restroom. At noon, we ate our sack lunches and relaxed for a half-hour. During the morning and again in the afternoon, we were allowed a five-minute break. Each time we left the work floor, we wrote our names in a notebook along with the time we signed out and signed back in. We tried to look innocent when we cheated by a minute or two.

Until my classmates and I were capable of taking care of customers, we spent afternoons observing the more advanced class at work. Standing for hours at a time was part of our training. Mrs. DeBella warned, "Be sure to relax your knees. Locking them could cause fainting."

The steamy, summer weather made us thirsty. Any time we weren't working on customers, we could drop a nickel in the red machine in the northwest corner of the room to buy a 6.5 oz., glass bottle of Coke. A wooden carrying case sitting next to the dispenser waited for the empties. They would be returned for a refund of the two-cent deposit charged for each of the twenty-four when purchased.

Ten days after I started school, Mom began getting a return on her investment. After she'd shampooed her hair, she sat on a kitchen chair while I made waves and pin curls. Mrs. DeBella stressed that we washed clothes but shampooed hair.

Two days later, I gave my first customer a shampoo and set. I did my best to disguise my shaking hands while making waves and pin curls. I didn't want the tall, slim, brown-haired, woman to know I'd never worked on a stranger before. I called Mrs. Bodley to check my work before sitting the lady under the dryer for half-an-hour. When I combed her out, she was pleased with the look and gave me a quarter tip. I was delighted.

By the end of the first month, I knew I'd made the wrong choice. I hated styling hair. My mother had urged me to first try a clerical job because in high school I took typing, shorthand, office practice and bookkeeping, but I was sure I knew best. I didn't like to admit I made a mistake, but I said to Mom, "You were right. Beauty school isn't for me. I'm ready to quit and look for office work. I thought I'd feel satisfaction at the end of the day, but I don't. My customers apparently have no complaints. Some of them have given me a quarter or a half-dollar tip. Today at noon, a woman treated me at Woolworth's lunch counter downstairs."

"Well, you're not going to quit," Mom said emphatically. "We've already paid part of the tuition money."

I resigned myself to finishing school in January. At least, I liked the girls.

Thursday afternoon, I played hooky to relieve my discontent. The movie *Not as a Stranger* opened at the nearby State Theater. I had devoured the best-selling novel by Morton Thompson and looked forward to seeing the medical drama on the screen. The matinee would begin at one twenty-five. Shortly after eating my lunch, I tried to look distressed when I said to Mrs. DeBella, "My stomach's upset. I need to leave."

While walking the two blocks east to the theater, I hugged the buildings. I didn't want my instructor to see me if she looked out a second-story window.

The movie disappointed me. A lot of things in the thick book were ignored or changed. Still, it cost only sixty-five cents to spend the afternoon sitting in air conditioning instead of standing in that hotbox above Woolworth's.

A week later, I stopped at the landlord's farm on my way home from Durand to pick out a puppy. Last spring, his female and our Rocky rendezvoused. The resulting litter of four was now two months old. I chose a male that looked like his father and named him Jeff.

Saturday was a real scorcher in a long, hot summer. At school, we put in a miserable, busy day. When I cut hair, the snips stuck to my sweaty hands and forearms. Our customers sat under the hair dryers and wiped perspiration from their faces with handkerchiefs.

When I returned home, Mom said one of their eight sows died from the ninety-plus heat. Losing the female animal that would have given birth to eight or ten baby pigs cut a hole in the farm's profit. Each year selling sixty to seventy butcher hogs added seasonal income to our balance sheet.

A farmer's fate depended on the weather, the animals' health and the markets. Most followed the old saying, "Don't put all of your eggs in one basket." By diversifying, if the pigs caught erysipelas and died, the fluctuating price of milk might be high at the same time.

My day ended on a bright note when Ken phoned from New York. He said, "We're doing a shakedown cruise to be sure everything's operating correctly. The carrier was recently repaired and modernized in the New York Naval Shipyard after an explosion a year ago last May. A 103 men were killed and more than two hundred were wounded. I don't know what caused the blast while the 'Big Benn' was moored at Quonset Point in Rhode Island."

Before we said our good-byes, I thanked him for the compact he'd recently sent from Haiti.

After I was in bed, a badly needed rain pounded the windows and cooled things off.

At the end of July, I lost my ride with Diane. She no longer wanted to drive the extra miles into Durand from her parents' farm northeast of the village.

Luckily, I found an opening with Betty, who always kept her late model, Ford sedan full of passengers. I considered the thirtyish, tall, thin, female who lived in the village with her mother, the epitome of a career woman. She dressed fashionably with her ash blonde hair cut stylishly short. I figured she made a good salary working as an underwriter for Rockford Life Insurance Company. On the way to her East State office, she dropped me off in front of my school. In the afternoon, I walked a couple blocks to Hobson's Drug Store and waited half-an-hour for her to pick me up. Her sense of humor kept the commute lively.

Labor Day weekend coincided with my eighteenth birthday. The State of Illinois considered me an adult female who could drink alcohol or marry. Neither of those things was going to happen while I lived with my teetotaling parents and my boyfriend sailed the seas aboard a navy aircraft carrier.

Friday night, Dad and Mom gave me a card and eighteen dollars before we went shopping in Beloit. I spent half of it for a pair of rust colored heels that I spotted in Stanton's Shoe Store window. The next day, I treated my schoolmates to chocolate chip cookies Mom baked. On Sunday, my actual birthday, my parents and I ate dinner at the Frontier located on the north side of Highway 75 at the west edge of Rockton. The restaurant included a bar and the area allowed Sunday liquor sales, but my ordering a cocktail was only a random thought. We then went on to Beloit where Dad and I saw the movie *Pete Kelly's Blues*. Mom wasn't interested in the Prohibition era tale starring Jack Webb, so she just drove around the area for a couple hours. The gangster drama and the lively jazz music thrilled me. From time to time, I glanced at Dad's face in the dark. It looked like he was enjoying it, too.

The following holiday afternoon, my cousin, Doris, took me to New Glarus, Wisconsin, to see *The Wilhelm Tell* outdoor pageant. Swiss immigrants, my father's ancestry, settled the rural community north of Monroe. I'm not usually interested in history, but I was fascinated by Switzerland citizens on horseback wielding swords battling for their independence from the Austrian Hapsburgs six hundred years ago. When Wilhelm Tell, a marksman who symbolized the struggle for political and individual freedom, used his crossbow to shoot an apple off his son's head, a collective gasp arose from all of us sitting on the wooden bleachers. I'm sure the actor didn't actually do that, but it certainly looked like he did.

The next day, Ken's letter said the Bennington started a fourteen-thousand-mile voyage from Jacksonville, Florida, around the Cape Horn of South America to San Diego, California, which would be their home port. The ship, one of the most modern carriers afloat, was too large to pass through the Panama Canal.

On the first Saturday evening in October, Mom drove me to Esther's to spend the night. Her neighbor, Raymond, gave us a ride to Theodorff's Barn, a dance hall located on a blacktop road east of Pecatonica. Esther and I wore flat shoes and cotton, gathered skirts.

Several years earlier, Harry Theodorff erected a sheep shed. Before moving the animals inside, he followed local custom and held a dance in the new building. The neighboring Black family provided the old-time music. Ray tucked a fiddle under his chin, his wife plunked the piano, older son, Russel, tooted a saxophone and younger son, Allen, beat time with his set of drums.

The crowd enjoyed the evening so much that the farmer continued the weekly gatherings. To convert the structure into a public building, he added restrooms, installed a furnace, covered the cement floor with hardwood and made other improvements to the premises. I don't know what the man did with the sheep.

During the evening, Esther and I ran into Bill and Jon, who'd been a year ahead of us at Durand High School. The former basketball players were good looking guys, about six feet tall and thin with light brown crewcuts. Bill farmed with his father and Jon worked at Sundstrand, a Rockford factory. They were there to meet girls, but rarely ventured onto the dance floor. They called themselves 'good sitter-outers'.

At the end of the night, Esther was thrilled when Bill asked to take her home. That was often a fellow's first move toward steady dating. Esther snuggled next to Bill on the front bench seat. Jon and I, who were old friends from our school bus riding days, were tagalongs. Like prize fighters in a boxing ring, we went to opposite corners in the back seat.

If my father had been there, I could not have climbed into Bill's new, pale yellow Mercury with a black vinyl top. Dad took a dim view of boys who attended dances to take girls home. He said, "They're cheapskates. If I pay eighty-five cents for you to get in, I'll take you home."

As we passed through Durand on our way to Esther's house, Jon said, "Hey, Bill, I've got to see a man about a dog."

At the edge of town, Bill pulled over to the side of the concrete street and stopped. We were in front of Ditzlers'. I was horrified. Jon grabbed the right rear door handle of the four-door sedan, jumped out and hustled across the yard toward the dark outline of a large bush. At any minute, I expected to see Ken's dad wearing pajamas and carrying a flashlight come around the corner of the house to investi-gate who was trespassing at 1:30 A.M. All stayed quiet. Jon climbed back into his corner. He gave a sigh of relief and so did I. Bill pulled away and we continued on our way to Es-ther's home. The boys walked us to the door and we all said a quick, "Good night."

Inside the house, Esther and I quietly climbed the stairs, changed into pjs and crawled into the twin beds in the room she had shared with her sister before June was married. We rehashed the evening. The last thing Esther said before saying goodnight was, "I've got my fingers crossed that Bill will call me."

With winter coming closer, I skipped school on the last Friday of October to shop in the Beloit stores that were closed Sun-days and evenings. I wanted to spend the remaining nine dol-lars of my birthday money at Stanton's Shoe Store for a pair of the new shoe boots to wear when it snowed. Pulling my stadium boots on over my burnt orange, slip-on, work shoes with their thick, rubber soles would be impossible.

November first, my birthday present from Ken finally arrived. I'd spent two months thinking he forgot my birthday. Like an on/off switch, my emotions kept flipping between mad and broken-hearted. The rhinestone necklace, bracelet and earring set was blue, my favorite color. I fastened the jewelry in place, looked in my dresser mirror and grinned from ear to ear.

The accompanying letter said the Bennington left Cali-fornia for Pearl Harbor. They were on their way to join the Seventh Fleet in Asiatic waters. I didn't even have a globe to follow his travels as he sailed farther and farther away.

A couple of days later, I sent Ken a three-pound box of Fannie May chocolates for his twentieth birthday coming up 8 November. His next letter, written from Japan, thanked me for the candy that he'd shared with his buddies.

By the middle of November, I'd learned to do permanents. I paid Mrs. DeBella thirty-five dollars for a kit to use at home. On a Sunday afternoon, Mom shampooed her hair and I cut it with the razor. Then we began the process. I parted her hair into small sections, dipped the little black brush into a cup containing a small amount of permanent solution, dabbed the tress, folded a paper over the ends and rolled it on a plastic rod. The strong smell of ammonia permeated the kitchen. When I'd finished rolling, I saturated each rod with waving lotion and she sat for twenty minutes while her hair curled. Mom moved to the kitchen sink and spent fifteen minutes bent over while I applied neutralizer and let it drip from her curls. After I removed the rods and rinsed her hair, she went back to the chair so I could make waves and pin curls. It took me three hours to do my mother's hair. She then started supper. Her hair would dry overnight.

The first Saturday in December seemed more like spring with the temperature in the forties, fog in the morning and thunder showers predicted later in the day. The inclement weather prompted Mom to drive me to Rockford and pick me up after school. In between trips, she finished last-minute preparations for the evening card party to celebrate Dad's forty-third birthday. By night, the weather cleared, which made my father happy. He loved playing Five Hundred with friends. At eight, the party started with the Weaver clan plus mutual friends, Bus and Hazel, who farmed south of Rockford. With three tables of participants, only four hands were played at a time. The winning couple moved up to the next table and switched partners.

During the eight rounds, players kept track of their scores on individual tallies. Prizes were awarded to men and women for the highest totals and the lowest. Mom topped off the evening with ground pork sandwiches, a white birthday cake decorated with pink roses and the words 'Happy Birthday Alex,' vanilla ice cream and coffee.

Monday at school, we took the first of three weekly final tests. My class would take state board exams in Chicago during January.

On the Sunday before Christmas, Dad and I did some holiday decorating. While he put lights on the little fir in the front yard, I trimmed our small, short needle tree sitting in the living room. I also drew a small picture of Santa and his reindeer flying through the air, colored it with pencils, cut it out and hung it in a shoe box.

The following Saturday, Christmas Eve day, the roads were slippery. Mom drove me to school. On the way, we saw a milk truck tipped over in a farmer's field. She waited to drive me home again.

In the evening, we ate our usual celebratory ham supper. I opened the presents my parents gave me: a table radio, which could also be used as a portable; fur lined, black leather gloves and a white, tailored blouse. The bronze, bridge lamp Dad and Mom bought as their gift wasn't wrapped.

Christmas Day after church, we ate left-overs and saw the Martin & Lewis comedy *Artists and Models* at the Majestic Theater in Beloit.

New Year's Eve we were invited to a party at Jack and Helen's rural Wisconsin home. I was included in the Five Hundred games with the adults instead of having to play Monopoly with their kids. At midnight, everyone said, "Happy New Year," and went home.

Chapter 5

1956

A week after New Year's Eve, Ken's letter said he'd spent the festive night at sea. It was a dull beginning of a new year for both of us.

Three days later, a phone call from our family friend, Mary, secured my future. She asked, "Would you like to work for me after you take your state boards?"

"Yes," I answered immediately. I admired Mary Weaver Dahlberg as a businesswoman who managed the Winnebago County Agricultural Stabilization and Conservation Office in Rockford. It was a local division of the U.S. Department of Agriculture that assisted area farmers to take advantage of government programs. During Dad's December birthday party, Mary and I discussed my disenchantment with styling hair, but I never thought she'd offer me a position. I immediately sent for a Social Security number so I'd be ready to be an employee. What a relief. I wouldn't have to look for clerical work or settle for a job doing hair.

Monday began our last week of beauty school. Tuesday night, Mrs. DeBella treated our class and the teachers to supper at

Jack's or Better on West Jefferson Street in Rockford. To attend the party, Charlene, my petite, classmate, came home with me after school and would stay overnight. Her short, dark-blonde hair was temporarily red because she'd served as Mrs. DeBella's model to demonstrate the old-fashioned dye made from the henna plant. After we changed clothes, my parents drove us back to the city. It was a cold night, but the roads were clear. Not much snow so far this winter.

Dad and Mom dropped us off and went to a cheaper restaurant while the two of us attended the party. Charlene and I joined the group waiting to be seated in the upscale restaurant. The women all looked so pretty wearing heels and colorful frocks instead of clunky, work shoes and white uniforms that reminded me of flour sacks. Sonny was dashing in a coat and tie. We were seated at our reserved table and served tossed salads followed by chicken breasts with rice covered by a sauce.

On the following Sunday, Dad and Mom took me to Charlene's house in Harvard, a medium-sized town fifty miles east of us. It was the first leg of a trip to Chicago to take state board exams Monday and Tuesday mornings. Our classmate, Sandra, who lived in Harmony, a spot in the road about fifteen miles south of Harvard, joined us. She stood just over five feet with short, curly, black hair, sharp, brown eyes and a good figure. Butterflies whirled in my stomach in anticipation of the tests.

Charlene's mother faced little Sunday traffic when she drove the three of us to the Loop and dropped us off. She'd made our reservation at the Washington Hotel, which she called 'cheap but clean'. We checked in at the front desk, climbed the stairs to the second floor and found our assigned room. I thought the place bordered on crummy with faded drapes, worn carpets and threadbare spreads on two double beds. After getting settled, we walked to a nearby diner for cheeseburgers, fries and Cokes. On our way back, we strutted like women of the world out on the town. When we passed a tavern, Charlene said, "Let's stop and have a drink."

Charlene, who often visited her aunt and uncle's cocktail lounge in Harvard, was comfortable entering the establishment. I felt like I was stepping into perdition. I'd never crossed the threshold of a saloon before. Several old guys sitting at the bar turned around on their stools and glared at us like we invaded their men's room. The three of us glanced at one another and silently agreed it wasn't the place for us. We bought a bottle of Mogen David to take back to our room and scurried out. After drinking our red wine from plastic tumblers, we slept soundly.

Monday morning, we took our written tests. We were nervous, but the men and women in the classroom tried to put us at ease. Afterward, we discussed our answers to the test questions and agreed we did well.

The rest of the day, we saw the city sights. At the Union Station, Charlene and I stepped onto an escalator and rode to the bottom. Sandra remained at the top of the moving stairway and called, "I can't. I'm scared."

The train depot was awash with young men in uniform from the nearby Great Lakes Naval Station. Two sailors approached Sandra, offered their arms and escorted her down. Sometimes being a damsel in distress reaped rewards.

The next morning, we checked out of the hotel and carried our bags with us to the salon. After completing our practical tests given by friendly examiners who served as models, we emerged as state registered cosmetologists.

Mrs. DeBella had told us, "If you pass the final tests at my school, you'll have no problem in Chicago." She was right. She also advised those of us who weren't going to work in a shop,

"Be sure and send in the dollar to renew that license each year. Just because you're not using it now, you might need to sometime in the future. It's good insurance." I followed that advice.

Charlene's mother was parked along the curb waiting to drive us back to their home in Harvard. My two classmates then gave me a permanent before Dad and Mom picked me up in the evening.

The next day, I rested at home. I was pooped from my ordeal in Chicago.

Thursday, 26 January, was my first eight to four-thirty day at the ASC office. I donned a calf-length, gray, straight skirt and a harmonizing, long sleeved sweater along with nylons and red loafers. My high school wardrobe sufficed for my new job. The only change was stockings instead of bobby socks.

I skipped breakfast. With my stomach full of butterflies, I was afraid adding food would make me car sick while riding to Rockford. To keep warm on the frigid, sunny morning, I wore the sur coat I'd bought when I was a junior in high school, fur-lined gloves and my new snow boots. A large, black purse hung from my left shoulder. I carried two brown, paper bags—one contained my red loafers and the other my lunch.

Betty maneuvered her Ford through the morning rush hour traffic to drop me off in front of The Rockford Post Office at 401 South Main Street. Nine tall, fat columns stood next to the double-door, entrance of the stately, two-story, concrete building.

The first person I saw in the high-ceilinged, entryway was Henry, the elevator operator who stood with the car-door open. The elderly man, who was about my height, had thick, white hair and dark eyes. He wore a white shirt with a navy blue suit and tie, but no smile when he said, "Good morning," as I entered.

I exited the elevator on the second floor. The first door on the left opened into the ASC suite. Beyond that, a long hallway led to restrooms and offices for the FBI, Soil Conservation Service and Internal Revenue Service. To the right of the elevator were the Social Security department and the federal courtroom where bankruptcy cases were heard periodically. All walls were painted government-issue beige and the floor was shades of brown terrazzo.

Mary was the first to welcome me. My middle-aged employer, who wore glasses, was a big woman, nearly six feet tall in pumps. The tailored dress covering her broad, well-padded frame reflected her executive position. A weekly salon appointment kept her short, graying, brown hair permed and her fingernails painted red.

I knew the other three employees. Donna and Diane were the sisters who provided my ride to Rockford the previous summer. Mildred, a tall, slender, gray-haired woman, was married to Mary's brother, Bob, and often played Five Hundred with my family.

Each woman was assigned regular tasks. Donna was the bookkeeper and Mary's 'right hand' who took charge when the boss was gone. Diane administered the corn loan and the wool support programs. Mildred did mundane tasks that didn't require typing, an office skill she lacked. My first duties were stamping our return address on envelopes, typing or filing when needed and studying the government program books.

The large, main room where the four of us worked at our olive green, metal desks was on the northeast corner of the square edifice. During hot weather, we cranked open the tall windows to let in breezes from the two directions. We talked with farmers at a counter sitting atop a bank of three-drawer, brown, metal file cabinets that separated us from the entrance. A doorway in the west wall led to Mary's office. Beyond that, a third room was used for monthly meetings of the farmer-elected, community committee who oversaw our work. The chairman was John from Seward Township with members Ken from Roscoe Township and Elmo from Durand Township. Except for that one day a month, the third office served as our lunchroom. Every day at twelve-thirty, we locked the front door, made ourselves comfortable in the padded, leather office chairs, opened our brown bags and relaxed for a half-hour.

At 10 A.M. and 2 P.M., Mary handled the office alone while the four of us walked kitty-cornered across the street to spend our fifteen-minute breaks at Cummings Coffee Shop.

Sometime during each day, Harry, the janitor, stopped by to chat and see if we needed anything repaired or replaced. He was a short, wiry man with thinning gray hair. Large tattoos on each of his forearms attested to his twenty-year career in the navy.

At four thirty, I walked five blocks to Hobson's Drug Store to meet Betty. While I waited half-an-hour for her to pick me up, I sat on a stool at their soda fountain and ordered a glass of chocolate milk. I avoided pop because I'd gotten sick from drinking too much of that during my summer at beauty school.

My first monthly paycheck taught me about federal income tax and F.I.C.A. deductions. My salary of a $1.25 per hour came to forty dollars for my four days' work in January. After withholding, I received $35.91. Saturday my folks and I discussed wages while driving to Brodhead to cash my check at the bank. I said, "I wouldn't work for less than a dollar an hour."

Dad retorted, "I cut wood for fifty cents a day when I was your age."

"But, Dad, that was in the thirties during The Depression."

On March first, I received February's salary, $171 after deductions. Mom said, "Now that you're earning a paycheck, you'll have to pay fifty dollars a month room and board." No discussion. No negotiation. Nobody else I knew paid nearly one-third of her take-home pay to live with her parents.

Doing a little hair styling for family and friends filled a few of my empty hours and earned extra cash. Customers bent forward over the kitchen sink for shampoos and sat on a hard, wooden, chair for haircuts, sets and permanents. I knew I was breaking the Illinois law requiring a separate, state inspected beauty parlor in the home. I didn't worry about someone reporting me.

Besides warmer weather and longer days, another sign of spring was the Davis Hatchery's delivery of three-hundred White Leghorn pullets that were three weeks old. I loathed chickens. In the henhouse, their stink aggravated my allergies and made me sneeze. When I retrieved eggs from under a bird sitting on a nest, she'd peck my hand with her sharp beak. I don't know if Mom liked the fowls, but the landlord allowed her to have them on her own without splitting fifty/fifty. She wouldn't pass up the opportunity to make a little extra money selling eggs.

On a Friday night in the middle of the month, the girls from my class were invited to a bridal shower for Corky who married

Roger, another classmate, in a private ceremony two weeks earlier. Her new sister-in-law, Dorothy, who lived in Davis, was our hostess. Esther came to our farm and I drove the rest of the way. On the northeast edge of the village, I slowly pulled off of the blacktop street to park in the grass opposite Dorothy's house. I heard a dull clunk and the right, front corner of our Chevy dropped several inches, I stomped on the brake.

"What happened?" Esther asked in alarm.

"I don't know," I replied. I feared our two-door would tip over but the sedan seemed stable. I slipped the transmission into Park and turned off the key. We both carefully slid out on the driver's side and checked the front of the Chevy. The right wheel hung off a cement culvert, which was shrouded by tall, dead weeds. I needed my vehicle pulled out. We went inside, found Corky's brother-in-law, Bob, sitting in the kitchen and told him about my problem. He called Louie, who operated a tow truck along with the Hilltop Gas Station at the mile-corner south of Durand.

While waiting for help to arrive, I called home. News traveled fast in rural communities. I didn't want Dad and Mom to hear someone else's exaggerated report about my predicament. They understood that it was an accident.

Bob, Esther and I waited outside for Louie. It was a clear, cold night and we could see our breath when we spoke. The wrecker arrived about half-an-hour later. Johnny, one of the community's biggest gossips, was right behind it. The middle-aged farmer climbed down from his pick-up, looked over the situation and said, "She must have been going like hell to go off the road like that."

I bristled like a porcupine. I wanted to tell the man, "If I'd been going like hell, my car would have rolled over," but I didn't. I just grumbled to Esther. She went inside while I paid

Louie four dollars for the rescue. I was relieved to see that our fifty-two wasn't damaged. I carefully parked and joined the other gals in our hostess's living room.

Two weeks later, our office, like all businesses in downtown Rockford, closed from 12:00 M. to 3 P.M. in honor of Good Friday. I ate my sack lunch quickly and attended the one o'clock service sponsored by the city's Lutheran churches at the Times theater. It was a five-block trek in heels, my black suit and large, Copen blue hat.

At the end of the workday, I bid Diane good-bye and wished her well. She was quitting her job.

The following Monday, I took over Diane's responsibilities handling the corn loans provided by the federal government. The Commodity Credit Corporation's price supports, exports and storage protected farm income and maintained a balanced supply of commodities.

The corn program was our biggest job. During the second week of January, Donna sat at a large Friden calculator and used individual crop histories to compute an acreage allotment for each of the more than eighteen-hundred farms in Winnebago County. As she figured, she created large, hand-written, record books. When she finished, we all pitched in to type and mail the information to farmers before spring fieldwork began.

Growers who chose to qualify for the government program could plant no more than allowed. After crops were in, Chandler, a tall, thin, gray-haired man, hired a seasonal helper to hold the other end of his steel tape measure while he diagramed the corn fields. After Chandler submitted his figures, Donna returned to the Friden to calculate the acreage. If a farmer inadvertently exceeded his allotment, the overage needed to be plowed under.

In the fall, most farmers harvested their ear corn using two-row, tractor-mounted pickers. If a man's fields produced more grain than he expected to need to feed his livestock, the surplus was placed in a separate crib and measured. I issued him a loan check based on a guaranteed price to purchase the extra corn. An eight and a half by eleven inch paper seal was attached to the designated crib to remind the farmer not to use that corn, which was collateral for the cash advance. During the following summer, the producer could repay the money or deliver his sealed corn to be shelled at Rockford Grain Co. on Cedar Street, a few blocks from our office. Some of the grain would be shipped out in railroad cars. The rest would be placed in large, round, metal bins at several CCC owned sites around the county. To keep the stored corn from spoiling, Mary hired Cal, an Owen Township farmer, and his crew of neighbors to stir it regularly.

Our office personnel also handled the sign-ups and the subsidy payments to farmers for soil preservation practices such as applying limestone and phosphate to enrich cropland or using contour farming around hills to prevent erosion. Two soil conservation technicians, Lyle, a thin, dark-haired man in his thirties and Glenn, a short, chubby, balding older man, supervised those projects.

I loved my job right from the start. I was comfortable talking to the men who came into the office because I knew about farming firsthand and had been trained in the government programs. My high school business courses prepared me to do the paperwork. I should have listened to my mother and tried employment before enrolling in beauty school.

A couple of weeks later in mid-April, my parents and I were kicking up our heels at the Wigwam on a Saturday night. My friend, Dick, and I had just finished the waltz quadrille, which was performed with four-couple sets like a square dance, but the pace was slower and the calls simpler. It was always scheduled right before the band took a half-hour intermission at eleven, but the guys lined up their partners early in the evening. Dick, a short, stocky, brown-haired fellow, who was cute in a boyish way, said, "Would you like a Coke?"

"Yes, thank you," I responded.

We stood in front of the lunch counter at the edge if the dance floor in the rough-hewn building. We were drinking our pop and visiting when he asked, "Would you like to go to a show on Wednesday night?"

Without hesitation, I replied, "Yes."

We finalized details and adjourned to the dance floor when the band returned to the stage and began playing a waltz.

Later, at home in my bedroom, I reflected on my rash commitment. I thought it would be fun to spend an evening with a nice guy that I'd been dancing with for several years. I didn't consider going to a movie a big transgression because Ken and I weren't married or engaged. Still, I wouldn't mention it in my daily letters to my boyfriend.

I missed dating since Ken boarded the aircraft carrier last May. A year with letters our only contact was proving to be a very, long, lonely time. It would have been so much easier if I hadn't fallen in love with him until after his hitch in the navy.

I didn't sit at home looking at four walls every night. I attended dances, card parties, community events and visited friends with Dad and Mom. I also did things with my cousin,

Doris, and my friend, Esther. Nothing compared with going out with a fellow and being the center of his attention for an evening.

The night Dick and I went to the show, I made sure I mentioned the sailor whose class ring I wore. I wanted it clear that I wasn't looking for a new boyfriend. We went to a couple more movies and then Dick didn't ask me out anymore. I think the frugal, farm boy, who lived a few miles north of the Wigwam, was looking for a girlfriend. He probably decided he was wasting his gas, his money and his time with me. Apparently, there were no hard feelings. He continued to ask me to dance and I accepted, which was best.

Wednesday, 30 May, was Memorial Day. I enjoyed sleeping late on the holiday. In the afternoon, I helped Dad wash and polish our Chevy. Afterward, I made a batch of fudge to send to Ken. It wouldn't get stale in the mail because the Bennington had returned from the other side of the globe to their home port, San Diego, California.

A couple weeks later on a Friday afternoon at work, I cleared my desk and waited for the clock to creep along the last five minutes to four thirty. Mary called from her office, "Lolita, can you come in here a minute?" I complied and she said, "Why don't you come with Henry and me for fish tonight? We always get together with the same bunch. Your mother could bring you to our house by six thirty." Like most wives, she used her husband's formal name. Everyone else called the brown-haired Swede 'Hank'.

"Thank you," I replied. "I'd like that." An evening out with my boss, her husband and their friends sounded more exciting than sitting at home listening to the radio with Mom and Dad.

At The Ranch in Beloit, Hank, Mary and I joined the group seated around a long table covered with a white cloth. Mary introduced me to the others and I sat down in the vacant captain's chair beside Clarence.

The previous March, my folks and I met Mary's friend, Clarence, when she hosted a card party to celebrate her birthday. Since then, the short, dark, good-looking guy came to the office a few times to do various odd jobs and we chatted. I learned he was ten years older than I, divorced and lived with his father on a small farm a few miles north of Shirland, an unincorporated village about ten miles east of Durand. Besides helping his dad, he owned a stock truck and hauled his neighbors' cattle and hogs to Milwaukee markets. I silently wondered why this single man in his twenties was included in a gathering of four, middle-aged couples, but he seemed to be well-acquainted. I guess he was a stray the same as I was.

Each of us ordered the dollar perch special. While we waited for our food to be served, it sounded like everyone was talking at once. After finishing supper, we all moved on to someone's home in Rockford to visit for a while. I sat quietly in the kitchen and listened to the other women talk about 'housewife things' such as plants and washing powders. The men gathered in the living room. When the crowd broke up about ten o'clock, Mary told me, "Clarence will drive you home."

During the trip to our farm, I chattered about Durand's upcoming centennial in July. The community contracted with a company to help local committees mark the milestone by compiling a history booklet, writing a pageant and arranging other activities to celebrate. The women formed the "Sisters of the Swish" and sewed long, calico dresses with matching sunbonnets to wear for events. The men, who were normally clean shaven, organized the "Brothers of the Brush" and grew beards, mutton chops and mustaches to look like citizens did in the 1850s. I said, "About a week ago, I received a letter stating I was a nominee to be centennial queen. Last night, I attended the informational meeting and found myself in a room full of local girls. The woman in charge said, 'The queen will be the one who sells the most coupons.' I immediately decided not to be a candidate. I didn't want to sell coupons."

"Too bad," Clarence responded. "You would have made a beautiful queen."

"Thank you."

Clarence pulled in our gravel driveway and stopped at the end of the cement walk. I thanked him for the ride, got out of his maroon coupe and strolled toward the house. He turned around in front of the garage and drove out.

The following Monday, we kept the ASC office open until 8 P.M. to give busy farmers extra time to sign up for the corn program before the deadline. When we closed, Mary arranged for me to climb into Clarence's '46 Ford for an uneventful ride home.

Early the next morning, Mom faced the glare of the rising sun as she drove me to the office to meet Mary at seven. My boss and I needed to be in DeKalb by eight for an all-day, training session that included employees from several area counties. The instructional meetings were held periodically to bring everyone up to date on the latest changes in government programs. When we arrived in the designated classroom at the Northern Illinois University, Mary greeted friends and intro-duced me. It was late afternoon when she and I returned to her home in Harrison. She phoned Clarence and asked him to drive me home. On the way, I told him about our long, boring day of speakers going over the manuals we could read for ourselves. For the third time, he dropped me at the end of the sidewalk and drove away.

When I entered our kitchen, my parents were seated at the oilcloth covered table finishing supper. Mom said emphatically, "You are not to be dating Clarence. He is too old for you and divorced. There are married men with wives and married men without wives." The set of Dad's jaw told me he agreed.

Without saying a word, I turned my back on supper, stomped into my bedroom and slammed the door behind me. My mind was spinning like a tilt-a-whirl ride at a county fair. I didn't know what she meant by married men with and without wives, but I was supposed to figure it out. I stripped off my work clothes, threw them in a pile on the floor and donned shortie pajamas. I flopped onto my bed muttering, "I'm not dating Clarence–he's just been my ride home three times. I'm an eighteen-year-old adult. My parents shouldn't be running my life, but they say, 'You put your feet under our table–you abide by our rules.'" It took me several hours to cool off enough to sleep.

A week later on Saturday, the last day of June, the temperature was expected to hit the nineties. In the morning, Mom and I went to Brodhead where I cashed my monthly check at the bank and opened a savings account. My mother urged me to deposit money for the future instead of buying things to place in a 'hope chest'.

Some of my friends' parents gave their daughters cedar chests as high school graduation gifts. The young women filled the wooden boxes with expensive china and sterling purchased one place setting at a time.

Mom said, "After you're married, a vacuum cleaner and a washing machine are needed a whole lot more than fancy dishes and silverware."

I agreed.

Sunday evening, we were finishing supper when Ditzlers' green Nash pulled in the gravel driveway and stopped at the end of the sidewalk. I was dumbfounded. Ken didn't tell me he was coming home. At least, I was still wearing my church clothes. I jumped up from the table, ran across the porch, down the wooden steps and out the sidewalk. When he stepped out of the car, I threw my arms around his neck. For me, it was Christmas in July.

Ken hugged me with his right arm and gave me a big kiss. Under his left arm, he carried a maroon, jewelry box that was embellished with illustrations of oriental landscapes. He handed it to me and said, "This is for you. The wood's been stained that color with pigeon blood." That was a gruesome thought, but the small chest was finished with several coats of lacquer so I wasn't actually touching the blood.

Inside the kitchen, Ken greeted my folks sitting at the round oak table. I displayed my present. When I lifted the lid, the tune, " China Nights, " tinkled. I'd admired music boxes for years, but I'd never mentioned it. He had a knack for choosing gifts I treasured. After visiting for a few minutes, we left to go to a show.

As soon as we pulled out of the driveway on our way to Rockford, Ken began telling me how close he came to being aboard one of the two planes that collided while flying over the Grand Canyon the day before. "Yesterday morning, at L.A. airport, I had my ticket home. I called Mom from a pay phone and told her I would be leaving a little after 9 A.M. California time on United flight 718 to Chicago. After I hung up, another sailor approached me. He said, 'My mother's dying and I'm afraid I'll be too late to see her if I don't leave on the next plane.' I let him have my ticket and I took the later flight.

In Chicago, I was walking away from the gate when I overheard a pilot and a stewardess talking about a plane crashing in the Grand Canyon. It must have happened while we were in the air. I went to a pay phone and called home to have the folks come and pick me up. When I said, 'Hi, Mom,' she started to cry. She'd been afraid I'd been killed. That's when I found out all about the plane crash. I felt bad for the guy I'd given my ticket to."

After hearing Ken's story, I said, "I'm glad I didn't know you were on your way home."

Saturday, I felt sad when radio newsmen described the greatest air tragedy in U.S. aviation. One-hundred-twenty-eight passengers and crew were killed. If Ken was aboard United's DC-7 flight 718 when it collided with TWA's Super Constellation flight 2, my world would have ended. I offered a quick, silent prayer of thanksgiving.

Ken was home on a thirty-day leave after being gone for fourteen months. A lot happened to each of us since we danced at my senior prom last May. He boarded the aircraft carrier and travelled to the Orient. I matured from a schoolgirl to a working woman. During the year, our letters held us together like butterfly tapes applied to the edges of a wound.

When we arrived at the air-conditioned theater, it didn't matter what was on the screen. We were content sitting in the dark with his arm around me and my head on his shoulder. On our way home, the night cooled enough that we were comfortable parking and necking on Weber Road.

On Wednesday night, the Fourth of July, Wayne and Gloria joined us watching the stock car races from the bleacher seats on the back side of the asphalt track at the Rockford Speedway. Gloria recently graduated from high school and worked as a file clerk at Retail Credit, a finance company in downtown Rockford. They were engaged. In a few days, she would be eighteen, the lawful age for women to marry. Their wedding would be 20 October, the day after Wayne turned twenty-one and could legally tie the knot.

The races were followed by fireworks. We ooh'd and ahh'd at the colorful spectacle, which reminded us of the line, "the bombs bursting in air," in "The Star-Spangled Banner."

The next afternoon, Ken called me from a pay phone at the Wisconsin Dells, a tourist attraction a couple hours' drive north that his family was visiting. His leave coincided with his folks' annual two-week vacation from their office jobs at Globe Imperial. I wanted to monopolize my boyfriend's time while he was home, but I realized his parents and Tommy missed him, too. His brief call assured me that he was thinking of me while spending time with his family

During the weekend, we saw shows Saturday and Sunday and parked on Weber Road on our way home each evening.

The following Wednesday night, Ken and I went to the Grange hall for the Ball that kicked off Durand's hundredth birthday celebration. My classmate, Lorraine, a petite, dark-haired girl of Irish descent, sold the most coupons and was crowned Queen of the Centennial.

Friday night, I went with Wayne and Gloria to the first of two evening performances of the outdoor pageant, *Days of Durand,* which dramatized the settlement of the community. Ken was asked to participate in the program's finale. Seeing him wearing his navy uniform and standing at attention amid flag waving and patriotic music gave me goose bumps. Afterward my boyfriend joined us to take Gloria and me home.

Saturday was warm and sunny, just right for the Centennial Parade. When Dad and Mom left after dinner to go to town, I waited for Ken to pick me up. Apparently there was a miscommunication. He didn't show up and I missed the parade.

Sunday, I slept until noon. Having Ken home was exhausting. In the afternoon, with the temperature in the nineties, we drove north two hours to Lake Mills with Wayne and Gloria. It always seemed cooler by the water. The glut of cars in the parking lot was a portent of the beach. We walked carefully through the clusters of people to avoid accidently stepping on someone sprawled on the Wisconsin beach. It took ten minutes to find a bare spot big enough to spread our blanket. We rubbed tanning lotion on our bodies and stretched out in the sun. I felt like I was in a dream lying beside Ken. The water was so crowded that we never bothered to get wet.

Thursday morning on my way to work, I left our Chevy parked in Durand with the doors unlocked and the keys stashed above the sun visor for Ken. My parents and my boss, Mary, had approved my spending the afternoon with my boyfriend. He picked me up at noon. We ate cheeseburgers at a drive-in on South Main and went for a ride in the sedan.

That evening and again Sunday night, we went to shows in Rockford. The air-conditioned theaters gave us a welcome respite from the heat wave. By the time we parked on Weber Road, it cooled down a bit. With the windows rolled down, a slight breeze kept us comfortable necking and listening to popular music on WGN.

The following Wednesday night, Ken's sister, Lola Mae, invited us for supper. She wore a white, sleeveless blouse and red shorts with white sandals when she greeted us at the front door. She was nearly as tall as Ken and slender as a teenager.

We walked into the living room where her husband, Joe, sat in an easy chair. A short-sleeved shirt was his only concession to the hot weather. 'Uncle Kenny' was waylaid in a mass hug by his young nieces and nephews–Judy, six, Suzie, four, Jimmy, three and Stevie, a year-and-and-a-half. The kids were barefoot and wore shorts and tee shirts. Ken lifted Stevie high in the air and the baby squealed with delight. A chorus erupted, "Do me, Uncle Kenny! Do me!"

Uncle Kenny complied moving up from the youngest to the oldest. By the time he lifted Judy, his arms were growing weary and his grin was close to a grimace but the giggles of each child made his moves worthwhile.

I smiled watching my boyfriend. He was definitely father material. He told me, "I used to be Judy's babysitter."

Lola Ma opened the windows and the back door, but there was no air movement when we gathered in their small kitchen. The table was set with avocado-colored, cloth placemats, paper plates, stainless steel tableware, and plastic tumblers. Once we all sat down around the blonde-wood table with the leaves extended and the highchair as a permanent fixture, nobody could move.

Our hostess was a good cook who had plenty of practice with her large family and extra men for dinner during the growing season. She served potato salad with her mother's recipe for homemade dressing to give it extra zest, cole slaw, hamburgers and hot dogs for the kids. Apple pie with ice cream topped off the meal.

While we were eating, Jimmy held up his empty glass and requested, "More." Ken was in position to open the refrigerator door, grab the gallon milk jug, reach across the table and pour a refill.

After the meal, I helped Lola Mae clean up the kitchen while the men and kids went to the living room. A short time later, we left. The kids wouldn't want to go to bed with Uncle Kenny there. We took a short ride that ended in our driveway.

Saturday night, we saw a show and lingered on Weber Road. July was ending and so was Ken's leave. On Monday, he would fly back to California and board the Bennington. His final good-bye while parked in our driveway was a repeat of last summer. He kissed me and said, "Bye. See you next year."

I didn't want Ken to see me cry so I managed to hold back my tears until I was inside my bedroom. Another lonely twelve months of going to work and coming home stretched ahead of me.

A couple of weeks later, Dad and Mom enjoyed milking in the remodeled barn that held forty cows instead of twenty-four. Mr. Lunde, the landlord's carpenter, and his crew had torn off the horse stalls that we no longer needed, replaced them with an addition on the west side of the existing building and renovated the old structure. The men also installed a pipeline system that carried the milk directly from the animals to a bulk cooler sitting in a new, small, white building adjacent to the barn. No more lifting full pails and cans.

Dairy cows are docile animals that thrive on routine. Like Lutherans claiming pews in church, the bovines stand quietly in the same stanchions at milking time. During the two months of construction, my parents contended with a skittish herd in a makeshift setup. Dad and Mom moved very carefully to avoid startling the cattle. They talked softly when they squatted down beside the animals to fasten the milkers to their teats. A nervous cow's kick could break a person's arm or leg.

The day after Labor Day, I turned nineteen. Dad and Mom gave me a hood-type hair dryer that could be placed on the kitchen table. It was a boon for me and my customers.

Ken's present, a silver necklace and earrings with exotic, Si-amese figures on a black background, arrived in the Wednesday morning mail. I always considered his gifts tangible proof he loved me and was thinking of me.

The following Sunday morning, the sun was shining when my cousin, Doris, picked me up at six thirty to begin our vacation trip to Mackinac Island, a tourist mecca in northern Michigan. We stowed my big, light blue suitcase and small navy one alongside hers in the trunk of her Chevy. I'd always tagged along with Doris like a baby sister, but after I grad-uated from high school, the fourteen-year difference in our ages melted away. She recognized I was an adult capable of making my own decisions and paying my own way. We each put a hundred dollars in a kitty for our joint expenses such as gas and motels. To avoid carrying a lot of cash for individual purchases, we'd each obtained traveler's checks from the bank.

As Doris pulled out of our driveway, I asked, "Would you please go to Rockford first? I need to stop at the office." She obliged without complaint.

Earlier, I'd been dressing for comfort in jeans, a red-plaid, short-sleeved shirt and tennis shoes, when my boss, Mary, phoned. "Would you mind meeting me at the office to sign some corn loan checks before you leave in case some are needed during the week while you're gone? I should have had you do it Friday, but I didn't think about it." The checks needed both my signature and hers.

Complying with my employer's request delayed us about an hour but, instead of being annoyed, I felt indispensable.

While we spent the day driving north, I thought about things my cousin taught me that my mother didn't do such as applying eye make-up and drinking alcohol. When I was a child, I sat on the edge of Doris's single bed and intently watched my grown-up relative preparing for a date. She leaned in close to her wall mirror to fill in her eyebrows with the light brown, Maybelline pencil. If she didn't have a glass of water sitting on the dresser in her upstairs bedroom, some spit worked just as well to moisten the bristles of the little, red-handled brush she used to apply the black, cake mascara to her lashes.

After my eighteenth birthday, Illinois's legal drinking age for females, Doris counseled me, "Some people expect everyone in a group to drink alcohol. If you're in that situation, order a Tom Collins. It's gin in a tall glass with lots of mix and ice. You can sip on that all evening with the ice melting. If anyone asks if you want something more, just reply 'I still have some.'"

We spent the night at a small motel in Escanaba, Michigan. The next morning, we drove to Sault Ste. Marie to board a sight-seeing boat. We travelled though the Soo Locks and experienced the twenty-one-foot drop between Lake Superior and Lake Huron.

The following day, a smaller craft took us from the city of St. Ignace across Lake Huron to Mackinac Island. To begin our tour of the premises, we climbed aboard a wagon pulled by a team of horses because no motorized vehicles were allowed. The Grand Hotel was too expensive for our budgets, but we went inside to look around the lobby at the splendor. The ornate light fixtures and furnishings were like stepping into a movie set from the 1920s. We then visited the historical sites including the blacksmith shop and Fort Mackinac, which stood on a stone bluff since the American Revolution.

Before the boat left the island to return us to the mainland, we perused the souvenir shops. We saw nothing within our price range that we wanted.

Back on Michigan's Upper Peninsula, we boarded a car ferry to travel to Mackinaw City. While sitting in her sedan, we observed the bridge being built to span the strait between Lake Michigan and Lake Huron.

On the Lower Peninsula, we checked into a 'Mom and Pop' motel. After showering, we donned dresses and walked to their restaurant to eat supper. The hostess seated us at a booth next to a large window overlooking the work site. As day became night, we admired the lighted view. While waiting for her red snapper and my fried chicken to be served, we sipped glasses of Virginia Dare Pink Wine.

A stocky, guy with a dark buzz cut who looked to be about Doris's age, arose from a barstool, walked over to our booth, pulled up a chair to the end of our table and sat down. He wore jeans and a long-sleeved, dark blue T-shirt. He said, "Hi. I'm Bill and I work out there. That will be one of the longest suspension bridges in the world when we finish it next year. Its center span is thirty-eight-hundred feet long."

I was surprised my cousin was cold and non-communicative. Usually she's congenial and talkative. I'm always quiet.

After a few more remarks about the work, the man stood up, replaced his chair at the nearby table and said, "Have a nice night, ladies." He returned to his bar stool.

Doris explained, "If we'd been friendly, he'd have phoned a buddy to join us." Another lesson, how to handle a strange guy trying to pick up women in a bar.

By lunchtime Wednesday, Doris and I were tired of eating diner food. On our way south from Mackinaw City to Muskegon, she stopped at a little, country grocery store along Highway 31. Inside, three aisles divided five rows of shelves stacked with basic items. Refrigerated storage with glass doors covered the right half of the back wall. The proprietor, wrapped in a full-length, white apron, stood behind the counter to the left of the front door. He greeted us with, "Can I help you, ladies?"

Doris told the thirtyish fellow, "We need a loaf of Sunbeam bread, four slices of big baloney, a pound of butter, a jar of mustard and a small bag of potato chips."

The man sliced the meat and gathered the rest of my cousin's order. Doris bagged half-a-dozen, small, chocolate chip cookies contained in one of the glass-covered, boxes sitting along the right side of the center aisle. I grabbed two bottles of Coke from the red cooler stashed in the back corner. Doris used the 'kitty' to pay for our food and we left the store. We continued south on 31 until we came to a roadside picnic table and stopped. I carried our groceries and Doris brought the box containing the tablecloth, paper plates, napkins, silverware and bottle opener she'd packed in the trunk. We sat down on the wooden benches and enjoyed our 'homemade meal'.

About four o'clock, we used the outhouse at a primitive rest stop to change from our comfortable jeans and tennis shoes to dresses and heels. We needed to be appropriately attired to eat supper at an upscale restaurant in Muskegon.

After dining, Doris drove onto a large ferry boat that would take us across Lake Michigan and arrive at Milwaukee about two-and-a half-hours later. After turning her Chevy over to a valet, we joined other passengers seated in the waiting room. Doris curled up in a lounge chair and dozed. I stood staring out the large windows at the calm, turquoise expanse while the ferry got underway. It was the first time I'd been on a body of water so large that I couldn't see land. When it grew too dark to see anything beyond my reflection in the glass, I sat down and read magazines that were lying on a table.

When we landed on the Milwaukee side about midnight, Doris said, "I'm not feeling very good. Why don't you drive home?"

We reclaimed her sedan stowed below deck. Doris took the passenger side of the red imitation leather bench seat and I slid behind the wheel. My cousin didn't opt for power brakes or power steering on her '53. I needed to apply a little more muscle for stops and turns than I did with our '52. With little traffic on Highway 15, we reached my house about 2 A.M. Thursday. Doris headed home and I went to bed.

Thursday afternoon, Doris phoned to tell me about her visit to their family physician. He shared quarters with two dentists above Tallackson's Grocery Store in Durand. She said, "This morning when I got up, I was still tired, feverish and sick to my stomach so I went back to see Dr. Schwartz. Last Saturday, he'd given me a routine injection for lock jaw after Smokey broke the skin on my arm while we were playing.

Today the doctor said I was having an allergic reaction to the tetanus shot he gave me and warned me to never have another one. He said I'll feel better in a day or two. I don't have to be back to work until Monday."

"I'm glad you called. I hope you're better real soon." We said our goodbyes and hung up.

On Monday back in the ASC office, I met our new employee, Lois. She was a tall, thin blonde of Swedish heritage who recently graduated from Hononegh High School in Rockton. She was just what we needed in the office, another young, single farm girl.

Several months earlier, Lois's oldest sibling, Dorothy, who looked like she could be Lois's mother, replaced Mildred, who retired. The sisters were nieces of our boss's husband, Henry.

The next night, I started bowling in the Tuesday night league at the four-lane establishment in Durand. Eight, five-member teams sponsored by local businesses competed in two shifts on ladies' night. The first started at seven and the second between nine and nine-thirty, whenever the early ones finished. I entered the building a few minutes before nine. The swish of the balls rolling down the hardwood alleys, the clatter of the pins falling and the cheers of the players echoed fun.

Two weeks earlier at the organizational meeting, six of us were assigned to a new crew sponsored by the Bentley & Highland grocery store. My married teammates included Bernice, who was about my mother's age; Esther, who was like Doris; and three others who were a few years older than I–Shirley, Marj, and her sister-in-law, Norma, from Winnebago. Each week, one of our members would sit out and be available if needed as a substitute. With this our first year, we didn't bother with team uniforms like established teams wore.

After changing into my new bowling shoes, I searched through the black balls sitting on the two racks between the alleys. Most of the holes were drilled for men's hands. I finally found one that I could hold on to.

At quarter-after-nine, my team met Tracy's Tin Shop on lanes three and four. Wayne's father and his uncle, Chuck and 'Tip', sponsored the team that included his mother and his aunt, Dot and Lilas. Our skilled opponents wore red dresses with their name in black letters across the back.

When we finished the three-game series about eleven-thirty, my total for the evening was 246 giving me an average of 82. That was similar to my scores in high school, but a long ways from the perfect game of three-hundred. Team captains used pencil and paper to figure individual handicaps based on each woman's average. That gave teams with a beginner like me a chance against those with experienced bowlers like our adversary. We lost all three games, but I enjoyed the evening and looked forward to improving.

The following evening, Ken's sister called and invited me to end September with their family at the Brookfield Zoo near Chicago. Lola Mae and Joe picked me up at eight thirty on a warm, Sunday morning. I crawled into the backseat of their two-door Chevy and squeezed in with Judy, Suzie, and Jimmy. Baby Stevie sat on his mother's lap. They dropped him off with Grandpa and Grandma Ditzler in Durand.

It took nearly three hours of driving along U.S. 20 to arrive in the parking lot of our destination. After paying our admission, Joe rented a bright, orange pushcart for the kids to ride on. We then strolled for miles along tree-shaded walkways looking at the creatures from all over the world.

The animals roamed free in their recreated, outdoor habitats instead of being confined to cages. Moats separated the people from the beasts and allowed interaction between the two groups. The monkeys on their island seemed to perform for the audience who laughed at their antics.

Three large polar bears stood on their hind legs with front paws ready to grab marshmallows tossed by visitors. Joe bought a handful of the white bits from a coin-operated, vending machine sitting in front of the area. The kids clapped their hands and cheered each time their dad tossed a morsel and an animal caught it.

At noon, we found a shaded, picnic table and enjoyed the ground baloney sandwiches, potato chips, oatmeal cookies and grape Kool-Aid Lola Mae had packed. It was too expensive for the family of five to buy lunch from a stand.

By four o'clock, we were worn out and ready to head home. Joe parked the orange cart and we entered an aviary. After viewing the colorful, squawking birds, we exited at the opposite end of the building and walked toward the parking lot. Joe abandoned the conveyance to avoid returning it and paying the fee.

As we left the edifice, Judy, their oldest child, said, "Dad, you forgot our cart."

"That's alright," Joe responded. "We don't need it now."

"But Dad, we have to take it back to the man."

Lola Mae then quietly silenced her daughter by saying, "Shh, it's okay. Don't worry about it."

Three weeks later on a Friday afternoon in the office, the four of us cleared our desks and watched the big hand on the clock slowly creep along those last few minutes before quittin' time. Mary stepped to the doorway and said, "Girls, please come in here for a minute." She returned to her large, office chair.

Donna, Dorothy, Lois and I gave one another puzzled looks while doing as our boss asked. We sat down in the same straight chairs surrounding her wooden desk that we occupied each morning to review the day's mail. Mary said, "Henry and I are getting a divorce. I have rented an apartment here in Rockford on Logan St. just east of the cemetery at Auburn and North Main. I'll be moving this weekend. That's all. I'll see you Monday morning."

We left Mary's office, grabbed our light coats from the closet and entered the elevator. As soon as Henry, the operator, closed the door, we began gossiping about her announcement. We weren't surprised. For months, a pink Lincoln picked up our boss at lunchtime while we surreptitiously watched out the windows. The driver was Kenny, the married man who operated Rockford Grain where the corn in the government program was shelled and transported. The two worked closely together every summer when farmers delivered their sealed corn. Mary's recent raise probably made her move possible. Federal law required employees' salaries to be posted on the wall where anyone entering the office could view them. Our boss made more than five-thousand dollars a year, which was considered high pay, especially for a woman.

The next afternoon, my family attended Willabea and Duke's wedding and reception held at Luther Valley Church located near her parents' farm. In the evening, a public dance was held at Bluff View hall near Brodhead.

Duke had worked at the General Motors car plant in nearby Janesville for the past two years. He'd accompanied Willabea to the Wigwam since they started dating when he was still in high school. He reminded me of Ken. They both had light brown hair, an average build and gentlemanly ways.

Back home at the end of the night, I cried. The Wigwam gang was no more.

Willabea was married. Janice and Joyce attended the University of Wisconsin in Madison studying to be teachers. My girlfriends entered new phases while my life remained on hold.

The first Friday of November, I stayed overnight with Esther and the next day, we shopped in Beloit. Before we left the city, she stopped at Mrs. Hogan's home on Sixth Street to pursue a newspaper ad offering to rent a bedroom with kitchen privileges.

Esther, who checked out customers at Bonnie Bee grocery store on Broad Street, was looking for a place she could afford to live on her own. She hit it off with the little old lady living in the two-story house and arranged to move in with her cookware.

Transportation wouldn't be a problem for my friend. Public bus service was available and her boyfriend, Sheldon, who lived in the city, owned a car.

Sometimes when I was disgusted with my parents' rules, I daydreamed about moving out, but I wasn't ready to follow Esther's example.

November eighth, Ken turned twenty-one and the State of Illinois considered him a man. He could marry, drink alcohol and vote. I had mailed an Old Spice shaving set, but I didn't know how long it would take the package to reach the Bennington. On 12 October, the ship left for the Far East.

Two days after Ken's birthday, my month-old cough pushed me to visit Dr. Hein, a young, physician who took over Dr. Stovall's practice in Brodhead. The tall, thin, black-haired, family-man prescribed a bottle of wild cherry flavored syrup to replace the over-the-counter remedies that hadn't cured me.

The following Monday, I went to work, but stayed home the next day. My hacking was worse when I lay down so I didn't sleep very well. The medicine wasn't helping so I returned to the doctor Wednesday and he prescribed stronger syrup. I was too tired to go to the office the rest of the week.

A couple of weeks after Ken's birthday, I received his letter that said, *Thank you for the Old Spice. That's something I can always use. I spent my birthday aboard ship. I'll have to wait for liberty to celebrate. My first drink will be a glass of fresh milk. We just have powdered milk aboard ship so fresh milk is a real treat when we go ashore.*

We're in Japan now, but I don't know where we'll be going from here.

To celebrate Thanksgiving, my folks and I were invited to dinner with the Weaver clan at Jack and Helen's rural Wisconsin home. While on our way along the blacktop roads, I sat in my usual place in the back seat of our Chevy. Dad was behind the wheel and Mom sat beside him holding a dish of fruit salad on her lap. She said, "I think they include us to prevent fighting among the brothers and their sister. When outsiders are there, everyone is on their good behavior."

At noon, the wooden dining table covered with a white cloth and set with good tableware overflowed with a traditional turkey dinner. Before ten adult members of the Weaver family plus my folks sat down, David, Margie, Nancy and I filled our plates and gathered around a card table covered with a white cloth.

In the evening, we took my cousin, Doris, and my friend, Esther, with us to the Auburn Theater on the northwest side of Rockford. We saw the new, singing sensation, Elvis Presley, in his first movie, *Love Me Tender*. Early in the year, when he crashed the hit parade with his recording of "Heartbreak Hotel," his unique vocal style was dubbed rock and roll. His dyed black pompadour, long sideburns and gyrations while he sang shocked TV variety show viewers. Of course, my parents and I didn't see him because we don't have television. After watching the black and white Western that took place during the Civil War, we all agreed the singer was no actor.

On Monday morning, I began December in Dr. Hein's office instead of the ASC office. He prescribed cough syrup that contained the opiate, codeine, and it helped. Tuesday I went to work after a good night's sleep.

In the evening, I walked into the bowling alley carrying my new red and black bag containing my tan shoes and a twenty-five-dollar ball. I'd followed the example of the other women and purchased equipment fitted to me. My initials were embossed in white so I could easily distinguish my black, sixteen-pounder from all of the identical ones sitting on the rack. I ended the night with a total of 319 giving me a 106 average, much better than my low nineties.

Two days later, I ate lunch at work and then felt like I might throw up. I blamed the new cough medicine. Five o'clock seemed like a long time to wait to go home. I called Ken's mother, Hazel, at Globe Imperial and asked, "Would you and Rolland please pick me up when you leave town at three thirty? I think my cough medicine has made me sick."

She quickly agreed and I began counting the minutes. When I arrived home, I skipped supper and went right to bed. The next morning, my queasiness was gone.

During the holiday season, stores in downtown Rockford stayed open evenings. Betty, my driver, told her riders she planned to Christmas shop after work Friday and wouldn't leave the city until six fifteen. With no gifts to buy, I had an hour and three-quarters to kill. I asked my new friend, Clarence, to meet me for supper. Last summer my parents decreed I was not to date him because he was ten years older than I and divorced. I believed I was an adult who could make my own decisions–my folks didn't always have to know what I was doing. Clarence met me in the office at four thirty and the two of us walked a block up the street to the Redwood family restaurant. We ate a leisurely meal and chatted about his trucking a neighbor's hogs to the Milwaukee market, my new bowling team and Mary's divorce. Afterward, he drove me to Hobson's Drug Store to catch my ride home with Betty.

Over the weekend, I rested at home. Monday, I felt better but that didn't last.

Three days later, during a coughing spell at work, I felt a sharp pain in my right side. It continued to hurt every time I inhaled. Saturday, I saw Dr. Hein who told me I'd pulled a chest muscle. He prescribed aspirin for the discomfort and time for it to heal.

Tuesday night, I was still sore. Dad drove me to Marj's house in Durand to join our team Christmas party before late bowling. A week earlier, Bernice and I drew each other's names for the gift exchange. She gave me Blue Waltz cologne in a heart shaped bottle and I gave her three handkerchiefs in a box. Marj served Christmas cookies and punch before the others went to the bowling alley and Dad took me home.

Friday morning, I was looking forward to the Christmas party Mary had talked about since I started my job. I donned dark gray, sling-back heels and my one-of-a-kind dress with an off-the-shoulder bodice and a gathered skirt. Before Aunt Frannie cut into my expensive pale-blue brocade with a gold and turquoise flower design, she made a muslin prototype and fitted it to me.

All day at the office, the five of us served our homemade cookies, sandwiches, punch and coffee to the other workers on the second floor, farmers and friends. Early in the afternoon, Dad and Mom picked up Mary's parents and drove through the fog to attend.

I enjoyed the party but, by the time I returned home, I was exhausted. I skipped supper and tumbled into bed. Saturday morning after breakfast, I went back to bed and spent the rest of the day. I just couldn't shake my cough and it wore me out.

Monday was Christmas Eve, a day off for me. The only package under our decorated tree in the living room was mine from Ken. After breakfast, I opened his gift, an opalite necklace and earrings set. I'd mailed him a black, leather billfold.

Our family Christmas present would be a '57, ivory over coral Chevy that we ordered at Iverson's, the dealer in Brodhead. The hard-top would be made to our specifications and delivered from the factory in early January. The four-door-sedan would cost $2,112.50 after deducting the trade-in allowance of $875 for our '52.

In the evening, we joined the Weaver clan at Jack and Helen's rural home for a traditional holiday supper. Mom took a plate full of bratzelies, the wafer-thin, Swiss cookies my parents baked on a special electric iron similar to a waffle iron.

Christmas day, I was invited to the Ditzlers for the first time. Mom drove me and a plate of bratzelies to Durand shortly before noon. I joined the family sitting in the living room waiting for the turkey to finish cooking in the electric roaster. Ken's mother left the kitchen for a few minutes respite and plopped down on her husband's lap. My boyfriend's family was a warm, friendly group and much more demonstrative than my parents.

When we all gathered around the kitchen table to eat the traditional dinner, I was relieved when Hazel's dressing tasted similar to my mother's. There were so many variations. Some of my friends told tales of having to choke down a mother-in-law's specialty such as oyster.

After eating, the grandkids impatiently waited while the grown-ups enjoyed coffee and cigarettes. We women cleaned-up the kitchen before joining the others in the living room. Tommy knelt beside the Christmas tree and began handing out presents. Ken's parents gave me an imitation gold necklace and earring set.

During the afternoon, Hazel took lots of pictures to send to Ken including one of me prominently holding Joe's Schlitz beer can. I tasted the brew once when Ken was drinking it with his brother-in-law. I thought it was awful.

After a supper of leftovers. Joe and Lola Mae drove me home. Stevie sat on his mother's lap while Judy, Suzie, Jimmy and I squeezed into the back seat of their two-door Chevy.

Spending the day with four little kids under seven years of age, pooped me out. They'd been like wind-up toys that never ran down. It made me wonder whether I really wanted to get married and have a family. I thought that four children would be ideal, but that might be too many. I definitely wanted more than one.

The day after Christmas, my cough seemed better. I was surprised when Ken's buddy, Bill, who was home on leave from the navy, called. He asked me to join him visiting Wayne and Gloria who were living in Rockford. It would be the first time I saw them since their wedding last October. I hated to miss their ceremony at the Durand Methodist Church, but it was the same time as Duke and Willabea's.

In the evening, Bill parked his uncle's two-toned blue, Ford along the curb on Seminary Street in a residential neighborhood on the city's east side. To reach the couple's second floor, furnished apartment, we climbed an outside stairway built on the side of a big, old house that had been converted to a two-family. Visiting them in their own home seemed as odd as my being with Bill without Ken. After greetings, Gloria made coffee and we gathered around their kitchen table to catch up on our lives. Our hosts showed us their wedding pictures. I told about Ken's travels to the Far East. Bill talked about his navy adventures. He said he didn't have a steady girlfriend since breaking up with my cousin, Marilyn, after boot camp nearly two years ago. city We gossiped a bit about Marilyn's church wedding I attended last June. A week after Gloria and Marilyn graduated from high school last spring; Marilyn married Jack, an Army veteran. At 10 P.M., Bill and I went home. The next morning would be a workday for everyone but Bill.

Later in the week, Dad and Mom received a letter from Ken thanking them for his greeting cards. He wrote about his Christmas as a duty daddy with kids from a Hong Kong orphanage. *There were about sixty kids who would probably be grade school age who came aboard. We had all pitched in money to buy food and gifts. They were all boys except for one little girl who had a twin brother. An officer escorted the two of them. Each of us had just one. I had a little boy about ten, who seemed quite shy. I couldn't understand what he said, but he gave me a lot of big smiles. Before they left, we gave them a tour of the ship, except for the restricted areas. I enjoyed the day as much or more than the kids did.*

He added, *The Bennington won't be back to the States until the middle of May.*

Five more months before I would see him seemed like a lifetime of loneliness.

My folks and I ended the year with a double dose of our old friends, the Weaver family. Saturday night, Mary entertained her siblings and several friends including Clarence for a card party at her apartment in Rockford. Before anyone left the gathering, her brother, Bob, said, "You're all invited to our house New Year's Eve for oyster stew and chili supper." On the festive night, the same group ate the soup and played Five Hundred at Bob and Mildred's large home in Harrison. At midnight, everyone shouted, "Happy New Year!" and went home.

Chapter 6

1957

New Year's Day, my cousin, Doris, invited me to watch the Rose Bowl parade on their television. Outside their old, two-story home, bales of straw banked the crumbling stone foundation to keep out the winter cold. Inside, their appliances were new. Although TV was only black and white, the floats made of flowers and the celebrities in their finery were still impressive. I enjoyed every minute of the extravaganza. I don't know why my parents continued to live in the radio age.

The rest of the week, I continued to cough, but I went to work. On Saturday, I saw Dr. Hein for the fifth time. He prescribed a stronger bottle of cherry syrup for my hack that plagued me since October.

My parents and I then drove on Highway 81 to Beloit. Half an hour later, before Dad and Mom did their shopping, they dropped me off to spend the night with Esther in the room she rented from Mrs. Hogan. I had connived with my best friend to stay with her so I could go out with Clarence without my folks knowing about it. I wasn't crazy about Clarence. I was rebelling against my parents' decree last summer that I couldn't date him because he was divorced and ten years older than I was.

I didn't feel guilty going out with fellows I considered friends. I wore Ken's class ring wrapped with adhesive tape and tried to make it clear to the guys that I wasn't looking for a new sweetheart–I just wanted to have a little fun. A year between my boyfriend's thirty-day leaves was a long, lonely time for me.

Early that evening, Clarence picked me up. He parked in the Ellis Theater lot and we walked across the street to eat supper at Plumb's, a family-type restaurant. We recrossed the street to see the movie *Anastasia* about the Russian Tsar's daughter.

Afterward, we returned to Mrs. Hogan's house. He walked me to the door, which was unlocked so I could get in. My coughing was all I needed to avoid a possible goodnight kiss.

Esther spent the evening with her new honey, Donnie, one of my Uncle Buck's nephews. I'd known who he was for years, but I wasn't acquainted with him. I thought he resembled our mutual relative although he was shorter, only about five-eight, with a reddish tint to his dark hair.

The next day, Donnie's mother, Mary, invited Esther and me to join their family for Sunday dinner. She was Buck's sister and like him, oozed the West Virginia hospitality they'd been raised with. Her husband, Dale, was a Durand native. Donnie picked us up at 11:45 A.M. After the table was cleared and dishes washed, we played charades with Donnie's younger siblings plus a couple of his sisters' boyfriends. The game brought out our acting talents. At the end of the afternoon, my friends brought me home and I went right to bed. It was only six o'clock but I was exhausted from coughing. The new medicine Dr. Hein prescribed wasn't working any better than the old one.

On the first two days of the new week, I didn't have the energy to go to work. Mom called Dr. Hein, who made an appointment for me to see a specialist at the Monroe Clinic on Wednesday. The trip to Monroe was my first ride in our new Chevy with Dad behind the wheel and Mom in the passenger seat. I slumped in the back seat, too sick to appreciate our Christmas present.

My clinic visit began with a chest x-ray. I undressed my top half, donned a paper gown and wrapped myself in a blue and white striped, cotton robe. I felt like lying down, but I sat on a bench with other patients until it was my turn to stand in front of the machine. I dressed and rejoined Dad and Mom in the waiting area.

Soon I was called into an examining room where I climbed up on a table and an aide measured my vital signs. A few minutes later, Dr. Davis, a tall man with glasses and thinning dark hair, entered. He used the stethoscope hanging around his neck to listen to my heart and lungs. He called my parents into the room and used a light box to show us my chest x-ray. He said, "I believe Lolita has tuberculosis. She should go right to the hospital. If it is TB, she'll need to be treated in a sanitarium."

His diagnosis left us all speechless. My mind's eye flashed scenes from an old movie showing people in robes and pajamas spending years in a TB sanitarium. They coughed and dragged themselves from their beds to a dining room, to lounge chairs on a veranda and back to their beds. Was that my future? I wanted to scream, "No!" but I remained silent.

After a few seconds, Mom asked, "Couldn't I just take care of her at home?"

"No, she really should be in a sanitarium," Dr. Davis responded. "You may think you're able to do it at home, but you aren't."

In our family, feelings weren't usually discussed. Each of us was lost in our own thoughts during the short drive from the clinic to the hospital.

I was immediately admitted and isolated in a small, private room with institutional green walls and that distinctive antiseptic smell. I undressed, put on the backless gown laying on the hospital bed and crawled between the stiff, white sheets.

The staff and my parents donned blue, cotton gowns and white masks before entering. Dad muttered, "This seems kind of silly after we've been living together all of this time." My parents left about five thirty.

No other visitors were allowed. Nothing could leave my room including letters to my sailor. I felt like a pariah.

I faced my reflection in the large mirror atop the brown dresser standing against the wall beyond the foot of my bed. I was the sickest I'd ever been and it showed. My face was ashen and gaunt. Exhaustion showed in my dull eyes and my shoulder-length hair was tangled. I turned onto my left side so I would hack less. The tears I'd been holding back rolled down my cheeks, but crying made me cough more, so I stopped.

A supper tray was brought to my room, I just picked at the chicken noodle soup, tuna salad sandwich and cherry Jell-O.

A radio was fastened to the wall above my bed. An attached cord brought a speaker with control buttons to my pillow. I searched for music to raise my spirits. Later, Art Linkletter once again proved *People Are Funny. Amos and Andy's* humor followed, but I was much too depressed to laugh. I couldn't believe that I didn't just have a cold that would go away. A sanitarium seemed scarier than a haunted house.

The next day before breakfast, an orderly wheeled me to the lab for the first of a series of three gastric tests. The technician inserted a small plastic tube through my nose, pushed it down my throat and into my stomach. He then attached a syringe to the tube to extract fluid. That liquid obtained would be used to grow cultures to determine if my illness was TB. Additional torture sessions followed on Friday and Saturday mornings.

After returning to my room, I tuned the radio to Monroe's WEKZ. The announcer said overnight the temperature dropped to zero and seven inches of snow fell. Plows cleared the roads before Dad and Mom came to visit me in the afternoon. I was glad they brought some magazines for me to read. Bed rest made me feel a little more energetic.

Mom told me talk about my illness swirled around our community like the wind-whipped snow. Mrs. Potter, a middle-aged farmer's wife who lived on the southeast edge of Durand, phoned her friends and said, "I saw Lolita Tschabold at the Monroe Clinic Wednesday afternoon. She looked like she was at death's door."

I was incensed. I wasn't dying. I hated gossips.

Saturday morning, get well cards came in the mail. Later, a nurse brought in a plant sent by my bowling team. I received two bouquets of flowers—one from my cousin, Doris; the other from Mary and Clarence, my boss and a co-worker at the ASC office. I felt better knowing people were thinking about me and praying for me.

Dad and Mom came in the afternoon. They'd seen Dr. Davis at the clinic the previous day. He said I should go to the Rockford sanitarium next week, although he wouldn't know for sure if it's TB until the cultures came back. That would take weeks.

On Sunday, my appetite returned. The hospital food wasn't too bad. There were a few menu choices such as roast beef or pork and mashed potatoes or French fries.

The zero temperature froze water pipes and complicated doing chores on the farm, but Dad and Mom visited me in the afternoon.

In the evening, my boss, Mary, Dad's sisters, Aunt Marion and Aunt Elnora, plus my boyfriend's sister, Lola Mae called Mom to ask about me.

Mom replied to each one that I'd be going to the TB sanitarium in Rockford later in the week. There would be no charge for treatment at the facility that served several northern Illinois counties.

Tuesday when my parents talked to Dr. Davis, he told them he was 99 percent positive I had TB. He advised them to have chest x-rays to be sure they didn't have it, too.

On Wednesday morning, 16 January, my parents picked me up about eleven thirty to go to the sanitarium. I crawled into the four-door sedan's back seat and lay down. I was exhausted from taking a shower and getting dressed. By the time we crossed the state line a half-hour later, I'd rested enough to sit up and look out the side window the rest of the way to Rockford. The landscape of sunshine on the, sparkling, white snow was beautiful—completely opposite my black mood. We didn't stop for dinner. Nobody felt like eating.

A little after one o'clock, we pulled up in front of the Rockford Municipal Sanitarium, 1601 Parkview Avenue, on the northeast side of the city. The 104-bed, three-story, brick building opened in 1916. The single-story entrance and offices were added at the secondary level in 1950.

A young, brown-haired woman wearing a black, straight skirt and a long sleeved, white blouse brought a wheelchair to the car and pushed me into a small office. She sat down behind a wooden desk and proceeded to admit me. She began with my health history. I was nineteen years old with no bad habits.

I didn't smoke; I didn't drink coffee or alcohol; and I didn't keep late hours. I didn't know how I'd contracted TB, which is transmitted from person to person by coughing, sneezing, speaking or spitting. The germs can float in the air for hours, especially in tight places with little sunlight or fresh air.

She then wheeled me along the lengthy corridor past offices on both sides. My parents, who'd been sitting in the waiting area, followed along with Dad carrying the suitcase Mom packed for me. After my isolation in the hospital, I was amazed at the openness. No one wore gowns and masks, visitors were unlimited and I could mail daily letters to Ken.

We continued through the first half of the second-floor men's dormitory. Males occupied the lower two levels of the aged building with the third reserved for females. While waiting for the self-service elevator, I noticed there was no antiseptic odor like the hospital, but I could smell smoke. In the adjoining communal area, guys clad in robes and pajamas sat in lounge chairs watching TV. I was surprised to see several of the fellows holding lighted cigarettes.

We exited on the third floor. Women wearing nightclothes were watching TV in the common area the same as the men with one exception–no cigarettes. I learned later that only one woman smoked; but, out of consideration for others, she did it in her room.

The day nurse took over pushing my wheelchair and greeted us, "Good afternoon. I'm Miss Uke." The short, chubby, older woman was all white—white shoes, white stockings, white uniform, pale skin with no make-up and short, curly white hair topped by a white cap. She didn't bother with small talk while propelling me to the east end of the corridor.

My single room was on the north side of the building. A steam radiator sat below a large window that overlooked stark, bare trees and an extensive, rolling, snow-covered lawn. Like the rest of the building, the walls were painted institutional green and the floor was gray terrazzo. Dad set my bag inside the clothes closet next to a sink.

My furnishings included a modern, adjustable table, an old-fashioned, metal, hospital bed and dresser painted brown. A box of tissues and a glass, rectal thermometer in a container of alcohol sat on top of a matching night stand with a bed pan concealed inside.

Miss Uke said, "You'll take your own temperature morning and night and leave the thermometer in the container."

That was a disgusting thought. I said, "I can't do that."

She replied, "We have a seven-year-old patient who takes her own temperature. I'm sure you can, too."

I did, but I still thought it was gross to stick a thermometer up my butt, pull it out, wipe it off with a tissue and put it back in the container. Later, when I was sure I didn't have a fever, I often used the radiator to raise the mercury to a healthy 99.6, one degree more than the normal 98.6 orally. If I wasn't watching carefully and the number shot up too high, I 'accidentally' dropped the glass thermometer on the floor to break it.

Before Miss Uke left my room, she showed me how to fold an old newspaper to make a disposable, 'bug bag' for used tissues. I stuck it on a wire hook fastened to the side of the night stand.

Dad and Mom left about two thirty. Their walking out of my room was like removing a Band-Aid from a wound. It was best done quickly. We were all still in shock trying to adjust to my staying in the facility. From time to time, I'd thought about moving away from home, but this was not what I had in mind.

I traded my clothes for a pair of pajamas, my wardrobe for the foreseeable future, and crawled into bed. There were no bars on my window and the door stood wide open, but I felt like I was in solitary confinement. My sentence complete rest, no getting out of bed for any reason. I used a bed pan and nurses gave me sponge baths. It didn't seem reasonable to me that walking down the hall to the communal toilet and shower would endanger my health, but I would abide by the rules. I was mad at the world, but all I could do was scowl. Crying wouldn't do any good. It just made me cough more.

A short while later, I heard a weak voice next door groaning, "Oh, nurse. Oh, nurse, please come. Oh, nurse. Oh, nurse, please come." When we passed that room, the little, old woman I saw sitting in a chair pulled up to her bedside table reminded me of a sparrow. Her muted cries continued and my apprehension grew. What kind of a place ignored an elderly person's pleas for help?

With no bedside call button like the hospital, I was forced to wait about half-an-hour for Miss Uke to return to my room. I greeted her with, "That old lady next door has been calling for you."

"Oh, that's just Miss Statler," Miss Uke replied. "Don't worry about her. She's fine. She just doesn't know what she's saying."

I did my best to ignore the moaning. Thank heaven, an old lady tires easily and sleeps a lot. A few days later, the senile female died. After listening to her lament for hours on end, I considered it a blessing.

At three o'clock, Miss Uke was replaced by Mrs. Whitford, a tall, thin, gray-haired nurse who wore glasses. She bristled with efficiency as she emptied my bed pan, brought me a basin of warm water to wash my hands and face for supper and refilled my water glass. "Is there anything else I can get for you?" She asked.

I said, "No, thank you," and she left.

I did not like the woman from that very first day. I learned later she rushed through her beginning-of-the-shift tasks so she could sit down at three thirty to watch the popular, half-hour, TV soap opera, *The Edge of Night.* After I was freed from my bed, I enjoyed breaching that sacred thirty minutes. Once in a while, I'd enter the booth at the east end of our hallway, drop a dime in the slot of the pay phone, dial and wait for her to say, "Third floor nurse's station, Mrs. Whitford speaking." I'd hang up and smile knowing she left her beloved program.

The next morning, I met the director, Dr. Bryan. He and his wife lived on the grounds in the white, clapboard bungalow provided. He was an older man with thinning, dark hair and jowls that reminded me of my English bulldog. He said, "I have looked at your x-rays and you won't have to have surgery. We'll wait and see how long your treatment will take."

I guess he meant to put my mind at ease, but I didn't know they ever did surgery for TB. He seemed nice and I liked him.

Later, Dad and Mom brought me more pajamas. They'd visited the second floor lab and received skin tests. The teachnician used a needle to insert a small amount of TB protein under the top layer of skin on the left forearm. If a firm, red bump formed after three days the TB germ was in the person's system. A chest x-ray determined whether the person had TB. Everyone who was in contact with me during the past four months was advised to be checked.

Until I was diagnosed with TB, my knowledge of the malady was limited to Christmas seals with their familiar red, double-barred cross in the corner. I learned the disease was identified as contagious during the 1020s and named tuberculosis in 1839. At that time, TB, which was sometimes called consumption, was the most feared disease in the world.

Sanitariums originated in Germany in 1859. The first TB hospital in the United States was opened in 1884 by Dr. Edward Livingston Trudeau. He'd contracted the disease in 1871 when he was twenty-three years old. He recovered after spending long hours resting in a cottage in the Adirondack Mountains in northern New York state. The young doctor was convinced that TB could be cured with bed rest, nourishment, fresh air and lots of sunshine. By 1907, sanitariums were springing up around the country, but each one could only care for a few patients at a time. In 1946, development of the antibiotic, streptomycin, made a cure possible. A patient's stay in a sanitarium was shortened from years to months.

An injection of 'strep' was my wake-up call every Monday and Thursday morning. 'Turn the other cheek' took on a whole new meaning. Before the night attendant went off duty at 7 A.M., she entered my room and roused me with her perfuctory, "Morning," It was the only time I saw the fat woman with cropped brown hair who wore a peach-colored uniform, I responded with, "Morning," and flipped over on my belly.

The aide pulled down my pajama pants and administered a shot in the butt. To be so painful, I thought the needles she used must have beeen rejects from World War II.

The well-managed institution ran on routine. Shift changes and meals punctuated my days. I greeted visitors Monday, Wednesday and Saturday evenings from seven to eight thirty and Sunday afternoons from two to four. My parents, my cousin, Doris, Uncle Buck and Aunt Elnora, my boss, Mary, and my best friend, Esther with her boyfriend, Donnie, came often. I was egotistical enough to expect their visits.

A few people avoided the place. My father's younger brother, Bobbie, told Dad, "My wife's afraid of TB. She won't let me go see Lolita."

A couple of days after I was admitted, the three young women I'd glimpsed walking in the hallway stopped to chat. The teenage spokesman said, "Hi, I'm Sue. This is Rosie and Florence. We hesitated to come in because you looked so sour. You never smiled at us when we passed your room."

I grinned and replied, "I'm Lolita and I'm really glad to meet you. I'm just not happy to be here. I guess it shows."

My new best friends were: Sue, a lively sixteen-year-old with brown hair and eyes, who was missing her junior year of high school; Rosie, a married woman in her early twenties with black hair, brown eyes and a dark complexion; and Florence, a woman of color. I was surprised to learn Florence was a forty-year-old widow with three children. I thought she looked about my age. Her little sister was the seven-year-old patient Miss Uke referred to during my orientation. During our conversation, I learned none of them had ever been confined to bed. I assumed the restriction was routine when a patient entered the san but my three friends weren't as sick as I was. When the girls left, they promised to return soon. Suddenly my days looked brighter. I never dreamed there'd be other young people here. I expected all of the patients to be old fogies.

Talking with those three young women made me realize if I was destined to have TB, this was the best time in my life for it to happen. I was through high school, my office job was waiting for me and my boyfriend was aboard an aircraft carrier on the other side of the world. I wasn't missing anything important while I recuperated at the 'san', my new friends' term for the institution.

The next day, I met Sue's parents, Clarene and Joe, who were also patients. Sue and her mother shared the only double room on our floor. Joe was assigned to the men's second floor. Clarene was a petite woman of Italian heritage with brown eyes, black hair streaked with a little gray, and a hot temper. Her family having TB embarrassed her. She considered it a poor people's disease that should afflict only the Mexicans who worked in the factory where her husband was a supervisor. Joe, a blond-haired fellow with the beginning of a middle-aged paunch, provided the voice of reason in their family. Sue's sisters, nineteen-year-old Nancy and fourteen-year-old Jolene, remained alone in their home in Sterling, a medium-sized town about an-hour-and-a-half southwest of Rockford.

Saturday night, I expected my first visitors. At 6 P.M., the moan of an air raid siren heralded the evening. The weekly blast was a check on equipment, just like Durand's daily blowing of the fire whistle at noon. At seven, I welcomed Dad and Mom, my cousin Doris and my boss Mary, who was riding with her friend, Clarence. My parents, who arrived first, politely greeted the others as they entered my room.

The following afternoon, Mom brought my stationery and art supplies that I'd requested. I still coughed quite a bit, but I felt pretty good and needed things to do.

After my parents left, I drew three elephants on pink construction paper, cut them out and taped them so they walked along the foot of my brown, metal bed. My conception of a sanitarium was a place for alcoholics to dry out. Seeing pink elephants was a standard reference to their DTs.

In the evening, I wrote to Ken, my first letter since being diagnosed with TB. It was several pages long with details of my illness and my new residence.

During the six weeks I was bed-ridden, I devoured books. Doris brought some of her collection of *Reader's Digest Condensed Books*. Each anthology included four or five popular novels. My favorite non-fiction book was a controversial best seller, *The Power of Positive Thinking*, available from the sanitarium's library. Author Dr. Norman Vincent Peale, a New York pastor for The Reformed Church in America, believed the mind influences our physical wellbeing. I agreed.

Monday morning Dad and Mom returned to the san to have their skin tests checked. Red bumps on their forearms showed positive reactions requiring chest x-rays. Those results were sent to our family physician. The following Saturday, Dr. Hein told my parents they were okay, but they should continue to have an x-ray every year.

Saturday evening, my parents brought Uncle Buck and Aunt Elnora plus a fourteen-inch, Motorola, black and white, portable television. Although my folks remained in the world of radio at home, my uncle convinced them I should have a TV in my san room.

I felt a special kinship with Buck, a six-foot-tall, thin, dark-haired, in-law who sported a Clark Gable style mustache. When Dad's quiet, slim, dark-haired, youngest sister married the fellow from West Virginia, I was a four-year-old strutting around in white cowgirl boots. I fell in love with him, too.

The set wouldn't work in my room so Buck, an electrician, took it home to adjust it. The following afternoon, he again placed the 'boob tube' on my dresser, plugged it in and it worked perfectly. A metal ring antenna pulled in Channel 39 WTVO and the rabbit ears WREX Channel 13, the two Rockford stations available. He also attached an extension cord to bring an on/off switch within my reach. When I wanted to change stations, I ignored my restrictions, got out of bed and took four steps to the dresser to twist the dial.

After my Sunday afternoon visitors left, I noticed Mom's pocketbook sat on the window sill. She NEVER forgot her purse. That lapse made me wonder how much my being sick was upsetting her.

Later, I enjoyed watching *The Ed Sullivan Show* for the first time.

Monday morning I turned on my new TV. I soon decided the daytime line-up of game shows and soap operas didn't appeal to me. I continued writing letters to my boyfriend, reading, drawing pictures or visiting with my new friends. In the evenings, my favorite programs were *Zorro, Mr. Adams and Eve, I Led Three Lives*, and Phil Silvers as Sgt. Bilko.

The girls told me I was the only one on the third floor to have my own TV. Everyone else watched the set in the communal area.

The next time Dad and Mom came, they finally brought a letter from Ken, his first since Christmas. Each time my parents visited without bringing a letter for me, I worried a little more. I wondered if my steady was busy working, had nothing to write about or, worst of all, if he didn't want a sick girlfriend, but hesitated to tell me. I tore the envelope open and scanned both sides of the sheet of paper. When I read that he wished me well and closed with his usual, *All my love, Ken*, I sighed with relief and laid his letter aside to savor later.

Get well cards began arriving in the mail and added rays of sunshine to my days. Everyone who sent a card or visited passed along tidbits of neighborhood news. I knew more about what was going on in the community than when I was at home.

Flowers decorated my room during my first month at the san. Although there was no grand plan, it seemed as soon as one bouquet wilted and was thrown out, another arrived. I also received some other gifts. Food was always welcome. Our meals were small and I didn't like some of the things that were served, especially corn soup.

On Saturday night, visitors besides my parents included our pastor, Rev.

Thompson, who rode with Trinity member, Mrs. Kinney, and Clarence, who was alone. I didn't know it at the time, but that was Clarence's last visit.

Mom didn't say anything in front of the church people, but the following Wednesday evening, she laid down the law to me and her old friend, Mary. When my folks entered my room, my boss was already there. Mom looked at me like I'd burped at a tea party and stated, "Clarence is NOT to come to see you anymore." she then turned to Mary, who introduced the fellow to us, "And YOU can tell him so." Last summer, my folks blackballed Clarence as a date for me because he's divorced and ten years older than I am.

With that out of the way, we all chatted like the old friends that we were. At eight thirty, Mary invited my parents to eat at the nearby Sweet Shoppe to celebrate their twenty-second anniversary, which would be the next day. On visiting nights, Dad and Mom started chores early and skipped eating supper at home to arrive at the san by seven.

After I was alone, I thought about Mom's decree. I didn't care whether I saw Clarence again or not. Early in January, I stayed with Esther to go out with him in defiance of my parent's rules. TB changed my thinking. I just wanted to get well by summer when Ken would come home on leave.

The following Monday at noon, I was surprised to see Donna, an old friend from high school. She wore a white, nurse's uniform and carried eight, caramel apples, one of my favorite treats. She worked in the portion of the building that had been converted to a regular nursing home for the elderly. Since antibiotics drastically shortened the treatment time for TB patients, they needed less space.

While Donna was in my room, I asked, "Would you please get my make-up kit out of my suitcase in the closet and put it in the drawer of my night stand?"

"I sure will," she replied. "Asking for make-up sounds like you're feeling better."

"Yeah, I am."

Donna continued to visit me often during her lunch hours.

In the evening, Dad and Mom brought Ken's graduation picture in the three by five, gold frame and my musical jewelry box as I requested. The two items sitting on my dresser proved my boyfriend loved me.

The first of every month, each patient received a chest x-ray and a gastric test. Frank, a short, wiry fellow in a white uniform, did the gastric painlessly. After inserting the tiny, plastic tube through my nose, the lab man gave me a small cup of sterile water to swallow. The liquid and the tube easily slipped down my throat into my stomach. No more torture like I endured in the hospital.

Frank's wife, Ruth, was the petite, dark-haired receptionist at the front desk. She greeted phone callers with a lyrical, "Sanatorium." The friendly pair, who met here while they were being treated for TB, were parents of a teen-age son. Their love story assured me that a normal life could follow treatment for TB.

Dr. Bryan reviewed the tests. As each patient's health improved, he assigned different levels of activities as defined in the handbook. A few days later he came to my room and said, "I'm promoting you to 2B. You may go to the bathroom and take showers. Your x-ray looks better, so I think you'll be going home by August."

I could have kissed him, but I just gave him a big smile.

After he left, I immediately walked down the hallway to the bathroom just because I could. I then stopped at the communal area and introduced myself to the eight female patients sitting in lounge chairs watching TV. They ranged in age from seven to around sixty. As I became better acquainted with two of the older ladies, Pauline and Maybelle, I learned they were 'retreads'. During the 'bad old days' before antibiotics, they spent years in the TB sanitarium. Now they were being treated for a recurrence of the disease.

I looked forward to sharing the news of my promotion with my Monday evening company. At six thirty, I looked out my window and saw fog as thick as whipped cream. For the first time, Dad and Mom missed visiting hours, but my cousin, Doris, braved the weather. I greeted her with, "No more bed pans! I can finally go to the bathroom."

"Good for you," she responded.

The next day at noon, when I was sure my parents would be in the house, I phoned home. "Hello, Edith." After the preliminaries, I added, "Dr. Bryan promoted me to 2B. Finally, I can go to the bathroom and take showers. I'll probably be home in August."

"I'm so glad to hear that," she said. "I'm sorry we couldn't come last night but we'll be there Wednesday night."

Although I couldn't see my mother's face, I could tell by her voice that she was as elated by my progress as I was. We said our good-byes and hung up.

When I was a grade schooler, my mother taught me to use the phone by saying, "Hello, Edith," instead of "Hello, Mom." Otherwise, with several mothers on our party line, I might get a wrong number and have a conversation with somebody else and never know the difference.

The following Saturday night, Mom handed me a package Ken sent from Japan. I ripped it open and lit up like a jack-o-lantern.

I held up a beautiful, blue, silk kimono with flowers painted on it. Slipping it on, I could imagine my boyfriend's arms wrapped around me.

My parents also brought three hamburgers and malts from Sam's diner for my buddy, Sue, her mother, Clarene, and me. We were always ready for an evening snack because our light supper was served in our rooms at four thirty. Once in a while on non-visiting nights, I solicited several women to chip in and share a pizza, a new treat sweeping the country. I phoned our order downtown to Dolly's Chicken on Wheels and then met the deliveryman at the front door forty-five minutes later.

After the weekend of visitors, Monday turned into moving day. The staff shifted Clarene into my single room, while my TV and I joined Sue in the double one at the opposite end of the hall. I didn't know who instigated the trade, but I think the mother and daughter were ready to be separated.

As an only child, I'd never shared my bedroom with anyone except a friend spending the night. At first, I missed having time alone, but Sue was fun to live with and I soon adjusted.

Three days after the room change, a pall hung over the women's floor. Miss Uke told us that Lorna, a permanent patient on oxygen, was dying. The woman's mother, two sisters, and brother were called to be with her during her final hours. We talked softly and walked quietly. Early that evening, an undertaker wheeled Lorna's body out the rear door. Her mourning family followed.

Prior to the room switch, I was across the hall from Lorna and visited with her several times. She contracted TB before antibiotic treatment and was sick for nearly half of her forty-seven years. Seeing a patient her age die from the disease left me with a knot in my stomach and a lump in my throat.

Although our circumstances were different, I wondered if the disease would shorten my life. That thought never left the back of my mind.

Sunday morning, I was the only white person attending the church service conducted by a Baptist preacher in the second floor rec room. The ten worshipers welcomed me. Their boisterous 'hallelujahs' and 'amens' were quite different from the solemn, Lutheran liturgy I was accustomed to, but I enjoyed it.

My friends and I often went downstairs to the large, room to play Chinese checkers, Life, Monopoly or other board games. Jerry, a tall, dark-haired, single guy who was my age and two middle-aged, married men often joined us. Hank, who lived in Dixon about forty miles southwest, could pass as a black-haired Jeff Chandler, the handsome, gray-haired movie star. Wally, a tall, ash blonde man with glasses, lived in Rockford and knew Clarene from high school days. The two World War II vets often entertained us with their version of the radio show *Can You Top This* telling humorous anecdotes from their time in the service.

Like any community, we were not one big, happy family. Petite, sandy-haired Francine looked down her freckle-dusted nose at me for using the Monopoly money and dice to shoot craps, a game Mom taught me. The Arkansas native's twang came through that same nose when she said, "Ya'all shouldn't be doin' that. That's gam'lin'."

I immediately responded, "You all shouldn't be going out at night with Charlie." Everyone gossiped about the thirty-something, married mother accompanying the bald, smooth talking, man of color to The Lush Heads, a night club in south Rockford.

In mid-March, my nurse friend, Donna, ended our lunchtime chats with a final good-bye. She said she was moving out

West, but didn't elaborate. I figured it would be nosy to ask questions. I would miss her popping in at noon.

The following Saturday night, my cousin, Doris, and my parents listened to my roommate, Sue, fume about one of Dr. Bryan's decisions. "It's not fair!" she ranted and I agreed. "Rosie and Sako are only on 2B and they've gone home for the weekend. I'm on 2C and I can't leave. That's just plain wrong. Just because they're married shouldn't make any difference."

Sako, a petite, black-haired, Japanese woman in her twenties, joined our group a few weeks earlier. She met her husband, Howard, when he was in the Air Force and stationed in her homeland. Her family was sure the brown-haired, muscular, good looking fellow would forget her when he got back to the States, but he didn't. When his enlistment ended, he returned to Japan, married her and brought her to his parents' farm near Paw Paw, a small town about forty miles south of Rockford. The outspoken, young lady talked a lot, but I couldn't always understand her because of her accent and the slang she'd learned while working with American GIs.

The first of April wasn't a Fool's Day for me. At last, Dad and Mom brought three letters from Ken. When a month or more went by and I didn't hear from him, I was irate. The problem was, I never knew whether I should blame the postal service, the navy or my boyfriend. Of course, the saying, 'a sailor has a girl in every port', nagged in the back of my mind. Ken said that didn't apply to him. I wanted to believe him, but I couldn't imagine his going on liberty and ignoring females. I knew young women were attracted to sailors. After the guys spent time at sea, I assumed they were attracted to the gals, too.

After my parents left, I read Ken's letters and learned how busy he was. He wrote, *The Bennington is participating in the 'Beacon Hill' operation from March 14 to April 1. The powerful armada of sixty thousand men and seventy-five ships is the largest amphibious operation to be held in the Far East since World War II. When I look out, all I see is ships.*

The beginning of the month also brought my promotion to 2C, which allowed more daily exercise. I told Dr. Bryan about my beauty school training and he agreed I could be the resident hair stylist. Mom brought my permanent kit and picked up supplies from Mrs. DeBella's school. My initial customer was Stella, a tall, gray-haired woman who growled like she'd gotten up on the wrong side of the bed every morning. I hoped a new hairdo would improve her surly attitude for her first weekend visit home.

Wednesday night was April third, but my parents, Buck, Elnora, Esther and Donnie drove though blowing snow to visit me. Esther showed everyone her new, diamond engagement ring and said, "We're getting married in a small ceremony Saturday. You're all invited to our reception Sunday afternoon at Dad and Mother's."

The next day, I discovered Dr. Bryan's soft spot for his patients. I asked to attend Esther and Donnie's reception and he approved.

Sunday at 3 P.M. Dad and Mom picked me up to go to the party at Nelsons' farm. I was thankful I could sit on the turquoise, sectional sofa in their large, newly-remodeled living room and eat wedding cake with my friends. They spent so much time visiting me.

Afterward, I rested at home while my folks did chores. It was three months since I enjoyed the luxury of lying in my own bed. Although my room looked the same, Mom had sanitized it after I was diagnosed with TB. Dad helped her carry the springs and mattress outside to air in the sunshine. She then scrubbed the brown underlayment that covered the worn, wooden floor. While the floor dried, she washed the lace curtains and all of my bedding including the white chenille bedspread and the peach throw rug that lay on the floor beside my bed. Before making my walnut, double bed, she used furniture polish to wipe down the headboard and footboard, the matching chest of drawers and the dresser. She then vacuumed the blue wallpaper with rows of peach flowers and my small, wood-framed, cardboard closet.

When Mom returned to the house, she fixed one of my favorite suppers–round steak, johnny cake and peas with bacon. We finished up on chocolate chip cookies. How I missed her cooking.

At 8 P.M., I entered the front door of the san. The outing made me feel like I was returning to normal.

A week later on Sunday morning, Rosie and I played the board game, Sorry, in the second-floor rec room. About ten thirty, Jerry, a tall, dark-haired patient who was my age, entered and asked, "Girls, how would you like to go for a ride? Larry let me borrow his car."

"Sounds good," we replied in unison. We jumped up and abandoned our game to its box.

Everybody liked Larry, a forty-something fellow who permanently lived in the room next to the exit from the second-floor men's dorm. Lung surgery for TB during the 'bad old days' left the thin man standing a little crooked. During the day, he worked in a hardware store. At night, he was tied to a large oxygen tank. After supper, he lounged in his hospital bed and patients gathered around for a bull session. Once in a while, Sue and I stopped by to join the confab.

Rosie and I followed Jerry out to the two-toned, green Buick parked in the lot behind the building. The unseasonably, warm, mid-April morning and the smell of blossoms on the trees gave us spring fever. We rolled down the windows and slid into the front bench seat with Rosie in the middle. Jerry drove the 30 MPH speed limit on city streets and the breeze ruffled our hair. We returned in time for lunch.

In the afternoon, my parents brought Dad's Aunt Grace and Uncle Fred to my room. Earlier in the week, when Aunt Grace phoned from their home in Monroe to ask about visiting me, Mom invited the tall, lean, spry pair for Sunday dinner. We enjoyed a lively two-hour chat. Uncle Fred, who recently turned seventy-five, told stories about the old days when he ran an ice business. He delivered twenty-five-pound blocks to the city's housewives who kept food cold in the wooden, storage boxes before refrigerators were common. Aunt Grace bragged a bit about their only child, Gerald, who taught high school music.

On Thursday afternoon, I was surprised by a childhood friend, Sandy, who carried a bouquet of pink carnations. Seeing the people who made the effort to visit me was like watching a holiday parade. I never knew who might come through my door next.

I'd seen in the newspaper that the cute, skinny blonde with a few freckles across her nose recently married and was living in the city. She held out her left hand to show off her rings. I would have assumed they were white gold, but she bragged, "They're platinum."

Sandy and I had a lot of catching up to do. The last time I saw her, we were sixth-graders attending similar country schools. At that time, our families attended the public dances held every other Friday night at the New England Grange hall in Durand. Besides the changes in her own life, Sandy told me about her older brother's marriage, her younger brother's upcoming graduation from high school and her parents' divorce.

Although divorce was happening more often in my parents' generation, Sandy's news shocked me. Years ago, when I spent occasional weekends at their home in Harrison, they appeared to be such a happy family.

Saturday began Easter weekend. It seemed like everyone went home except Clarene and me. We could only go outside to enjoy the beautiful weather. A croquet court was in place on the spacious lawn, but it took four people to make a competitive game. We just sat on a wooden bench and basked in the sunshine.

Sunday Dad and Mom brought a letter from Ken that said the Bennington was headed from the Orient to Australia on 18 May. As he sailed farther and farther away, I felt like a deserted island in the sea of loneliness.

My folks also brought an Easter lily from a neighbor's burial. I thought those plants were ugly and that flowers from a funeral were a bad omen, but I kept my opinions to myself. Aloud I said, "Tell the family thank you."

After my parents left, I immediately took the plant downstairs to my friend, Jerry, who seemed glad to get it. I told him, "I can't have this in my room. It aggravates my allergies."

The next time Dad and Mom came, she brought some homemade, beef stew.

Each delicious bite reminded me what a good cook she was.

I suppose our food was healthy because nourishment was an important part of the early treatment for TB, but the meals delivered to my room were tasteless. If I closed my eyes, I couldn't tell if I was eating mashed potatoes or squash, roast beef or roast pork. I kept a jar of sweet pickle sticks on my nightstand for flavor.

The month of May brought another promotion. Dr. Bryan said I could dress and join Sue eating meals in the dining room next to the kitchen on the second floor. The following morning, I shucked my pjs and put on a purple print, cotton skirt and harmonizing blouse with bobby socks and loafers instead of slippers.

The dining room for patients and staff was a little larger than our living room at home. The walls were painted white and gray plastic tile covered the floor. Gray Formica topped the dozen, chrome-framed tables for four. Matching chairs were upholstered with with red and white vinyl A black speaker high in one corner piped in popular music.

Hearing "Four Walls" by country singer Jim Reeves takes me back to that time.

I celebrated my elevated status by drinking my very first cup of black coffee with breakfast. Like all new things, it would take a while to develop a taste for it.

At noon, McVeigh, the janitor, sat at a table alone. The brawny, toothless, bald-headed man was a former TB patient who huffed and puffed when he cleaned our bathroom. A tattoo on his left forearm branded him a former seaman. He looked to me like he could have been a pirate, but he probably joined the navy when he was young like Ken.

At the end of each meal, someone passed the toothpick holder. The first time I did that chore, I stopped at each table and asked, "Would you care for a toothpick?" My fellow diners didn't let me forget I offered a toothpick to McVeigh, a toothless man.

My upgrade in status included a weekend at home. Friday evening, my parents picked me up and we shopped in Beloit. The next day, 18 May, Mom turned forty-four. I gave her a card, a pair of imitation pearl earrings and a permanent.

Two days of eating Mom's cooking and sleeping in my own bed seemed more luxurious than spending a weekend at a fancy hotel. Sunday night coming back to Rockford, I drove our new, '57 Chevy for the first time. It was another step on the path back to normalcy.

I noticed another improvement in my health. My hack was finally gone. Before I was diagnosed with TB, I could have filled a book with all of the old family cough remedies people gave me. Some were downright disgusting such as swallow a ball of Vicks Vapo-rub rolled in sugar.

The following Saturday night, Mom brought a letter from Ken that he'd written from Pearl Harbor. At last, he was on his way back to the States. I could almost feel him moving closer to me.

Sunday afternoon when my parents came to visit, I rode home with them. While Dad and Mom did chores, I drove over to see Ken's sister, Lola Mae. She was expecting their fifth child in about a month. She said,"With two girls and two boys, it doesn't matter to us if it's a boy or girl. We just hope for a healthy baby."

She told me about seven-year-old Judy being treated for nephritis, an inflammation of the kidneys. She got sick about the same time I went to the san. "She's fine now," her mother said.

I returned home at six. I expected my parents to be done chores with Mom preparing supper in the kitchen and Dad cleaning up in the bathroom, but they were still in the barn. When they did come inside, they were grumbling about everything that went wrong. They quickly bathed and dressed. We skipped eating in an effort to meet my eight thirty curfew. By the time we pulled up in front of the san, my watch showed eight forty-five. I jumped out of the car and practically ran into the building, across the empty lobby, down the deserted corridor and through the men's hall to the elevator.

Mrs. Whitford met me as I stepped onto the third floor. She glowered worse than my mother when I was tardy getting home from a date. "It is eight fifty. You should have been back here twenty minutes ago. If you can't get back on time, you won't be allowed to leave."

I knew if I said anything, it would be wrong. I kept my mouth shut, went to my room and vented to Sue. "Dear Mrs. Whitford bawled me out for being late. I would have liked to tell her that things on a farm twenty-five miles away don't always stay on schedule, but I kept quiet. I didn't want to jeopardize my chances of going home again."

On a cool, sunny Tuesday during the last week of May, the staff loaded about a dozen of us into cars and took us to nearby Alpine Park for a picnic at noon. Although we needed light jackets, we enjoyed the fresh air and change of scene. The food from the kitchen even tasted a little better outside.

When we returned, the institution treated all patients to cake and coffee served in the rec room as a farewell for Miss Wong. The young, occupational therapist of Chinese heritage was leaving her job to be married.

The next day, Sue went home with her sisters and their dad, who had been released a month earlier. I was happy for her, but our double room seemed as large and empty as a ballroom after the band has played the last dance. At least, I hoped to go home soon, too.

In the evening, Dad, Mom, Buck and Elnora took me to Sam's for sandwiches. It was like rare cologne to smell the coffee and grease in the familiar hamburger joint on

Auburn St. After Mrs. Whitford's scolding on the weekend, we made sure I was back to the san by eight thirty.

The June reclassifications also sent my friend, Jerry, home. But our group wasn't without a young man for long. Eddie, a black-haired, brown-eyed, stocky teen-ager of Mexican descent, soon joined us in the rec room. Billy, a skinny, blonde-haired, blue-eyed, eleven-year-old clung to him like a shadow. When the newcomer discovered the current hit, "Eddie, My Love," was on the free, juke box, he practically wore the record out. He missed his girlfriend. I knew the feeling.

The following Wednesday morning, I was called to Dr. Bryan's office. He sat behind his large wooden desk with my records open before him. A light box sat on the left front corner. I walked across the carpet and took the straight chair facing him. He turned the light box so we could both view my chest x-rays from the previous Friday. "They look good," said the physician. "You may have one hour of exercise every day and go home every weekend. It won't be too long now before you can go home for good."

"That's great." I left his office feeling like a kite flying high. Home was such a beautiful word. Before I contracted TB, I often wished on a star that I was any other place. Now I was anxious to return. I could hardly wait until evening to tell my visitors the good news.

At seven, Dad and Mom walked into my room. I greeted them with, "I can come home every weekend."

"That's good," they said in unison and smiled.

Friday afternoon, Dad and Mom picked me up at three o'clock and we stopped at nearby North Towne Shopping Center before leaving the city.

Saturday, I spent the day finishing my stole, a craft project Miss Wong, the occupational therapist, provided. I used a long needle to weave black yarn through the holes in a strip of white, synthetic material that reminded me of a lace curtain. The finished wrap matched my new white, sleeveless dress trimmed with black and the spectator pumps I would wear to an evening wedding. Attending friends' marriage ceremonies was a major part of my social life. I looked forward to the day I would walk down the aisle wearing a long, white gown.

At 7 P.M., I sat in the Shirland Methodist Church watching the beautiful candlelight ceremony uniting my co-worker, Lois, and her fiancé, Don, in marriage. I decided right then that Ken and I would have an evening, candlelight service.

Afterward, I joined the other guests gathered on the concrete steps and sidewalk outside the front door of the small, wooden building painted white. We waited to throw rice at the newlyweds who were inside signing documents and posing for pictures. The sun was setting but it was still warm. I recognized my former classmate, Skip, and he remembered me, too. Thirteen years ago, the two of us were first graders riding the yellow bus from our rural homes on Highway 75 to the Rockton School until my family moved away from the neighborhood. He was still about my height with the same freckles across his nose and mischievous grin. After the usual greetings, we caught up on our lives. He said, "Don and I graduated from Hononegh together. Now I'm farming with Grandpa and Uncle Al."

I briefly told him about my school, my sailor boyfriend, my job at the ASC office and my stay at the san.

The bridal couple emerged from the church and we showered them with rice before they ducked into the basement door. I told Skip, "I'm heading home instead of going back inside for the reception."

He asked, "Would you like to go to a movie next Saturday night?"

"Yeah. That'd be great." I gave him directions to our farm.

I enjoyed the evening with Skip. He took me to a couple more movies and that was it. I heard no more from my former classmate. I think the fellows who asked me out were looking for a steady girlfriend. Three dates convinced them I wasn't available and they moved on.

Thursday, 13 June, was just another day until Dr. Bryan came to my room in the afternoon and said, "You may go home tomorrow."

I could have run up and down the hall shouting hallelujah, but that wasn't my style. Instead, I called home. Mom answered with her usual non-committal, "Hello."

With no preliminaries, I exclaimed, "Dr. Bryan just said I can come home tomorrow!"

"Well, I'm glad to hear that. We'll pick you up in the afternoon. Bye."

Friday morning, after a restless night, I finished packing and said farewell to everyone. I would miss the people who were part of my daily life for the past five months. It was the first time my friends were different from me including Sako, who was from Japan, Florence, a woman of color, Eddie, who was of Mexican heritage plus

Clarene and Wally, who were my parents' generation. It wasn't only politics that made strange bedfellows—so did a shared affliction.

At lunch, I told the kitchen staff good-bye. I was too excited to eat much. It amazed me that going home could be so thrilling.

To pass the time in the afternoon, I sat with the other women watching soap operas on TV. When my folks finally arrived at three o'clock, we loaded the car trunk and the back seat with my TV, suitcase and boxes filled with clothes, art supplies and books. I climbed in front between Dad and Mom and we headed for the farm. My parents' relieved expressions told me how happy they were that this was their last trip to the san.

Home remained the same as when I left except we now watched television like everyone else. To have good reception in the country, the ring and rabbit ears attached to the set were replaced by a tall aerial installed on the roof by Buck and his friend, Mark. It felt odd for me to watch TV sitting in a chair after always lying cranked up in a hospital bed.

Saturday evening, I took Doris to supper at the Frontier in Rockton followed by a movie in Rockford. It seemed like so little to show my appreciation for all she'd done for me while I was in the san, but I couldn't think of anything else. When I stopped to pick up my cousin, I parked our sedan on their gravel driveway beside the dark-red, rough, lath snow fence that permanently circled their dooryard. I saw no sign of the small flock of sheep that sometimes grazed in the area out-side the enclosure. I passed through the gate and stepped onto the weather-beaten, front porch. Smokey, their large, black, shaggy dog, barked to announce my arrival. Looking through the screen door, I saw Aunt Frannie sitting in her chair that she'd covered with a maroon slipcover.

"Come on in, McGinty," she called.

It surprised me to hear my childhood nickname. I entered the living room.

Smokey recognized me and settled down at Aunt Fran-nie's feet. She reached for the shiny, metal piggy bank that sat on the lamp table beside her chair. When she handed it to me, it rattled. "This is for you. Every Wednesday while you were in the sanitarium, I dropped in a quarter."

What a thoughtful gift. In spite of the lump in my throat, I managed to say, "Thank you."

Doris came downstairs, we told her mother good-bye and the two of us were off in our Chevy hard-top.

My first week at home began with a shot in the butt, the same as when I was a patient. For the foreseeable future, I would drive to the san every Monday and Thursday morning to receive an injection. When I entered the sanitarium's lobby, Ruth, the petite receptionist, greeted me with an upbeat, "Good morning, Lolita." A nurse I didn't know met me in an examining room. She introduced herself as Mrs. Johnson and we exchanged small talk. I laid down on my stomach on the examining table. She pulled down my pants for the usual jab and I returned home. Once a month, I'd have a gastric and a chest x-ray.

The summer stretched before me. I felt fine, but Dr. Bryan said I wasn't ready to return to my office job. I spent the days alone in the house while Dad and Mom worked outside doing chores and baling hay. I missed my playmates at the san. To fill some of my time, I prepared our meals. I liked to cook and it gave Mom a break to have food on the table when she came in from helping Dad with farm work.

"Waste not, want not," was the watchword in our kitchen so we didn't have much trash. Garbage such as potato peelings was tossed to the hogs roaming on the north side of the woven-wire fence that enclosed the orchard adjoining our yard. Table scraps from supper went into the chipped, enamel cooking pan that was relegated to be the dog's dish. The only time Jeff ate Friskies from the box was when there weren't enough morsels left from our meal for his once a day feeding. Empty tin cans and other refuse were thrown into a box in the basement. From time to time, Dad dumped them in the ditch at the edge of a field.

I'd been home for two weeks when I finally received a letter from Ken telling me he was back in California. I wished I could fly there to see him, but my parents would never have allowed that.

The following Friday night, my family joined the crowd dancing to the old time music played by the popular Jack Busch's band in the Durand Grade School gym. The evening benefitted the medical clinic to be built in town beside the new bank that opened 1 February. The camaraderie developed during the Centennial celebration continued to enrich our community.

On Sunday afternoon at five, Doris picked me up for another new experience to broaden my horizons. Rise Stevens, a major performer at the 'Met' in New York City, was presenting a recital beside the Geneva Lake at Williams Bay, Wisconsin, an hour's drive away. We joined dignified men wearing suits and elegant women in their Sunday best dresses sitting on, wooden folding chairs in the outdoor amphitheater. I wore my sleeveless, white dress trimmed in black and matching spectator pumps.

When the program began, the sun was setting leaving behind a pleasant, calm evening. After the mezzo-soprano's first aria, I was amazed by how softly the opera devotees applauded. The evening was something new, but I preferred the country music at *The Grand Ole Opry* to grand opera.

The next day, I drove to the san for my shot and went to the third floor to give my Japanese friend, Sako, a permanent.

The following week when I went to the san for my Thursday shot, Ruth, the receptionist, was watching for me. "Good morning, Lolita. Dr. Bryan wants you to stop at his office after you've had your shot."

I looked forward to good news. Maybe I could go back to work at the ASC office.

When I knocked on Dr. Bryan's wooden door, I heard, "Come in." He was sitting in his large, brown, leather chair behind his wooden desk. My records lay open in front of him. I sat down in one of two straight chairs facing him. After the usual small talk, he said, "Your June gastric was positive. It happens sometimes and we don't know why."

It's a good thing I was sitting down. I felt like I'd been diagnosed with TB all over again. After a quick intake of breath, I responded, "Now what?"

"You don't have to be concerned about being contagious, but you won't be able to go back to work for some time."

I said a brief good-bye and closed the door behind me. I wanted to go home and crawl in a hole, but I'd brought homemade, chocolate chip cookies for the women upstairs. On the third floor, my friends were gathered in front of the TV in the common area. I told them about my setback. They commiserated with me as they nibbled on cookies.

By the time I returned to our farm, I was just plain mad. "It isn't fair!" I ranted to Mom. "I stayed in bed six weeks and used that cussed bedpan. I followed all of their rules. Why did this happen?" It was a rhetorical question. If Dr. Bryan couldn't explain it, I was sure Mom couldn't.

During the last week of July, doing beauty work helped take my mind off of my reversal. I gave my cousin, Doris, a haircut on Monday and the next day, my boss's mother, Amy, came to have her hair set.

On the first Saturday afternoon of August, a Buick with the distinctive portholes along the sides of the front fenders stopped in front of our house. My classmate, Ron, was behind the wheel of his parents' cream over maroon sedan. He was a tall, thin, good-looking guy, with dark, curly hair and brown eyes in a lean face. Riding shotgun was his buddy, 'Elmer,' a nickname that clung to Clifford since we were all in junior high. The fellows remained seated and I strolled out the sidewalk to talk with them. Ron, a soldier home on leave, knew all about my having TB. My friend, Gloria, who was also his younger sister, wrote to him about visiting me at the san. During a brief conversation, Ron and I agreed to meet Monday for lunch at the Tic Toc restaurant on West State Street. The boys left and I went back in the house.

On Tuesday afternoon, Ron and I sat in our living room chatting. He was bored at home during the day while his friends and family were busy working. I, too, had a lot of free time plus a devil-may-care attitude since Dr. Bryan's bombshell about my positive gastric. I wasn't looking for romance. I just wanted to forget about TB. We reminisced about our senior trip to Washington, D.C., including riding the roller coaster, climbing the Washington Monument and sitting on our suit-cases to talk all night during the train ride back to Chicago.

On Friday night, Ron and I saw a movie in Rockford. Sunday, the soldier and I picked up his cousin, Jim and his girl-friend, Joanne, for a picnic. I could see a family resemblance between the two tall, dark-haired young men. Joanne was also tall and thin with long, dark hair. The other couple provided a typical lunch–ham sandwiches, potato chips and chocolate chip cookies. I contributed baked beans and Ron brought a cooler of Coke.

We visited Lake Le-Aqua-Na, the new state park near Jim's family farm in Stephenson County. It had opened at the beginning of the season without tables or beaches. We spent the warm, sunny afternoon eating and visiting while lounging around on blankets spread under small shade trees. When it was time for Jim to do chores, we all went home.

The next day I again met Ron at the Tic Toc for lunch. After our preliminary greetings, he asked a question that made me blush., "Do you have chigger bites on your stomach and butt from sitting on the ground at the park yesterday?'

"Is that what it is? I've never had them before. When I woke up this morning, I wondered why I was so itchy."

We spent the afternoon riding around the Rockford area. When I returned home about five o'clock, Mom bawled me out for being gone so long. I didn't realize she'd be worried.

The following afternoon, Ron stopped by and asked me to go to the show, *The Ten Commandments,* Saturday night. The epic movie reflected the religious revival sweeping the country during the fifties. It would be our last date before Ron returned to his Army base.

My parents were glad to hear Ron was leaving because they didn't like him. Dad usually left it up to Mom to oversee my dating, but he spoke up, "Good riddance. Ron's in love with himself. Ken's a gentleman."

On Saturday night, the Biblical extravaganza starring Charlton Heston as Moses lasted four hours. Parting the Red Sea impressed us.

While I was at the movie with Ron, Ken came to our house at eight to surprise me, but his plan backfired. 17 August 1957, could have been the end for us.

The next morning, I didn't get up until 10 A.M. I wrapped a robe over my pjs, slipped my feet into my slippers.and slouched into the kitchen. Mom greeted me with, "Ken was here last night looking for you. I wasn't going to lie. I told him where you were."

"Damn." I grew up surrounded by women who swore, so I did, too. It was a time when gentlemen were cautioned to watch their language in front of the ladies. I guess the females in my family weren't ladies.

Aunt Frannie's favorite idiom popped into my mind. Instead of the usual, "You made your bed, now lie in it," she said, "You burned your ass. You'll have to sit on the blister." Boy, did I have a big blister.

Soon Dad and Mom left to eat dinner in a restaurant and go for a ride, but I stayed home. My stomach was doing flip-flops and I was hoping to see Ken. I loved him and I believed he loved me, but I couldn't imagine how he was feeling. Angry? Broken-hearted? I waited all afternoon and evening, but a Nash didn't pull in the driveway and the phone didn't ring. I didn't know what to think. Was he done with me?

The next morning, I left home at eight to get my shot at the san. I then stopped at the ASC office. I wanted to tell my boss, Mary, I wouldn't be back to work for a long time, but she wasn't there. The girls said they would ask her to call me so I could explain my health situation. While I was in Rockford, Ken came to our house again. Great timing.

After dinner, Dad and Mom went out to bale hay. I sat at the kitchen table trying to reproduce a picture of a rodeo cowboy astride a bucking bronco. I loved horses, but they were the only thing I struggled to draw. I thought the picture would capture my attention, but I couldn't concentrate when I was hoping to hear from Ken. The ringing of a long and a short broke the silence. I jumped up to answer the telephone. Ken said, "Hi Honey. Do you want to go to a movie at the Mid-City tonight?"

"Yeah. I can hardly wait to see you."

"Good, I'll pick you up at seven. Bye"

"See you later. Bye."

He sounded the same as usual on the phone, but I didn't know what to expect when I saw him. I considered peeling the tape off his class ring and wearing it on a chain around my neck in case he wanted to break up. Bad idea. Think positive like Dr. Peale's book. As a good luck charm, I wore the turquoise, sleeveless, cotton dress I'd bought for his farewell party three years ago.

At seven o'clock, Ken stopped his parents' new, blue and white Nash Rambler at the end of our front sidewalk and stepped out. Seeing him tanned and handsome in a blue polo shirt and black slacks gave me hope that everything would be okay. With my stomach feeling like a knotted hay rope and the first two fingers on my right hand crossed, I ran out to greet him. He gathered me into his muscular arms and gave me a big kiss. So far, so good—maybe he just needed time to cool off. I slipped into the compact sedan from the driver's side and stayed close beside him on the bench seat. After maneuvering out of our driveway onto the blacktop, he slipped his right arm around me and steered with his left hand. It took about half-an-hour to travel the back roads to the outdoor theater located on Wisconsin Highway 51 between Beloit and Janesville. On the way, we discussed the weather, which was clear and comfortable, his parents' Rambler with that distinctive new car smell and friends, who were married. At the theater, he pulled into a parking spot, grabbed the speaker that was suspended on a post, cranked up his window part-way and hung the device so we could listen to the music playing. The sun was sinking and a slight breeze kept us comfortable cuddling together. The movie wouldn't start until dusk, which gave us about an hour to wait.

Ken began telling me about the Bennington's last cruise. "While we were on our way to Australia, I checked into taking pilot training. I've wanted to fly ever since Jim Van Buskirk took me and my brother up in a Piper Cub Super Cruiser at the Cottonwood Airport. I was probably thirteen or fourteen and Tommy nine or ten. Mom introduced us to him in the telephone office back when she was an operator and he was a lineman. He said, 'How would you boys like to take an airplane ride?' Of course, we jumped at the chance.

"When I went in the navy, I took a battery of four tests, but my score on math wasn't high enough for pilot training. I talked to the senior medical officer about it and he agreed to give me the tests a second time. I passed, but I found out I'd have to sign on for two more years before I could go to the school. If I didn't pass the cadet training, I'd still be stuck in the navy for six years altogether. I decided not to do it because I want to get married and I don't think military life goes with being married. I'd be gone more than I was home. I thanked the officer for the opportunity."

The knot in my stomach started to relax when my boyfriend said getting married was more important to him than flying.

Ken continued, "I wish you could see the Southern Cross, but it's only visible in the Southern Hemisphere. I think it's the most beautiful constellation there is. Four stars make a perfect cross. At night after the bugler plays "Taps," the chaplain says a prayer and then he tells us where it is in relation to our position.

"I slept in a compartment that was down three decks below the waterline and the bunks were four high. After some guys left, I finally got a top bunk so there was nobody climbing over me. When we were in the tropics, it got really hot in there. I'm in charge of the tool crib, so I'd take my mattress up there and sleep on top of it. Then I had my head next to a porthole and got a breeze."

Ken didn't mention my Saturday night date with Ron.

I certainly wasn't going to bring it up. I told him about Miss Staler, the old woman who moaned for the nurse when

I was admitted to the san and a few stories that included my roommate, Sue.

Ken responded, "I wish I'd been here to visit you."

Porky Pig's antics on the screen ended our conversation. *The Quiet Gun*, a black and white B Western, followed the cartoon. We both liked 'oaters'. Debbie Reynolds, one of Hollywood's most popular, young females, starred in *Tammy and the Bachelor*. The romantic comedy ended with Debbie's naïve, young character getting her first kiss from the older, sophisticated Leslie Nielsen. I was way ahead of her on that score. The drive-ins were often referred to as 'passion pits', but Ken and I saw most of the movies. Still, by the end of the night, I was sure everything was okay between us.

I wanted to monopolize Ken, but I knew he needed time with his family. Since Tommy graduated in June and followed in his big brother's footsteps by going to work at the Barber Colman factory, the boys were now men with more in common.

Sunday night, Ken picked me up to join his family at Lola Mae's house to view the slides he'd taken while aboard the Bennington. During the fifties, a popular program at social gatherings was someone showing slides taken on a recent trip.

We entered his sister's hunter green living room. Rolland and Joe lounged in the two gold, Naugahyde easy chairs. I joined Hazel and Lola Mae sitting on the avocado, Naugahyde davenport. A mahogany coffee table and matching end tables topped with lamps and eight-by-ten color portraits of their first four children completed the setting. A brown, throw rug lay on the floor in front of each piece of furniture. Tommy plopped down in the middle of the bare, wide-board floor. Judy, Suzie,

Jimmy and Stevie surrounded him. Two-month-old Theresa was asleep in her parents' upstairs bedroom.

Ken set up the large, white screen at one end of the room, placed the projector on a small table at the opposite end and sat down beside it. Joe doused the lights.

Soon we saw jet planes soaring off the carrier deck, the most flexible airfield in existence. Ken began his commentary, "The Seventh Fleet, including the U.S.S. Bennington, furnished on-the-spot protection to United States foreign policy across the far eastern seas whenever and wherever required. We had drills every day except Sundays to learn lessons in time of peace because there is little time when at war and no time in battle. Our big computers electronically found solutions to the hypothetical problems that were presented.

"The closest I came to any enemy action was when we were in the Formosa Straits. We had two of our fastest jet fighters armed and ready on the two catapults with pilots aboard. One day our radar picked up two 'bogeys', unidentified aircraft. In less than two minutes, our pilots were airborne. We were able to see them chasing two MIG 17 Russian jets off our bow. There was no exchange of firepower and our jets returned. I realized then why we were there and always training.

"While we were on maneuvers, the replenishment fleet furnished ammunition, spare parts, men and fuel. One of the tankers had a yellow flag with a rooster chasing a hen and the words, Find'em, Fuel'em, Forget'em."

After watching multiple shots of a tanker ship next to the Bennington, Tommy said, "You sure did like refueling."

Ken then told about seeing one of my classmates. "When we were refueling in the Philippines, I looked over at the tanker, Ponchatoula, and saw this guy wearing a life preserver and hard hat that looked like Jim Schmerse and walked like him. I didn't know he was in the Navy. Paul was standing beside me with a pair of binoculars hanging around his neck, so I asked if I could borrow them. Then I could see for sure it was Jim. I hollered, 'Hey, Schmerse!' and waved. I don't know how he could hear me over all of the noise, but he recognized me and waved back. The next night I went ashore with a bunch of guys. When we got back, I was told that a guy named Jim from my hometown came out to the ship to see me."

Ken's pictures included the high jinx when the Big Benn crossed the equator on the way to Australia. Two years earlier, my boyfriend endured the hazing when the ship travelled from Jacksonville, Florida, around the tip of South America to San Diego, California. Shellbacks, sailors who had crossed the imaginary line before, initiated the pollywogs. The day began when the kangaroo court found the pollywogs guilty of all trumped up charges, ordered 'royal haircuts', and divided them into three groups.

Shellbacks walked 'duty canines' wearing collars and leashes. The 'kindergarten set' wrapped in diapers crawled around the deck. 'Bathing beauties' wearing long, yellow yarn braids and ladies' swimsuits paraded in front of the shellbacks, who greeted them with whistles and catcalls.

Ken added, "At the end of the day, the pollywogs stood to eat their supper after having evil spirits beaten from their bodies by the shellbacks wielding shillelaghs."

I'd laughed at the role playing in costumes, but walloping the young men with sticks seemed harsh to me. I suppose that's one of the differences between men and women.

Joe turned the lights back on. A lively discussion concerning the aircraft carrier followed while Lola Mae served coffee and chocolate cake. Ken took me home, walked me to the door and gave me a quick good night kiss. His parents and Tommy waited for him to drive them back to Durand.

In bed before going to sleep, I spent a long time thinking about the evening. Ken's slides and commentary helped me understand his dangerous work. I would be more patient when a lot of time elapsed between his letters.

The next night, Ken and I followed our routine of seeing a movie and parking on Weber Road. The following morning, I stopped in Durand to pick him up on my way to the san. While waiting for him to come out of the house, I scooted over on the bench seat of our Chevy so he could take the wheel. After my shot, we drove up Highway 2 to South Beloit where Esther and Donnie lived in the second-floor apartment of a converted house. Donnie was at work. Esther made a pot of coffee and the three of us sat around her small kitchen table and visited. Esther confided, "I'm expecting in January."

"Congratulations," Ken and I said together. "Are you hoping for a girl or a boy?" I asked.

"It really doesn't matter," Esther replied. "We just want a healthy baby."

After dropping Ken off in Durand, I was home in time to join Dad and Mom for lunch at the round oak table in the kitchen. I chatted about visiting with Esther while we munched ham sandwiches, potato chips and celery. Homemade chocolate chip cookies and coffee topped off our meal.

We half-listened to the WEKZ radio news in the background until the words "Durand family" grabbed our attention. The announcer said David, nineteen, was the second son of Anne and Keron to die from polio, the viral disease that inflames the brain stem and spinal cord. A year ago, his brother, Ed, seventeen, passed away. Both boys were confined to iron lungs since the summer of 1955 when the scourge of the age struck eleven of the family's fourteen children. At that time, our neighbors made national news headlines.

Dr. Jonas Salk recently conquered the dreaded malady with an immunization.

Last spring, Dr. Hein gave me the series of two shots in my arm.

As Mom and I cleared the table after the meal, I said, "It must be hard to lose a child, even when you have fourteen of them. Each one has to be special."

My remark prompted my mother to tersely explain what it felt like for her to have only one child. Up until that time, I only thought about what it was like for me to be an only child. Mom said, "Anne is still a mother. If your only child dies, you are no longer a mother." After a short pause, she added, "You know, you almost died twice."

I was dumfounded. I knew appendicitis and TB made me the sickest I've ever been, but dying never entered my mind. Even Mrs. Potter's remarks last January that I looked like I was at death's door didn't worry me. It just made me angry. Was I naive? Did doctors tell Mom more than they told me? Was she prone to thinking the worst?

I spent the afternoon in the house alone. I pondered Mom's statement and recalled her stories about her early life. She was only seven years old when her mother died at home. When she was twenty-one and still living with the father who raised her, he passed away after surgery in a Rockford hospital four days before Christmas. While I was in first and second grades, my parents lost two baby boys at birth. The shadow of death clung to my mother for as long as she could remember. No wonder she worried I would die.

The next day, I turned twenty. At breakfast, Dad and Mom gave me a card stuffed with twenty, crisp, dollar bills.

In the evening, we took Ken and my cousin, Doris, with us to Walt Williamson's Wagon Wheel for supper and the play, *King of Hearts.* It was a treat reserved for very special occasions because it was expensive.

When Ken walked in our front door late that afternoon, I could have swooned. He wore the black suit with white flecks through it that he had tailor-made in Hong Kong. His pink shirt, the latest rage for men, enhanced his tanned face. A narrow, black, knit tie and gold cufflinks completed his fashionable look.

I don't know what happened after Ken joined the navy, but it curled his hair. After his initial regulation buzz cut, his light brown hair grew out in ringlets. His photos in the high school annual show him having straight hair when he was a little boy and when he graduated.

Although it was September, the weather still felt like summer. I wore my white, sleeveless dress trimmed in black and spectator pumps. In case of a chill later, I carried the matching stole I'd made. Ken's gift, a small, black, velvet purse, completed my outfit. He and I were color coordinated.

My father drove blacktop roads to pick up Doris, who joined Mom and me in the rear seat. Ken rode shotgun. Standard division in the car, men in front and women in back. Dad then followed Highway 75 to the intersection of Highway 2 at the western edge of Rockton. He parked in front of the world-famous, rustic resort, which had been visited by several celebrities. We went inside and waited in the lobby to be seated at a table. I picked up a free picture post card that showed the various dining rooms in the rough-hewn restaurant. Printed on the back, *Only women are employed in the kitchen of the Wagon Wheel because women, through their innate sense of taste and daintiness, excel in the fine arts of cookery.*

We were seated in the Martha Washington room at a table covered with a white cloth. One of the waitresses wearing a long, colonial style dress brought menus and took our orders. While we waited for our meals, Ken told us about the people he met when the Bennington was in port in Australia. "The only time I went ashore, I was alone and wearing my 'whites' because our winter is their summer. I walked across the Sydney Harbor Bridge around noon and found a restaurant. An older woman was behind the counter and her husband was sitting in the back, but there were no other customers. I asked the lady, 'Should I sit at the counter to be handy for you?'

"She replied, 'Sit wherever you want.'

"I sat down at a table covered with a red and white checked table cloth. The old man came over to me and asked, 'Is it okay if I sit down to visit?' I assured him it was. He joined me and said, 'Where are you from?'

"In the navy, I always said Rockford, Illinois. Few knew where that was let alone Durand.

"The old man then said, 'Do you remember the old Palace Theater?'

"I was dumbfounded that he knew about that. I said, 'My parents took me and my brother and sister to vaudeville acts there.'

"The old man pointed to his wife and said, 'That lady and I played vaudeville there in the thirties and forties. We were originally from Peoria.'

"The woman brought my meal, but they wouldn't let me pay. The U.S. kept the Japanese out of Australia during World War II and the people have been very thankful for that. I thanked the couple and left.

"On my way back to the ship, I was walking under an overpass. A Volkswagen pulled over and the driver asked, 'Where are you headed?'

"'Back to my ship,' I said.

"The man then said, 'I told my family if I saw a sailor, I'd bring him home for dinner.'

"I was a little leery, but I decided to get in with him. He then stopped at a pay phone and explained, 'I have to call my wife that I'm bringing you home.'

"I ate with him, his wife, two children and his mother-in-law, who were all living in an apartment. On the way taking me back to my ship, he drove by the new home that he was proud that they were building."

After supper, we moved to the theater. Ken and Dad stood in the lobby while the three of us used the ladies' room. We then took our seats with Dad sitting on the aisle and Ken on the far end beside me. My boyfriend quietly filled me in on what happened during the time we were gone. "When a couple of women walked past me and your dad, a myna bird in a cage behind us gave a loud wolf whistle. The women immediately turned around and glared. I couldn't help but laugh when your dad's face turned red."

After we enjoyed the light comedy, Dad drove us home, stopping on the way to drop off Doris. In our driveway, Ken and I got out of the Chevy to sit in the Nash parked in front of the house. Dad wheeled our hard-top into the garage. My parents walked up the path and entered the house through the basement door. We said a long good night.

The following Friday night, Ken and I rode with Wayne and Gloria to the Butterfly restaurant on Highway 15 northeast of Beloit where we enjoyed the fish fry special. We returned to our farm and Wayne parked in the driveway at the end of the sidewalk. Ken and I necked in the back seat while the radio set on WGN played popular tunes. The married couple sitting in the front seat of their Ford were probably bored, but they were understanding of our plight. When I figured we were in danger of Mom turning on the porch light, I said, "I better go in." Ken walked me to the door and kissed me good night. I entered the porch and he left with our friends.

The next evening, Ken took me for a ride and parked in front of our house. I didn't think we were there very long when Mom turned on the spotlight aimed at the Rambler. We exited the Nash, walked up the sidewalk and paused in front of the wooden steps. He said, "Good night," gave me a quick kiss and turned on his heel to return to the compact sedan. I entered the quiet house.

Sunday morning at breakfast, Mom explained, "You can tell Ken the light wasn't for him. I heard a noise and turned it on to see if maybe a cow had got out, but I didn't see anything."

I called Ken later and passed along her message.

"I'm glad to hear that," he said. "I don't want your mother mad at me."

The next day after my shot at the san, I met with Dr. Bryan in his office. After the usual pleasantries, he said, "You may go back to work part-time."

"Thank you." That was the third best thing he'd ever said to me. Number one was, "You may go to the bathroom and take showers." Running a close second was, "You may go home."

While driving along the city streets to the ASC office to share my good news, I chimed in with Debbie Reynolds singing "Tammy" on the car radio. The title song from the movie brought romantic thoughts of my evening with Ken at the drive-in theater nearly a month ago. I'm glad that incident is behind us. I never want to lose my boyfriend.

When I entered the Post Office building, Henry, the elevator operator, said his usual glum, "Good morning."

Mary and the girls greeted me warmly when I strolled into the ASC office. My first words were, "I'm coming back to work."

My boss and I walked into her office. I took one of the three wooden straight chairs surrounding her desk and she sat down in the leather chair behind it. "Dr. Bryan said I could work three days a week."

"What days do you get your shots?"

"Mondays and Thursdays."

"How about working Mondays, Tuesdays and Thursdays?"

"That would be great. Ken's home on leave until Thursday. Can I start next week?"

"That's fine. Have fun and I'll see you next Monday."

I bid Mary and the girls farewell.

At home, Dad and Mom were pleaased about my upgrade.

Tuesday evening, when Ken came for our date, I greeted him with, "I'm going back to work next Monday."

"That's great news." He then picked up Lola Mae and Joe to treat them to supper at the Pink Pony on the east side of Rockford. Forty-five minutes later we were inside the upscale restaurant and seated at a table covered with a white cloth. Our silverware was wrapped in white cloth napkins.

A waiter brought menus and greeted us, "Good evening. My name is Charles. May I get you something from the bar?" He was about thirty, tall with dark hair and dressed in a black shirt and pants covered by a long, white apron.

Joe and Lola Mae ordered martinis, Ken asked for a bottle of Heineken with a glass, and I stuck with a Tom Collins. When the man went to get our drinks, Lola Mae said, "They have waiters so you know it's expensive."

While we were looking at the menus, Ken said, "Honey, try the lobster. I've eaten it in California and it's delicious."

Priced at $3.50, it was more than twice the cost of my old standby, fried chicken. I was feeling adventurous and ordered the twin tails accompanied by a baked potato with sour cream and a tossed salad with Thousand Island dressing. Lola Mae and Joe selected steaks. My first bite of the white meat dipped in drawn butter made it my instant favorite.

Wednesday night, Ken and I spent about an hour saying good-bye while sitting in the Rambler parked in front of our house. After our final kiss at the front steps, he said, "The next time I see you, I'll be home for good."

"That'll be wonderful." A happy thought, but July was ten long, lonely months away.

A week later, his letter stated that the following morning three of his navy buddies stopped for him on their way driving to California. They pulled into San Diego on Saturday with time to spare. They weren't due until Sunday.

Monday, 16 September, I started the week with my shot as usual. Instead of returning home, I drove the city streets to work and parked in a near-by lot. It was exactly eight months since I'd entered the san as a patient. I was humming as I entered the post office building. Henry, the elderly elevator operator, spoke his usual solemn, "Good morning."

I was so happy to be back, I could have kissed him. That would have shook the old boy up.

The girls in the office greeted me with smiles and welcoming words. I slipped back into the routine as though I was never away. Once again, I was earning a check and paying room and board at home.

On Friday, 4 October 1957, people around the world trembled with fear when Russia launched Sputnik, the first artificial satellite to circle the earth. Rockets used for space travel could also be used as guided missiles in warfare giving the Russians an important military advantage. Success in space became the measure of a nation's leadership in science, engineering and national defense. The Space Race within the Cold War between the two Super Powers was ignited.

Americans criticized their schools for not training more scientists and engineers. Ken and I thought we received a good education, but Durand High graduated farmers and factory workers, not physicists.

October also brought a personal milestone. The following Monday, I met with Dr.

Bryan after my gastric, x-ray and shot. The physician and I engaged in the usual preliminaries. He set a quart jar on the desk. It was filled with pills that looked a lot like M&Ms. He said, "You may discontinue the shots and take twelve of these a day, four before each meal. You also may go back to work full-time."

I could have jumped for joy, but, I didn't. Instead, I calmly picked up the jar and said a brief, "Thank you." After a quick farewell, I exited his office.

I would soon be plopping down in a chair instead of sitting carefully on one butt cheek or the other, depending on which side received the injection. I wanted to celebrate.

I went to the third floor to tell Sako my good news. My Japanese friend and I arranged to go shopping in the evening. The stores downtown stayed open until nine on Monday nights.

At the office, Mary and the girls shared my elation.

When I finished work at four thirty, I picked up Sako. We browsed the business district for a couple hours, but bought nothing. Supper at Mandarin Gardens capped our outing. The Chinese restaurant was a long-time fixture on Wyman Street, but I had never visited it before. The décor, the staff and the food made me feel like I travelled to the Orient. For my companion, it was an opportunity to eat a meal similar to those in her homeland. We returned to the san before the eight thirty curfew.

The first of November, I sent Ken a blue, plaid sport shirt for his twenty-second birthday on the eighth. He looked sharp in uniform, but I could hardly wait until he would pack it away and wear civvies.

Early in December, I attended a baby shower for Esther hosted by her mother-in-law, Mary. I gave my friend a car seat that hooked onto the front bench beside the parent. The child could sit and 'drive' with its little steering wheel.

First, wedding showers for my friends and relatives—now the baby showers followed. The parties made me feel like everybody's old maid aunt. I consoled myself that my turn would come.

On the following weekend, Mom was so sick with a cold that she didn't dress, which rarely happened. The previous Monday, she washed clothes and hung them on the outside lines to dry. When she took them down, she dampened those needing to be ironed and left them rolled up in the large, wicker basket. I spent Saturday afternoon pressing those garments so they wouldn't mildew.

The cold germs made the rounds. Dad got sick Thursday. By the weekend, my nose was stuffy and my throat scratchy. I rested a lot and by Monday I felt I could go to work. After TB, I was very careful when I caught a cold.

With the holidays approaching, I missed Ken more than ever. It seemed like years since he kissed me good-bye in September. The end of his enlistment was still seven long months away. A new song, "Blue Christmas" by Elvis Presley, fit my mood perfectly.

Each time I heard the record played on the radio at home, I stopped what I was doing to wallow in my loneliness. At work, during our morning and afternoon breaks, I took advantage of three plays for a quarter to listen to my theme song on the jukebox at Cummings Coffee Shop. The tune playing over and over probably drove my co-workers nuts, but I didn't care.

Early Christmas morning, it was raining and freezing making the blacktop too slippery for us to go to church. By eleven-thirty, it warmed up enough to thaw the ice on the roads. Mom drove me and a plate of homemade cookies to Durand to again spend the holiday with Ken's family. The day was exactly like last year except baby Theresa had joined the family in June. The five grandkids were tiring, but I felt so much better than a year ago, I weathered the event just fine. I began to feel like I belonged.

Later in the week, a letter from Ken described the ship's Christmas party in San Diego. The big city impressed the small-town boy. He wrote, *You should see the glass elevator on the outside of the Coronado Hotel where the party was held.*

I had my picture taken with Jane Russell, the movie star who was one of the celebrities that was there. Her figure is just as awesome in person as it is in the movies. I never saw a copy of the picture, which made me wonder if the photographer had any film in his camera.

A New Year's Eve snow storm cancelled our plans to celebrate at the Wigwam. Mom popped popcorn for the occasion, but we turned in after the ten o'clock news.

Chapter 7

1958

1958 began with the jangle of the telephone startling us awake from a sound sleep—a long and a short, our ring on the party line. Good news did not arrive at 2 A.M.

From my side of the closed door that separated our bed-rooms, I could hear my parents mumbling. Mom pushed back the blankets carefully so she didn't uncover Dad. She sat on the edge of their double bed, grabbed the flashlight from her night stand and clicked it on. After sliding her warm feet into cold slippers, she stood up, aimed the beam ahead of her and scuffed through the living room to the kitchen. Another long and short pealed. The old-fashioned, black, office-type instrument sat on the modern, walnut desk in the southeast corner of the room. I heard the snap when she pulled the chain to turn on the overhead light. The chair's wooden legs scraped against the linoleum as she pulled it out so she could sit down. Mom lifted the receiver, placed it against her ear and tentatively said, "Hello," into the mouthpiece. I held my breath so I could hear her better. After a short pause, relief surged in her voice, "Happy New Year. Just a minute."

I heard her lay down the receiver and slide the chair back so she could stand up. "Lolita, it's for you," she said loudly, her tone dripping with exasperation. She shuffled back to bed.

I knew it was Ken calling. I hopped out of bed, dashed to the kitchen and eagerly picked up the receiver. "Hello," I said breathlessly.

"Happy New Year, Honey!" said my slightly inebriated sailor. I heard revelers in the background. "I'm sorry. I forgot about the time. I suppose it's 2 A.M. there isn't it? Did I get you up?"

"Yes, and the operator and probably everybody else on our party line."

When Ken entered high school, his mother worked for the telephone company, but he'd forgotten that in Durand no one was at the switchboard between 10 P.M and 6 A.M. After-hours calls roused Nona, the middle-aged, corpulent, red-headed chief operator. She and her husband lived in the house where the system was located. I assumed our neighbors also crawled out of their cozy nests and lifted their receivers to learn about the Tschabolds' catastrophe.

Ken asked, "Did you go out to celebrate tonight?"

"No. It snowed all day and didn't quit until after Dad was done milking. About eight o'clock, Buck and Mike drove in with the snowplow. After township roads are cleared, Stan, the highway commissioner, directs his crew to open driveways for those of us who live on county roads. That gives us some benefit from our tax dollars. It was too late to get ready and go to a dance. Mom popped some popcorn and we just watched TV and went to bed after the ten o'clock news."

"Well, I'm here in San Diego at the Jade Room bar and I just wanted to wish you a Happy New Year. I'll see you in July. Bye."

"Happy New Year. I'm glad you called. Bye." I returned to bed feeling warm and gooey inside like a toasted marshmallow. After nearly four hours of sleep combined with the excitement of talking to my boyfriend, it took me a long time to return to dreamland.

On the second Thursday morning of the new year, I drove along Highway 70 on my way to Rockford to have my monthly gastric and x-ray at the san before I went to work. I wore sun glasses but the rising sun shone through the windshield below the visor and made me squint.

When I left the office at four thirty, the sun was sinking in the west. The days were slowly getting longer. I drove up Main Street to Wayne and Gloria's upstairs apartment. Gloria's folks, who lived downstairs, purchased the four-family building on the north side of Rockford when they quit farming a year earlier.

After the usual greetings, I made myself comfortable on the davenport in Gloria's living room. I stopped by to deliver a small dress for their baby girl who was a week old. My friends were becoming mothers while I sat in the waiting room of my life.

Gloria picked up her daughter from the bassinet and held the baby in front of me so I could see her. I said, "She's beautiful."

"Lori Lea weighed six pounds nine ounces and was nineteen inches long. The doctor had to use forceps for her delivery. That's why her head looks like a tube of lipstick, but it's rounding out. She's still got a small bruise on her cheek, too. Do you want to hold her?"

"No," I said quickly. I wasn't experienced with babies. I thought children should be at least two years old before I had anything to do with them.

Gloria laid her daughter back in her basket and went to the kitchen to make coffee. I moved to a straight chair painted yellow to match the small wooden table covered with a white luncheon cloth printed with flowers. My friend sat down and gushed on about motherhood. It would take a while for me to think of our friends as parents. By the time we'd finished the pot of coffee, I needed to use her bathroom and head home.

Ten days of typical, January weather complicated the twenty-five-mile commute to my Rockford job. On Tuesday morning, Mom drove me to Durand because she was more experienced with snowy roads than I was. By afternoon, the flurries turned into a blizzard forcing my driver, Betty, to leave the city early. I called to alert my parents and they met me in Durand at three o'clock. We were two miles from home when Dad got stuck on the curve north of our landlord's farm. More than a half-hour passed before a county plow came along and pulled our Chevy out of the drift. While we waited, my father griped about the weather.

The next morning, Dad put chains on the rear wheels of the sedan before Mom drove me to Durand. By Thursday, the snow was piled so high around the business district in town that there was no place to park the hard-top for the day. Inclement weather continued for the rest of the month, but I made it to the office every day.

Valentine's Day was only ten days away when my Christmas present from Ken finally arrived in the mail. The beautiful eight-by-ten headshot of him wearing his blue, navy uniform was worth the wait. He'd signed the photo, *To the sweetest most wonderful girl in the world with all my love, Ken.*

The accompanying letter contained an apology for the delay and the following notation, *Mine is one of the last traditional winter uniforms to have thirteen buttons on the blue trousers. Right after I enlisted, the navy updated and started using zippers. It may be inconvenient going to the bathroom, but I like having the buttons.*

A few days later, the Montgomery Ward spring and summer catalog brightened our mail box. While thumbing through the colorful pages of new offerings, a set of dishes called Moss Rose captivated me. The modern-looking, round, white plates were trimmed with pink roses and a gold edge. I ordered a set of eight to be delivered to our house. Ken and I weren't engaged, but I believed we would be married.

On Sunday, 9 March Dad and I joined his parents' golden wedding anniversary celebration at the New England Grange Hall in Durand. Jake and Jessie Hughes Tschabold were dressed in their Sunday best. Grandpa, whose full head of snow-white hair was freshly trimmed, wore a dark gray suit with a harmonizing tie around the neck of his white shirt. He would have been more comfortable in his everyday blue and white striped overalls with his Plow Boy chewing tobacco tucked into one of the bib pockets.

Grandma, whose dark brown hair was streaked with gray, replaced her usual cotton housedress protected by an apron with a navy blue, crepe frock. I had inherited her flawless complexion.

The extended family gathered in the basement for dinner at noon. Wooden picnic tables covered with white paper filled the large cement floor. In the kitchen at the rear of the room, the organization's women cooked a hearty meat and potatoes dinner and served all of us.

A few weeks before the event, Dad's youngest sister, Elnora, stopped by to tell us about the party plans and collect
money from Dad. Each of the five children kicked in a ten to
make a cash gift of fifty dollars. At that time, Mom told her
sister-in-law, "I don't want any job connected to the celebration." Sunday Mom stayed at home and ate her homemade
bean soup.

When my parents were first married, family difficulties
left hard feelings, but I didn't know what happened. While I
was growing up, sometimes we went to the Tschabold pow-
wows, Mom's term for the family get-togethers at Grandma
and Grandpa's house, and sometimes not. My only grandparents always sent a card with a dollar enclosed for my birthday
and exchanged Christmas presents with me, but I never spent
time with them.

After the meal, everyone moved upstairs to greet friends at
an open house. The hall floor was hardwood. White, sound-ab-
sorbing material covered the walls and ceiling. Several small,
decorative lamps were attached to the walls.

Nieces served coffee, punch and pieces of a large white
cake decorated with pink roses and the words, Happy 50th
Anniversary Jake and Jessie.

The short, chubby blue-eyed couple married in 1908 and
started farming in Clarno Township southeast of Monroe,
Wisconsin, where their Swiss ancestors settled. During The
Great Depression, they moved their family to the Durand area.
Twenty years later, their younger son, Bobbie, took over the
family farm on Best Road. His parents moved to the small
house on a few acres a quarter-mile south at the intersection
of Rock Grove Road. Early every morning, Grandpa drove
his little, gray, Ford tractor down the hill to help his son with
chores.

At the end of an afternoon of visiting with friends and family, Dad and I returned home. I put our five-by-seven, black and white picture of my grandparents in Mom's bottom dresser drawer with other photos and newspaper clippings. I didn't know if she wanted to hear about the day or not, so I kept quiet. She didn't ask any questions.

Dad had recently bought his first pick-up truck. He paid the Brodhead Allis-Chalmers dealer $250 for the twelve-year-old Chevy that the mechanic had driven on service calls. The last Saturday of March was warm enough for me to paint Dad's name and address on the vehicle's dark-blue doors. State law required the information to be prominently displayed to prevent rustling of farm animals.

When I was little, I secretly hoped Dad would include '& daughter' like other men included '& son' with their names. I loved wearing 'spender overalls and tagging after him. When he needed to go to town or the neighbors, he patiently waited for Mom to wash my face and comb my hair so I was presentable to go along. At twenty, I was still Daddy's girl, but I no longer wanted it proclaimed on the doors of his pick-up.

April brought Easter. With my own paycheck to spend, I bought a dozen of the pink, yellow and green Fannie May candy eggs our family traditionally enjoyed. I also purchased a billfold for Mom along with socks and a tie for Dad.

I treated myself to an outfit. When I prepared for church, I donned my new navy-blue coat dress with a full skirt that struck me mid-calf. I left the two bottom buttons open to show the ruffled, pink crinoline half-slip that I wore underneath. My accessories included long, pink gloves that met the dress's three-quarter-length sleeves and a large, pink, hat adorned with tulle and an artificial rose. My navy blue, patent-leather, sling backs were open-toed and trimmed with a bow. My parents gave me a small, matching purse.

A week later, I started getting a cold, which was always scary after TB, but I continued to work every day. On Saturday, Dr. Hein prescribed cough medicine and penicillin pills. The next morning, I went to church with Mom, but spent the rest of the day in bed. Monday, I felt tired but I went to the office. Tuesday, I stayed home to rest. Another day in bed did the trick and I returned to work Wednesday.

During May, we observed Mother's Day with dinner at Windy Acres restaurant near Monroe. Dad and I gave her an everyday, Timex watch with a stainless-steel case and black leather strap. It also served as her birthday present. It was practical for us to give her one big gift instead of two little ones for Mother's Day and her birthday, which was a week later. The following Sunday, we ate Mom's celebratory dinner from the smorgasbord at the Salad Bowl restaurant on the west edge of Rockford.

The month ended in tragedy on a hot, muggy Saturday. The storm we expected all day blew in about four o'clock. I stood in front of the living room window and watched the wind uproot a small apple tree in the orchard next to the house. A downpour followed. I jumped when a lightning bolt cracked followed by a thunder boom. If counting between the slash and the rumble indicated how far away it struck, it was close.

An hour later, the typical summer squall moved on and the setting sun cast a rainbow in the eastern sky. Dad went to the barn to milk and looked out the south door toward the pasture. His horse, Mickey, lay on his side in the grass and that wasn't normal. Dad walked out to investigate, discovered that the animal was dead and returned to the house with the news. "Mickey got struck by lightning," he said with a catch in his voice and tears in his eyes. He then went back to doing chores. I started to cry. Our dogs and horses were part of the family.

I remembered a farm auction on a fall day in 1941 when Dad bought the Morgan/Tennessee Walker cross that was broke to drive and ride. The bay horse had a black mane and tail, a white blaze down his nose and a touch of white on each of his hind feet. Dad opened the trunk of our Chevy and removed the saddle and bridle stashed inside. He and Mom changed off riding the horse the ten miles home. The young gelding walked nearly as fast as most horses trotted.

During the sale, Mickey was locked in a fox pen, a wire mesh enclosure with a roof. My parents assumed that was for convenience. After the horse was in our pasture, they learned he could stand beside a fence and leap frog over it.

Every morning and every night, my father straddled Mickey to round up the cows in the pasture. When needed, he hitched the gelding and our mare, Brownie, to the hay rack, the grain box or the corn planter. Dad was pleased with his purchase.

The following spring, when I was four-and-a-half, my dream came true. My parents bought a two-year-old, sorrel pony with four white stockings and a white blaze down her nose. Millie was a Shetland/Welsh cross making her a little taller than average. I soon realized I was allergic to Millie. I avoided watery eyes and a stuffy nose by never touching my face while riding. Afterward, I washed my hands thoroughly with soap and water.

When Dad and I rode our two steeds, he held a lead rope snapped to my pony's bridle to make sure she didn't run away. One summer day, while we were galloping along a makeshift road behind the farm buildings, I slipped out of the saddle, landed in a bed of sand and started to cry. I wasn't hurt, just scared.

Dad immediately stopped, jumped down from Mickey and checked that I was okay. "Come on, get back on and we'll go to the barn."

"No," I whimpered. "I don't want to ride Millie any more. She threw me off."

"You didn't get thrown off. You just fell off."

Dad sat me in the saddle and made sure my feet were firmly in the stirrups. I left the reins lay on my pony's neck and clung to the horn with both hands. Dad mounted his horse and we slowly walked the animals the rest of the way to the barn.

In the spring after I turned eight, Dad and Mom agreed I could ride by myself. That first afternoon at four thirty, Dad watched as I put the bit between Millie's teeth and slipped the bridle over her head. I threw the saddle on her back, bent over, reached under her belly, grabbed the woven girth and fastened it with the leather strap. I wasn't strong enough to tighten the cinch so the saddle wouldn't slip. I stepped back to let Dad give it a final tug. I mounted Millie and proudly rode off to round up our dairy cows in the pasture. We needed to cross a shallow creek and Millie balked at wading through it. She seemed determined to keep her milk-colored, legs sparkling clean. Fortunately, I was more obstinate than she was. After much urging, and a slap or two on her rump with the tail end of the reins, she attempted to jump across the water. We landed in the midst with a splash because it was too wide for her to leap over. She scrambled to the far side while I clung to the saddle horn with both hands. Although she was a young animal, her memory didn't seem to work very well. We went through the same falderal when we brought the herd back toward the barn.

In the spring after I turned twelve, I felt I was too big for Millie. I no longer imagined riding the range with cowboy movie stars Roy Rogers and Gene Autry. We put an ad in the daily newspaper and sold my pony to another family. I couldn't hold back the tears when Millie rode up the driveway in the back of a horse trailer pulled by a pick-up truck.

I began mounting Mickey to bring the bovines in from the pasture. Afterward, I left the cow yard through the wooden gate next to the barn. One sunny, summer afternoon, I decided to try jumping Mickey over the barrier that was about four feet high. With only a hundred and fifteen pounds on his back, he didn't need much urging. That first leap literally impressed on me the reason people I watched in horse shows used English saddles when vaulting fences. I was thrown against the pommel of our Western-style saddle and it hurt my lower body, but that didn't stop me. The next day, I braced myself better before the horse lunged. Jumping was a lot more fun than getting off the horse, pulling the heavy, oak gate open, leading him through, lifting the gate to shut it behind us and remounting.

Saturday night after supper, I rode with Dad to the Durand telephone office. The storm knocked our phone service out and we needed to call the rendering works to pick up the dead horse. I felt like we were contacting the undertaker to retrieve a relative.

The new week finally brought a letter from Ken after nothing for a month. He wrote from Hawaii, *I'll be in California by the end of June.*

My heart leaped like a bunny rabbit. He was getting closer to home.

With his next letter, Ken printed *42 days to go* on the back of the envelope. He'd be home 27 July. My hand shook with excitement when I circled the date on the calendar hanging on my bedroom wall.

At the ASC office, Donna left her job to move to Florida. Mary placed a help wanted ad in the newspaper, interviewed several ladies and hired Fran, a petite, gray-haired woman. The workload was reshuffled, but I continued to handle the corn loans.

The last Saturday morning in June was warm and sunny, a perfect day to wind up haying. The neighboring family we'd hired to bale our crop with their machine was making their last rounds gathering the windrows. A haze of dust and dirt surrounded Orville, the father, and Donna, their oldest daughter who was my age, as they rode steel seats on opposite sides of the implement. As each bale slid between them, they pushed two wires back and forth to tie it. Ruth, the mother, drove the tractor pulling the baler. A cushion softened her metal seat and a large umbrella protected her from the hot sun shining down on the open field. They finished their work by noon, ate Mom's hearty dinner and went home.

In the afternoon, I helped Dad and Ed empty the final two loads of hay that they gathered from the field during the morning. Whenever a job required two men, the neighbors 'changed work.

Ed was several years older than Dad. A flat cap covered the short fellow's thinning gray hair and waist-band overalls girded his paunch. He could fix most anything that Dad needed repaired, but it took a while because he always told a few stories from his past.

A wagon load of fifty-six, square bales sat in the middle of the second-story of the barn. A slight breeze wafted from the open south window. Ed climbed atop the hay to stick the tines of the large fork into eight bales at a time. A heavy rope was threaded through the mechanism that lifted the bales from the wagon to the track in the peak of the building and carried them to the mow. The other end of the rope was tied to the rear axle of the Allis Chalmers to provide the power needed to move the bales.

I perched on the metal seat of the running orange tractor stopped at the bottom of the driveway to the loft. I wore shorts, a sleeveless shirt and tennis shoes with no socks, but the sun beating down made me sweat. The light wind blowing through the driveway of the barn brought dust and the aroma of the alfalfa in my direction, but little relief from the heat.

When Ed waved his arm, I stuck my left foot against the clutch, shifted into reverse with my left hand and slowly backed up until Ed shouted, "Whoa." After he dumped the bales, I shifted into low gear and the tractor crept forward. Dad did the hottest job stacking the dropped bales neatly in the airless storage area. The three of us repeated our tasks over and over all afternoon.

After we'd finished the last load, Ed pushed the empty hayrack out of the barn and parked it under a shade tree. The two of us sat down on the edge of the wooden platform. He pulled a small, white bag of tobacco and a package of papers from the two breast pockets of his blue, chambray shirt, rolled a cigarette, lit it and said, "I don't know how you get anything done. You're blowing your nose all of the time."

"I can't help it. I'm allergic to hay dust. There's nothing else I can do."

The next afternoon, I was in the midst of giving Mom a permanent in the kitchen when Jack, Helen and their three kids stopped by. Dropping in at someone's house with no advance notice was a common practice among our friends and relatives, but it wasn't always convenient. It took me another hour to finish my mother's hair. She then joined Dad visiting with our guests in the living room.

David, Margie, Nancy and I went outside to play croquet on the lawn. I set up the nine wire arches and two wooden stakes for the court. Nancy and I teamed up against her older brother and sister and easily won the game. It wasn't a fair match. Last spring during our daily games at the san, I'd become a crack shot at hitting the wooden ball with the wooden mallet. At chore time, our company departed.

Doris and her short, chubby, friend nicknamed 'Pudge' picked me up at five thirty to play golf at the rolling, Windy Acres nine-hole course near Monroe. The two women brought their own clubs but I rented a set for my first attempt at the game. With the sun setting and no wind, it was ideal weather on the course. When we finished the round, we entered the club's bar and each ordered a brat, French fries and a Coke. While we ate, we rehashed our playing. Doris said, "You did all right for your first time."

"Thanks. You two were a lot of help, but I don't think I'll do it again." I didn't add that I thought it was a sport for older people.

Doris dropped me off at our house just before dark. When I entered the living room, Mom greeted me with, "Ken called about an hour after you left. He got home for good yesterday. He'll see you tomorrow night."

"Oh great. Why didn't he let me know he was coming?"

He'd arrived a month earlier than I'd expected. My emotions were entwined like a jelly roll. I was elated that he was here, but I was disgusted he didn't alert me ahead of time. I sat down to watch TV with Mom and Dad but I couldn't concentrate on the programs. I went to bed after the ten o'clock news, but didn't go to sleep. My mind spun like a top. At last, we would have unlimited time together.

Monday morning, I could hardly wait to tell the girls at the office that Ken was home. All day my mind wandered. I'd start a task and all of a sudden, I was thinking about my boyfriend.

I arrived home at six o'clock and supper was on the table. My folks wanted to get to Beloit before the stores closed at nine. Dad needed to exchange a new pair of slacks he'd bought at George Brothers because Mom found a flaw in the material.

After they left, I cleared the table and washed the dishes. It was about seven.by the time I sat down in Mom's easy chair in the living room to wait for Ken. I wore my work clothes– white sandals and a gold cap-sleeved, blouse with an olive green, pleated, cotton skirt printed with gold flowers. I turned the TV to Burns and Allen on Channel 13. I spent more time looking out the north window hoping to see a Nash enter the driveway than I did watching Gracie's inanities. "Arthur Godfrey's Talent Scouts" showcasing their discoveries began. Still no Ken–he didn't tell Mom what time he would come. At eight, I watched Danny Thomas and his family's adventures followed a half-hour later by Spring Byington, the "December Bride." I was getting more impatient by the minute.

Questions flitted through my mind like flies. What was taking Ken so long? Wasn't he as anxious to see me as I was to see him? "Amos and Andy" began their humor at nine o'clock. Soon Ditzlers' blue and white Rambler pulled in our gravel driveway.

The sun had set about half-an-hour earlier, but it was still comfortably warm. I dashed out to greet Ken when he walked around the rear of the compact sedan. He wore a black and gray striped polo shirt with black wash trousers. He wrapped his arms around me like he'd never let me go. His kiss made up for the time I cooled my heels watching the boob tube.

"Get in and we'll go see Wayne and Gloria," Ken said.

I looked at my watch, "It'll be going on ten o'clock by the time we get there."

"Nobody goes to bed until after the ten o'clock news."

He was right. Our friends were still up at quarter-to-ten when we arrived at their upstairs apartment in Rockford. The four of us spent about an hour catching up with each other. Gloria showed us a handful of snapshots of Lori Lea, their six-month-old baby who was asleep in her parents' bedroom. We then made plans to celebrate the Fourth of July Friday night at Buffa's bar in South Beloit.

After Ken and I returned to my house, we cuddled in the Rambler with popular tunes playing on radio station WGN. He talked about his disappointment with the navy that he'd been stuck in the rank of petty officer second class. "Three times I'd passed the tests to be promoted to first class, but it was frozen."

"That's too bad."

When we kissed goodnight, it reminded me his leaving was only temporary.

Four nights later, a '56 Lincoln entered our gravel lane with Ken proudly behind the wheel. I dashed out to see his expensive auto. "It's beautiful."

"When I first saw pictures of it, I decided that was the car I wanted," Ken said. "I knew it would be two years old by the time I could buy one, but I didn't care."

He located the cream over mint green, four-door sedan at a used car lot in Rockford. To protect the dark green, cloth upholstery, he purchased clear plastic seat covers decorated with little gold stars. Sitting on them proved to be hot in the summer and cold in the winter.

We picked up Tracys at their Rockford apartment and headed north on Hwy 2 toward Buffa's bar in South Beloit. During the trip, our friends sat in the back seat. "This is like riding in a limousine," Wayne said.

Inside the tavern, the four of us walked alongside the bar to enter a large room where live music blared. We seated ourselves at one of few vacant, small tables placed on the carpeting at the edge of the dance floor. When the young, blonde cocktail waitress approached, the guys and Gloria each ordered a beer. I followed my cousin's advice and chose a tall, Tom Collins. My three companions lit cigarettes joining the majority of the people squeezed around the tables crammed in the room. A cloud of blue smoke hung in the air above our heads. When the waitress set our order on the black Formica, Wayne raised his brown bottle and said, "Here's to Kenny." We all clinked our drinks.

The band began one of the new rock n' roll tunes, Jerry Lee Lewis's "Whole Lot of Shakin' Goin' On." Jerry Lee and his raucous piano threatened to topple Elvis as the king of rock n' roll.

Dancers jammed the parquet floor, which didn't look much bigger than our nine-by-twelve living room rug at home. A dark-haired, young woman wearing a tight red dress trimmed with fringe shimmied past. Ken hollered, "Shake it, baby, shake it!"

He embarrassed me, but I guess that was the sailor in him coming out.

When the leader announced the "Bunny Hop", the latest dance craze, the four of us joined the queue of young people on the floor. Gloria placed her hands on the hips of the last guy in the single-file line. Wayne and I followed her with Ken the new caboose. The music dictated the simple steps. Tap the floor twice with your right foot, then twice with your left, hop forwards, hop backwards and finally hop forward three times.

The rest of the time, we slow-danced cheek to cheek or listened to the loud music while savoring our drinks. Conversation was impossible except when the band was between tunes or took a break.

At 12:55 A.M., Ken and I squeezed into the crowd on the dance floor as the band closed with Frank Sinatra's "One for My Baby (and One More for the Road)," which was enjoying a new round of popularity. I remembered my cousin, Doris, playing the tune on her portable, record player when the song came out in the forties.

Saturday night, Ken and I went to a movie. I wore a new, blue and green swirled print, sleeveless, nylon dress lined with blue taffeta, the blue rhinestone jewelry he had given me and a new hairdo. Instead of watching summer reruns on TV in the evenings, I stood in front of my dresser mirror to practice winding my shoulder length hair into a French twist. It took a handful of bobby pins and a cloud of spray net to keep every hair stiffly in place. I hoped Ken would like my cool, calm and collected demeanor. On our way to the Mid-City drive-in theater, he said, "Honey, you look beautiful."

Wednesday night we watched Ken's former teammates win their softball game in Pec. Our unlimited time together was as sweet as gorging on a box of chocolates.

The following Friday night, we again visited Wayne and Gloria. The guys looked up the phone number in the book and Wayne called to have a pizza delivered to the apartment house. While waiting for the food, the fellows continued to peruse the large Rockford directory. When one of them saw a person's odd name, he read it aloud and then they both laughed. For the two of them, the tome was a joke book.

Later, Ken and I sat in front of my house and he told me about beginning his job search. Earlier in the year, business picked up after a recession in '57. President Eisenhower had been right to oppose a broad government spending program that he believed would lead to inflation. Ken said, "Every morning I check the pages of help wanted ads in the news-paper. I don't want to go back to the factory. Yesterday I went to the state police headquarters at Pec and started filling out an application to be a trooper. When I came to the question, 'Are you willing to move anywhere in the state at any time?' I knew I didn't want to do that. I threw the application away and left."

Eight years later, Ken began a twenty-five-year law en-forcement career with the Winnebago County Sheriff's Police. He used his navy training when the department created its first bomb squad to defuse homemade explosives.

At 1:30 A.M., the glare of the spotlight smacked us in the face. I might be a working adult, but I was still my parents' child. Ken gave me a quick goodnight kiss, walked me to the house, turned on his heel and left. When I entered the living room, Mom was back in bed. I flipped off the outside light on the way to my room.

A month after Ken was discharged from the navy, he started working as a collection agent for the Public Finance Company located in an office building at the corner of Church and Elm Streets in downtown Rockford. People who didn't have the collateral required to borrow money from a bank went to a finance company and paid higher interest rates. Every weekday, Ken dressed like a businessman and drove his Lincoln to chase down debtors who were delinquent in repaying their small loans.

Ken became friends with two other employees who were about the same age and single. Duane was built like Ken but with darker hair. Ross, who wore thick glasses, was short, pudgy and balding. Their boss, Jack, a short, dark fellow of Italian descent, was a few years older and married.

A month after Ken bought his Lincoln, he let me drive it. We'd spent Sunday afternoon with Tracys on the beach at Lake Mills, Wisconsin. After dropping our friends at their Rockford apartment, we were returning to Durand when my boyfriend said, "Why don't you leave me at my house and take the car home? Then I won't have to take you home, come home myself to clean up and then pick you up again to go to the Mid-City."

"That makes sense."

Ken stopped the sedan in their driveway, got out and entered the house. I slid behind the wheel, pulled the seat ahead, adjusted the mirrors, and backed out to the street. I was the queen of the road piloting his big car along the curvy, blacktop road to the farm and back to town. When I picked him up about an hour later, his skin was glowing pink after baking in the sun, but I was a deeper shade of brown. It irked him that I tanned easily while he burned. Nothing could be done about heredity.

Thursday night, Ken came to tell me good-bye. This time our roles were reversed—I was the one leaving. He stopped his Lincoln at the end of the front sidewalk and I joined him sitting in the sedan. He slid the bench seat back and we snuggled together with radio station WGN playing pop music in the background. I said, "Saturday morning we'll begin a nine-day trip to South Dakota, our longest vacation ever. August's the ideal time to be gone. The hay's baled, the oats are combined and it will be a month or two before the corn's ready to pick. Ed's agreed to do our chores for fifty dollars. His family can handle their milking while we're away." After a little more discussion, Ken kissed me good-bye and left.

Friday, I packed my shorts, shirts, underwear, pjs and makeup inside two, new pieces of molded, pearl-colored, lightweight Samsonite luggage. I thought of this as our farewell tour because I expected it to be my last trip with my parents.

The next morning, we left home at nine fifteen. Dad drove and Mom sat beside him with the road map in her lap to navigate. We picked up Doris who joined me in the back seat. Taking her along was like adding a little hot pepper to the stew. Dad squeezed her two suitcases plus a box of food alongside our luggage in the large trunk. He got back behind the wheel and we were off. The day was sunny and hot forcing us to ride along U.S. 20 with all of the hard-top windows rolled down. Doris and I tied head scarves to protect our hair. Mom preferred the old lady look of a brown, mesh hairnet.

In Dubuque, Iowa, Dad pulled into Strawberry Point Park, which overlooked the city. He carried Doris's box from the trunk to a wooden picnic table. She spread a cloth and distributed paper plates and plastic tumblers. We sat on the benches and enjoyed her lunch of chicken salad sandwiches, chips, oatmeal cookies and lemonade.

Our next stop, The Little Brown Church in the Vale at Nashua. A popular song had made the small, plain, country chapel famous and brought many couples there to wed.

Shortly after crossing into South Dakota, we stopped to admire the Corn Palace in Mitchell. Each year, local artist, Oscar Howe, decorated the exterior of the arena with murals created from kernels of corn, cobs and stalks.

About four o'clock, we looked for a place to spend the night. In the fifties, independent motels lined the highways in tourist areas. We only considered those exhibiting the Triple A sign indicating they were approved by the American Automobile Association. Before paying the twelve to twenty-four dollars in advance for two rooms, Mom checked the facilities. If everything didn't meet her approval, we continued on. Sleeping in air conditioning provided a welcome respite from the heat of the day.

The next morning, Mom got up with one of her sick headaches. She took a couple Anacin and made herself as comfortable as she could in a corner of back seat. She didn't eat anything all day, but we still stopped along the road a couple times for her to throw up. Doris took her place reading the map and navigating while Dad drove.

On Monday morning, Mom felt better. The sunrise cast a rosy tinge to the rocky pinnacles and buttes in the Bad Lands. We stopped at the world-famous Wall Drug Store and bought some candy to snack on. In 1931, the wayside began drawing tourists from Route 16A by offering free ice water.

We continued visiting attractions in the Black Hills including Mt. Rushmore and a gold mine. Black Hills gold jewelry was on sale every place we stopped, but I didn't buy any. At Crazy Horse Mountain, the guide estimated the huge granite sculpture of the Lakota warrior astride his steed would take twenty years to complete. I hoped to return when it was finished. In the evening at the dog races in Rapid City, we didn't pick any winners with our two-dollar bets

Tuesday in Deadwood, we visited the Mount Moriah Cemetery to view the side-by-side graves of Martha Jane Cannary-Burke, called Calamity Jane in tales of the Old West, and James Butler 'Wild Bill' Hickok, legendary gunfighter, scout and lawman. The hill leading to the graveyard was so steep, Dad had to slip the automatic transmission of our Chevy into low. That evening in Spearfish, the outdoor performance of the Biblical *Passion Play* telling the story of the final seven days in Jesus' life enthralled us all.

The next morning in Rapid City, we visited Dinosaur Park to see seven, life-sized animals sculpted from concrete molded over steel frames and painted a bright green with white underbellies. During the Great Depression, the creatures were part of the government's WPA projects providing jobs for unemployed men.

We moved on to the Cosmos Mystery Area, which was advertised on billboards as a magic spot that defied gravity. Dad and I stood at opposite ends of a cement platform. He was taller than I was, which was normal. We switched places and I looked taller than he was. "There's got to be a gimmick, but I can't figure out what it is," Dad said. "This so-called magic spot wouldn't just crop up in a tourist area."

Before heading back east, my father drove through Gillette, Wyoming, and Miles City, Montana, so we could say we'd been in both states.

Saturday, we drove in a gentle rain. We only stopped for gas and meals. That evening, we checked into a motel in Winona, Minnesota, before visiting Grandpa's youngest sibling, Dave, and his wife, Helen. Dad and his uncle were only a few years apart in age and could easily have passed for brothers.

The next morning, we women went to church in the rain. Dad visited another uncle, Herman, an elderly bachelor. By the time we were ready to leave Winona, the sun was shining making it another hot day.

Sunday afternoon, we arrived at our house at four o'clock, just in time for Dad and Mom to start chores. We'd covered twenty-eight-hundred miles.

I drove Doris to her place and then stopped at Ditzlers' to say hello. Ken's hug and kiss made me feel like I was truly home. In the evening, he and I saw a show and parked on Weber Road. We were back in the routine I adored.

Monday, I stayed home from the office and spent most of the day in bed. Dad and Mom did only the necessary farm chores. We'd all slept well in the comfort of the air-conditioned rooms, but being on the go every day took its toll. We needed a day to recuperate. Tuesday, we all worked as usual.

Thursday morning, 28 August, I drove to Rockford to meet with Dr. Bryan at his request. A slight shadow of dread clouded my optimism. I hoped to hear good news, but I couldn't forget a year ago he dropped the bombshell that my gastric was positive. I walked into his office, greeted him, shut the door behind me, took a chair and said, "I've been feeling fine."

Dr. Bryan was seated behind his wooden desk with my records open in front of him. After the usual preliminaries, he said, "You can quit taking pills and do anything as long as you don't get too tired."

I felt like jumping up and shouting, "Whoopee!" but I responded with a brief, "Oh, good." I was finally medication free after enduring nine months of painful shots in the butt twice a week followed by almost a year of swallowing a handful of pills every day. When I got up to leave, the doctor arose from his leather chair and walked me to the door. He gave me a peck on the cheek and said, "I won't be seeing you anymore. Good-bye and good health."

I floated through the day like a multi-colored soap bubble. Everyone in the office and at home shared my joy.

The following Wednesday after work, I baked a lemon filled, layer cake and covered it with white, seven-minute frosting. It would be my treat at the office for my twenty-first birthday the next day.

Later, Ken and I went to South Beloit to visit our friends, Esther and Donnie, at their upstairs apartment. We chatted and Esther showed photos of their eight-month-old baby, Pam, who was asleep in their bedroom. She also showed me the outfit she purchased for Lorraine's baby shower the following Friday night. I paid her for my half of our joint gift.

On the way back to my house, I said, "Tomorrow night, we're going for pizza at Maria's in south Rockford to celebrate my birthday. Do you want to come along?"

"I'm sorry, but I can't. I've got to work. The only time I can catch some of these people at home is in the evening."

I was disappointed, but I understood. Ken's job came ahead of me.

He parked in our driveway and we sat for quite a while talking and necking. In the background, WGN's Saxy Dowell was spinning records and tales from his days as a big band leader during the forties. When the Yale men's group began singing "The Whiffenpoof Song," the deejay's nightly sign-off at 2 A.M., I told Ken, "I should be getting inside."

He murmured in my ear, "Honey, will you marry me?"

"Yes," I responded immediately. I'd been waiting four long, lonely years to hear those words.

"I want to get you a ring for your birthday tomorrow."

We strolled to the door with our arms around each other's waists. He gave me a final goodnight kiss and left. All was quiet as I entered the house.

Ken proposed! I couldn't imagine sleeping, but it would soon be time to get ready for work. I tried to convince my body it was a normal night. I undressed, donned pajamas, washed my face, brushed my teeth and slipped between the sheets. It took the sandman a long time to come. It seemed like I just closed my eyes when Elvis's "You Ain't Nothin' But A Hound Dog" bellowed from the clock radio sitting on a small table beside my bed. I jerked awake, grabbed the off button with my right hand and twisted.

Ah, silence. I relaxed a few moments before crawling out of bed and putting on my robe and slippers.

I joined Dad and Mom for breakfast at the oil-cloth covered table in the kitchen.

They greeted me with, "Happy birthday."

I smiled a thank you and blurted out, "Ken's getting me a diamond for my birthday."

My parents said nothing. Dad continued to spoon his corn flakes and Mom chewed her toast. I knew they liked Ken and probably by now, they expected us to get married. I thought back to our first date and asked Mom, "How come you let me go out with Ken while I was in high school, but not the other guys that asked me?"

Between sips of coffee, she responded, "You finally got out of the bargain basement shopping for boyfriends."

I admitted to myself that, like a lot of teenage girls, I found some of the 'bad boys' appealing.

I opened the card lying in front of me on the table, found twenty-one, green backs inside and thanked Dad and Mom. I forced myself to eat a piece of toast and drink a cup of coffee before dressing for work. I left the house with the cake carrier in my hands.

When I entered Betty's car, she asked, "What have you got there?"

"Today's my birthday and I'm taking a cake to the office as a treat."

The carload of women wished me a happy birthday.

When I entered the ASC office, the girls greeted me with, "Happy birthday." Lois handed me a card signed by everyone. It contained a five-dollar bill.

I thanked them and added, "Ken proposed last night and he's getting me a diamond ring for my birthday."

A chorus of congratulations greeted my news.

When we broke for lunch, I cut five pieces of my lemon cake and served them on small paper plates with plastic forks that Mary provided. My co-workers complimented my baking.

In the evening, I enjoyed pizza with my parents at the Italian restaurant in south Rockford, but it would have been better if Ken could have joined us. When we returned home, we ate left-over lemon cake. My parents also complimented my baking.

The next night I dressed for a date with Ken, but he didn't show up. Apparently, we'd had a miscommunication, but I was perturbed. I skipped my classmates' baby shower for Lorraine hosted by Eva Jean at her home in Rockton. During the fifties, a date with a guy always took precedence over getting together with girlfriends.

Saturday, I was positive Ken planned to pick me up at 7 P.M. to go to the stock car races at the Rockford Speedway. The thought of my boyfriend bringing my ring was more exciting than when I believed in Santa bringing gifts at Christmas.

In the afternoon, I went with Dad and Mom to *The Johnny Cash Show* scheduled at two thirty in the Beloit College field house. A country music presentation always lasted about an hour-and-a-half, so I expected to be home in plenty of time before my date.

When it was time for the program to begin in the auditorium that seated four-thousand people, a man stepped out on the stage. He announced, "Johnny Cash and his musicians are running late. The program will start as soon as they arrive." As the delay stretched toward two hours, the crowd remained patient. I began to worry about getting home in time for my date with Ken.

Finally, at four thirty, George Hamilton IV and Marty Robbins, stars in their own right, kicked off the performance. George appeared regularly on the Jimmy Dean TV program that Mom and Dad watched every weekday morning while they ate breakfast.

Last year, Marty's recording of "White Sport Coat and a Pink Carnation" sold more than a million copies and earned a gold disc.

Johnny Cash accompanied by "The Tennessee Two," Luther Perkins and Marshall Grant, soon replaced the openers. The star began with his latest hits, "Ballad of a Teenage Queen" and "Guess Things Happen That Way." When he drifted into some of his older favorites, the audience sang along with

"Folsom Prison Blues" and "I Walk the Line." I enjoyed the music, but I watched the time.

It was six fifteen by the time we pushed our way out of the crowded auditorium. Mom drove sixty all the way to the farm. She was concerned about chores, not my date. I wiggled and squirmed in the back seat while watching the telephone poles whiz by. At home, I just had time to go to the bathroom, comb my hair and put on fresh lipstick before Ken pulled in the driveway promptly at seven o'clock.

I met him on the porch and led the way into the kitchen where Mom and Dad were seated at the round oak table eating sandwiches and drinking coffee. I impatiently waited while he greeted my parents and exchanged pleasantries before we left the house.

Strolling down the sidewalk, I'd have liked to challenge Ken to a foot race, but I didn't. As soon as we both slid into the Lincoln from the driver's side, my boyfriend handed me a small, black, velvet box and said, "Happy birthday, Honey. I knew from that first ride on the Ferris wheel I'd marry you."

I lifted the lid and diamonds sparkled. I removed Ken's class ring that I'd worn for the past five years and dropped it into my purse. I would peel the tape off later and return it to him. I slipped the white gold engagement ring on my finger and held out my left hand to admire it. I kissed Ken and said, "It's beautiful, thank you."

On our way to the Rockford Speedway, we stopped by Wayne and Gloria's apartment. Ken had showed them my ring right after he bought it, but I thought it looked much better on my finger than in the box. Their congratulations were the first of many we received.

After the races, we lingered in the Lincoln parked in our driveway. I didn't want to leave the man who would soon become my husband, but our evening needed to end. He walked me to the door and gave me a lingering kiss goodnight.

The next morning, I popped out of bed at seven o'clock to eat breakfast with my parents and display my birthday present.

"It's very pretty," said Mom. "Very nice," Dad added.

At church after the service, I shook hands at the door with Rev. Moen, our slender, balding, pastor. I took an extra moment to show him my ring and said, "There'll be a wedding coming up."

He responded, "Congratulations. I'll look forward to it."

In the afternoon, I shared my good news with Rowleys. When I entered their living room, Doris laid aside the Chicago paper she was reading and Aunt Frannie stopped cutting old garments into strips to be used in rugs. Smokey looked up from his spot at my aunt's feet. Uncle Hookie, a big sports fan, sat in his wooden rocker watching a baseball game on TV with another game tuned in on the small, brown radio sitting on the floor beside him.

I showed my ring to the women and sat down on the davenport. Aunt Frannie said, "Congratulations."

Doris asked, "When's the wedding?"

"We haven't discussed that yet," I replied.

Between innings in the TV game, Doris said in a loud voice, "Dad, Lolita's got something to show you."

Uncle Hookie looked up at me. I walked across the linoleum and stuck out my left hand. "Ken and I are engaged."

"Well, isn't that pretty. Congratulations." My uncle went back to his games and I returned to the davenport to continue visiting with the ladies.

In the evening, when Ken picked me up for our date, he came into the kitchen where Dad and Mom were finishing their supper coffee. He wanted to do the proper thing and asked for my parents' approval, "Do you have any objections to our being engaged?"

Mom replied with the archaic phrase, "She's free, white and twenty-one." Dad said nothing.

Ken was dumbfounded. He was a little afraid of my mother and didn't know what to do next. I grabbed his hand and we quickly walked to the car.

On our way to the movie in Rockford, I assured my fiancé, "Don't worry. That's just my mother. I know they're both pleased about our getting married."

At the office Monday morning, I greeted the girls with, "See what I've got," and held out my left hand. They gushed congratulations. I stepped into Mary's office and laid my left hand on the desk in front of her. She smiled at me and said, "Congratulations. I'm sure you're very happy."

"I'm floating on cloud nine," I assured her.

The following Thursday morning, I heard Dad and Mom rising earlier than usual. They were going to the little town of Forreston for "Sauerkraut Day." While doing chores, Mom slipped and fell on the dew-soaked, grassy bank surrounding the automatic water pump in the front yard. She got up by herself, but could barely walk. She'd twisted her left ankle. Instead of going to the festival, Dad took her to the new Durand Medical Center located beside the bank. Dr. Harvey, the young physician recruited for the facility, said she pulled a ligament. He advised wrapping her ankle with an elastic bandage for three weeks and using one crutch for the next five days.

About ten o'clock, Ken called me at work and asked, "Can you take the afternoon off and ride with me to Chana? I'm trying to chase down one of our customers."

Mary approved.

After I ate my sack lunch, Ken picked me up. It took about a half-hour to reach the street address in the little town southwest of Rockford. My fiancé rapped on the trailer door, but nobody answered his knock. He returned to his office with nothing to show for the trip, but we savored being together.

Saturday, with Mom laid up, I washed clothes in the morning and cleaned house in the afternoon just like the housewife I'd soon become.

In the evening, Ken and I went to a movie. When we returned and parked in the driveway, he asked, "When do you want to get married?"

"I think mid-April would be good. That'll be spring, but we shouldn't be too involved with field work yet. We'll have seven months to plan an evening, candlelight ceremony in our church and a dance. I'll have to check a calendar to pick a date. If we're married on a Friday night, we'll have two weekends and the week in between for a honeymoon."

"Where do you want to go for a honeymoon?"

"I think New Orleans would be nice. What do you think?"

"That's fine. Any place warm is okay with me."

I chose 17 April and Mom mailed announcements of our engagement to area newspapers.

Girls of my generation, even tomboys like me, dreamed of that life-changing event. When I was in second grade at the one-room, Dobson country school, my best friend, Karen, and

I played dress-up in her farmhouse attic. The fourth grader, who was only a year older than I was, had brown eyes and medium length, permed, brown hair that her mother wound into finger curls for special occasions. On weekends, we put on her mother's cast-off clothes and high-heeled shoes for dates with imaginary boyfriends.

Then we took turns being the bride draped in old lace curtains walking down the aisle we created by moving aside discarded furniture and boxes of memorabilia. We sang the parody, "Here comes the bride, short, fat and wide. There stands the groom, stiff as a broom."

At that time, my knowledge of big weddings came from movies about the wealthy, upper crust. My family didn't receive invitations to church ceremonies until the fifties after the country recovered from World War II.

On a Wednesday afternoon in mid-September, Dad had his fourth appointment with Dr. Mings, an ophthalmologist at the Monroe Clinic. When I returned from work, my father seemed down in the dumps when he told me, "Dr. Mings said my eyes won't get any better. I'm to continue to take the pills at mealtime and that should keep my eyes from getting worse."

"Don't you think that's good news?"

"I guess so."

Last spring, Dad was having trouble reading the newspaper and assumed he needed his glasses changed. Dr. Weinstein, a Rockford optometrist, examined Dad and said my father's condition was more serious than a need for new glasses and suggested a physical checkup. Our family physician, Dr. Hein, referred Dad to the eye specialist at the clinic. Dr. Mings diagnosed an eye disease, but my father couldn't remember the name of it. Dad could no longer pass the vision test for a driver's license. Although he considered Mom a good driver, relegating him to the passenger seat was a blow to his manhood. My teetotaler father grumbled, "I'll bet those drunks on the road can't see as well as I can."

I skipped supper and went right to bed. Having Ken around all of the time was as exhausting as running a marathon, but I loved it.

I wasn't asleep when the phone rang. Mom answered and called me. Ken said, "How about visiting Joe and Lola Mae?"

"Not tonight. I need my sleep." In my mind, I could hear Dr. Bryan's words, "You can do anything as long as you don't get too tired."

The next morning, I was still weary and stayed home from work to rest. When I rolled out of bed at 9 A.M., Mom managed to do the weekly washing. I hung the wet garments outside on the wire clotheslines. By early afternoon, the bright sun and breeze damp-dried the garments that needed pressing. I removed them from the line and finished the ironing in time to prepare supper. After the meal, I brought in the rest of the dried clothes, folded them and put them away in dresser drawers.

The following Friday night, Ken and I bowled with his co-worker, Duane, and his girlfriend, Bonnie, a cute, plump gal with dark hair. We met at the Hotel Faust on East State Street in Rockford. The name of the landmark stood atop the eleven-story building in fourteen-foot, red, neon letters that could be seen for miles around.

The six lanes in the basement featured automatic pin setting and scoring. It was sound-proofed so the area wasn't as noisy as Durand's four lanes.

In between turns on the alley, I listened to Ken and Duane discussing their workday. When Ken said he received one from somebody and two from somebody else, I thought he was referring to hundreds. As their conversation continued, I realized he meant a dollar and two dollars. The young men took any amount of money they could get from the customers who were behind in repaying their small loans.

When we finished, the four of us agreed it was a fun evening. A notice on the bulletin board announced a Friday night league of young couples was starting. We formed a team and joined.

The following Monday afternoon, Dad and I were seated at the kitchen table when the jangle of the phone interrupted Mom's serving supper. Her non-committal, "Hello," was followed by silent listening. I knew it was bad news when I heard her incredulous, "Your Dad?"

After hanging up, she turned to my father and me, "That was Doris. Uncle Hookie had a heart attack and died about three o'clock this afternoon. Aunt Frannie was there alone with him."

No wonder Mom sounded shocked. Aunt Frannie was the one who had been ailing for years. Uncle Hookie, who celebrated his sixty-ninth birthday earlier in the month, seemed in good health. The smoker's only apparent problem was the early morning coughing spells that woke me when I spent the night at their house.

After supper, we visited the bereft family. Greetings were somber. We weren't a demonstrative group. Hugs, kisses and tears were rare. The three of us sat down on the black, frieze davenport in the living room facing Aunt Frannie, Doris and

Sis, who sat in easy chairs. The odor of Uncle Hookie's cigarette smoke clung to the furniture and dusty rose drapes. My aunt's hand-braided, round rugs dotted the blue-patterned, linoleum floor.

Sitting listening to their discussing Uncle Hookie's death and funeral made me antsy. I got up and looked around for something to do. In the kitchen, I discovered the apartment-size, white, electric range needed cleaning. I found supplies in the cupboard under the sink in the adjoining pantry. Before starting, I set aside the little, metal frying pan sitting on a black burner. It waited for Uncle Hookie to fry his two, breakfast eggs the next morning. Scrubbing kept my tears at bay.

Doris and Sis entered the room. Doris grabbed the small skillet and stashed it in the cupboard above. "I don't want Mother to see that in the morning and be upset."

About ten o'clock, we went home.

The following afternoon, Dad and Mom ordered an arrangement of flowers at Chapin's Funeral Home and Furniture Store. The two-story, beige, stucco building that sat alone at the north end of the Durand business district also provided living quarters for the proprietor, a gray-haired, widow.

My parents then visited the mourning family. At four, Dad went home to milk the cows, but Mom remained with her sister and nieces. Neighbors helped Doris with their evening chores.

When I returned home from work, Dad was cleaned up and sitting on a kitchen chair waiting for me. I made baloney sandwiches. After we ate, we joined my mother.

The evening's conversation centered around funeral arrangements Aunt Frannie had made and plans for the next day. Before we headed home at ten o'clock, my mother grabbed the wicker basket sitting in the bathtub. It overflowed with a week's worth of the family's dirty clothes, which Mom would wash.

The next morning when I left for work at seven, Mom was hanging the laundered garments outside on our wire clotheslines. The bright sun and a southern breeze made it a perfect drying day.

My mother then went to stay at her sister's house while the family visited the cemetery. After a death, people didn't like to leave their home unattended. Friends might come to pay their respects or thieves take advantage of the situation.

In the afternoon, Mom returned home and removed the clothes from our lines.

She ironed the dresses, blouses, skirts and shirts and draped them on hangers. Handkerchiefs, slips and bras were ironed, folded and placed in the wicker basket atop the neat piles of overalls, men's underwear, women's panties, and socks. I would return the garments the next morning.

After chores and supper, my parents and I attended visitation from seven to nine at the funeral home. Flowers and people filled the large room. Viewing Uncle Hookie lying in his casket dressed in a white shirt and dark blue tie with his Legion cap clasped in his hands gave me a feeling of finality.

My uncle's only sibling, Aunt Florence, who was six years younger, flew in from her home in Los Angeles. The single, gray-haired, chain-smoker was tall and slender like her brother. She worked at a high-paying office job, dressed well and emitted a certain California aura that I admired.

The following afternoon, Pastor Moen conducted the Lutheran service at twelve thirty in the funeral home with burial in the nearby Durand Cemetery. It was warm and sunny at the World War I veteran's gravesite where the family and close friends gathered. After Pastor Moen's final words, the American Legion honor guard rifle squad riddled the air with their twenty-one-gun salute followed by the bugler's plaintive "Taps." The ritual released the tears I'd been holding on to so tightly.

After the funeral, I was pleasantly surprised when Dad and Mom joined the fellowship at Sis and Joe's farm home. Sharing the loss of a beloved family member overrode my parents' disapproval of their niece's husband. Several neighbor women provided sandwiches, Jell-O, cake and coffee for the family and close friends.

On Saturday afternoon, I gave Mom a permanent. My fingers rolled her hair, but my mind was on supper. Ken and I were invited to Tracys' to eat the squirrels the guys had shot in Stateline Johnnie's woods. I knew I would have to be polite and consume the meal Gloria served, but I certainly didn't want to.

Every fall while Ken was growing up, his family, including his mother who carried her own .22 rifle, hunted rabbits and squirrels in a friend's woods. Afterward, Hazel prepared the game in a pressure cooker and they ate it for supper.

My mother refused to cook rabbits and squirrels. The only wild things I'd ever eaten were a few pheasants Dad bagged during the fall seasons.

In the evening when Ken and I arrived at Wayne and Gloria's upstairs apartment, her parents, Jack and Ilene, were already there. They were middle-aged versions of their children, Ron and Gloria. Grandma was entertaining nine-month-old Lori Lea, who was installed in the high chair. Earlier in the day, Gloria placed a card table at the end of their small, wooden kitchen table and covered each of them with a patterned, luncheon cloth. She set out her good dishes, glasses and silverware. Her parents, who lived downstairs, carried up two extra chairs to seat the six adults.

I took a very small helping of the squirrel, tried to tell myself the meat was just like pheasant and choked it down. I filled up on mashed potatoes, tossed salad and green beans. While we were eating, Jack picked up the meat platter that matched the plates and turned to pass it around again. It slipped out of his hands, hit the floor and shattered. He was devastated, but his daughter was forgiving.

On 8 November, Ken and I celebrated his twenty-third birthday by going to a show. I gave him a gray, wool, waistlength winter jacket. The clothes he'd worn before joining the navy no longer fit and needed to be replaced.

The following Tuesday, 11 November, was Veterans Day, a federal holiday so I could sleep late. At ten o'clock, Doris brought Aunt Frannie for a permanent. When my cousin returned at noon to pick up her mother, Sis's kids, Donnie, five, and Pat, three, accompanied their aunt. Mom invited everyone to stay for dinner.

A few days later, the telephone company installed a modern, black, dial phone in our kitchen, but the up-to-date equipment was still attached to a party line.

At the beginning of the following week, I was a little hoarse and felt like I was getting a cold. Wednesday, I stayed home to rest, but worked Thursday and Friday. I probably shouldn't have bowled with our couples' team in the Friday night league at the Faust, but I wanted to be a normal person, not an invalid. The next morning, Mom took me to see Dr. Hein, who prescribed medicine. I spent Sunday in bed. Monday Mom took me back to Dr. Hein for more pills. I continued to rest at home.

By Wednesday night, I felt able to attend the high school Homecoming basketball game against Pec and the dance. It was the first time Ken and I returned as alumni. Old friends who were already married congratulated us on our engagement.

The next day, my mother fixed ham for our Thanksgiving dinner. She'd asked Aunt Frannie and Doris, but they declined. Mom's sister had been sick.

Late in the afternoon, Doris called to invite us to join their family for a supper of turkey sandwiches and Mom accepted. My mother understood the first holiday since Uncle Hookie died was a difficult time for them.

When we entered Rowleys' living room, the odor of Uncle Hookie's cigarette smoke still clung to the drapes and furniture. Their drop-leaf, dining table was pulled away from the wall and leaves added to accommodate the seven adults and two kids. We all took seats around the mahogany table, which was covered.by a white cloth and set with good dishes and silverware. Respect for the bereaved family overshadowed my parents' disapproval of Sis's husband, Joe. The atmosphere was thick with politeness.

December began with the in-laws-to-be getting together for the first time. Mom invited Ken and his parents, Rolland and Hazel, for a Saturday night supper to celebrate birthdays. Dad would turn forty-six on the fifth and Hazel would be forty-seven on the eighth. When our guests arrived, Ken and Rolland sat down in the living room with Dad so our fathers could get acquainted. Hazel joined us in the kitchen where Mom stirred gravy and I mashed potatoes. The smell of ham baking in the oven whetted our appetites.

Our mothers were best friends in high school, but as often happens, they lost touch after their marriages. Mom said, "Who'd have thought we'd end up with a son and daughter getting married? I remember stopping at your mother's to see you when Ken was a new baby."

Hazel replied, "When I first saw him in the hospital, I cried. He'd been born two months premature and I thought he looked just like a little monkey."

I thought he grew up to be a handsome, young man.

Mom called the fellows and we gathered around the oak table expanded with leaves, covered with a white cloth and set with good dishes and silverware. We feasted on Mom's usual company meal–ham, mashed potatoes with gravy, baked beans, fruit salad and coffee. Vanilla ice cream and a white bakery cake decorated with pink roses and inscribed, "Happy Birthday Hazel and Alex," topped off the meal.

After we'd finished eating, the three men returned to the living room and we cleaned up the kitchen. The two old friends reminisced while Mom washed the dishes in the sink, Hazel dried and I put them away in the cupboards. Hazel giggled like a schoolgirl and said to my mother, "Remember when you raced with 'Boob' whose '29 Dodge was just like yours? We were on our way back from Rockton after the school picnic at Macktown Forest Preserve right before graduation. Seventy-five was a brand-new cement highway. 'Boob' came up behind you, honked and pulled over into the left lane intending to pass. That's when you tromped on the gas. I excitedly watched the speedometer creep close to fifty. He never did get around you all the way to town."

Mom grinned at the memory and responded, "It's a good thing your folks didn't know about that. They'd never have let you ride with me again."

I loved that story. The first time I heard it, I was a nine-year-old playing with dominoes in Rowley's living room. I'd carefully stand each one on end and give the last one in line a push to watch them fall. Uncle Hookie returned from town and stood in the kitchen talking with Aunt Frannie. When he mentioned reminiscing with 'Boob', the local electrician, about his race with Edith, I was all ears. A little later, Mom picked me up and I confronted her with my new knowledge. She didn't deny it, but she tried to laugh it off by saying, "You know your Uncle Hookie is a great story teller."

When we finished putting the kitchen back in order, we went into the living room. Dad set up their old wooden, card table with black oilcloth covering the top. To play Five Hundred, Rolland and Ken teamed up against Hazel and me. Ken didn't know how to play so Mom pulled up a chair at the corner of the table and patiently helped him. Dad kibitzed.

Two things Ken had to do if he was going to marry me, play Five Hundred and dance. They were my favorite pastimes. I didn't want to give them up when I became his wife.

The next night, Ken and I visited Lola Mae and Joe. My fiancé told his sister and brother-in-law about our family get-together the night before. "Edith sat down beside me and helped me learn to play Five Hundred. I'd always been a little afraid of her, but that changed my mind. I think she likes me."

Then Lola Mae set up their card table and we played Five Hundred with the guys partners against the gals. That division always brought out my competiveness. His sister and I won two games to one.

Christmas Eve was the usual ham supper for the three of us. Then we moved to the living room to open the gifts surrounding the decorated, short-needled tree. I gave Dad and Mom a brown, metal, Cosco card table with four matching folding chairs. Their gifts to me included a steam iron, a silver-plated, table service for eight in my choice of Aloha pattern and $138.13 added to my savings account to make it an even thousand dollars.

The next morning while doing chores, Mom slipped on a patch of ice, fell and twisted her left ankle for the second time. She again wrapped it with the old, elastic bandage she used when she first injured it last September.

Later that morning, Ken came to exchange presents. His gifts to my parents were a green sport shirt for Dad and a box of Russell Stover chocolates for Mom. My folks gave him a red, plaid car robe in a plastic case.

My fiancé gave me a black and gold lipstick and compact set along with a stylish, beige, two-piece knit dress. He was right on with the size.

I gave Ken a large, charcoal gray, molded, light-weight Samsonite suitcase for our honeymoon trip to New Orleans. It would complement my two, new pearl-colored ones.

At noon, Dad and Mom dropped me off at Gaffneys' on their way to Beloit to eat pizza and see a movie. This year, Lola Mae prepared their family's traditional Christmas feast so the kids didn't have to leave their toys from Santa. She recently purchased a second-hand, Duncan Phyfe style, mahogany, drop-leaf, extension table, with matching chairs and a buffet to create a dining area in the north end of their large living room.

After stuffing ourselves and cleaning up afterward, we moved to the playroom at the west end of the house to open the presents that waited under the tall, decorated tree. My gifts to my future in-laws included a pair of pillow cases that I embroidered with flowers for Ken's folks, a box of Fannie May candy for Joe and Lola Mae and toys for the youngsters. Another baby, dark haired Colleen, had joined the family last summer. Six kids surrounded by new toys reminded me of a cage full of monkeys with a bunch of fresh bananas.

I received a black sweater from Ken's parents and a silver bracelet with matching earrings from the Gaffneys.

We ate leftovers for supper and Ken took me home. I was tired, but I looked forward to our becoming a family and providing cousins to play with his nieces and nephews.

Six years later, Ken and I celebrated our fifth wedding anniversary by eating lobster and toasting each other at our favorite upscale restaurant, the Red Coach, near Byron. Our children, Linda, four, Lisa, three, and Kurt, one, stayed at home with Ava, their teen-aged, baby-sitter. She heated a can of Spaghetti O's, which the kids considered a treat for their supper, and tucked them into bed while we were gone.

The following week on New Year's Eve day, I drove to Rockford to have my annual gastric and x-ray at the san before I went to the office.

In the evening, Ken and I were invited to his boss's house to celebrate. After eating supper at home, I donned my new, knit dress with the brown pumps and matching envelope purse I'd bought to wear with it. The outfit fortified me—I felt like I was on trial meeting Ken's employer. When my fiancé picked me up at seven thirty, he was wearing a sport coat, slacks, white shirt and tie.

Our hosts, Jack and Carol, were casually dressed in jeans and sweaters when they welcomed us into their ranch-style home on the west side of Rockford. Their easy-going manner helped me relax a bit. We spent the evening visiting and munching on snacks while the TV showed 1959 being welcomed around the world. At midnight, we all said, "Happy New Year!" Ken kissed me. Jack kissed his wife and then stepped outside to fire his rifle into the air. By the time we left for home, I was convinced Ken was his boss's favorite employee.

Chapter 8

1959

A new year and time to plan for our new life together. Our marriage would begin Friday, 17 April, with a candlelight ceremony at 7 P.M. in Trinity Lutheran Church followed by a reception in the basement. John Pela, the Chevrolet dealer in Rock City, and his band, the Bel Air Ranch Boys, would provide music for a public dance in the nearby New England Grange Hall from 9 P.M. to 12 P.M. A rushed evening but necessary to include farm chores and my dream wedding.

Ken and I decided to each have one attendant. I asked my cousin, Doris, to be maid of honor. She'd been my life preserver while my boyfriend was in the navy.

Doris's response, "I will as long as I don't have to wear blue. Blue makes me look sallow Do you want to borrow my Emily Post book of etiquette?"

"Yeah, that'd be a big help. I certainly want to do things properly." When I left her house, I toted the tome with me.

Wayne, Ken's long-time friend who'd instigated our first Ferris wheel ride, would be best man. Wayne's younger brother, Gary, and my cousin, Ronnie, who were both sixteen, agreed to serve as ushers.

Ken's brother, Tom, couldn't attend our wedding. A year ago, he and Denny, his boyhood buddy, enlisted in the army and he was stationed at Fort Benning, Georgia. During our honeymoon in the South, we planned to visit the soldier.

My husband-to-be was happy about our upcoming nuptials, but unhappy with his employment. After five months of trying to collect money from people who obviously didn't have it, he hated working for Public Finance.

On the first Saturday night in January, we were visiting Joe and Lola Mae. Joe asked Ken a routine question, "How's work going?"

"Not great. I'm thinking about looking for another job."

"How would you like to be our hired man?" Joe and his father, Earl, operated a five-hundred-acre hog and feeder cattle enterprise located about half way between my folks' place and Durand at the intersection of Rock Grove and Eicks Road. Their last full-time employee had left the first of the year and they needed another.

"That's a good idea." Ken had enjoyed working there summers when he was in high school.

"Give me a week and I'll have some figures together."

When Ken told his parents about the proposition, they responded in one voice, "You'd be nuts to work there." They loved their daughter's husband, but considered him too controlling to be a good boss. My folks and everybody else we told about the job offer concurred.

I believed my husband-to-be should do whatever made him happy because he would be supporting our family. I planned to quit my job when we had children. I thought four would be an ideal family. After our kids were all in school, I expected to return to office work. I knew I couldn't be content forever as 'just a housewife'.

Ken ignored his parents' misgivings and looked forward to farming. On a Sunday evening in mid-January, the two of us returned to Joe and Lola Mae's living room to discuss the position. Ken told me, "I want you to come along. It'll be your life, too."

Joe, who took pride in his Irish heritage, was pushing thirty. The wiry, average-size guy had dark curly hair and a short temper. He laid out the following particulars, "We'll pay you a hundred dollars twice a month on the first and fifteenth. You'll have every other Sunday off.

When it comes to holidays, we'll have to wait and see what we're doing. At the end of the year, you'll receive a bonus based on the farm's profit. That should be about a thousand dollars going by the last couple years."

The farm complex included three houses. A place to live would be provided as part of Ken's salary. We would move into the two-bedroom, story-and-a-half, white 'corner house' located next to the intersection at the south end of the long, faded, red barn. Joe's parents, Earl and Hazel, who were in their late sixties, lived in the big, two-story, white, clapboard dwelling sitting at the other end of the structure. Joe and Lola Mae's home, the largest abode, was about a mile north on Eicks Road.

The farm would also supply us with beef and pork. To store the meat that wouldn't fit into our refrigerator's freezer, we'd rent a locker where the animals were processed in Davis.

Ken said, "That sounds great." He looked at me and I nodded in agreement. "I'll need to give Jack at Public Finance, two weeks' notice. I can start the first of February." He and Joe shook hands on the deal.

On Wednesday, a big snowstorm with strong winds kept me home from the work. The next morning, Dad put chains on the rear wheels of the car before Mom drove me to Durand. By the time we arrived in town, Betty had already left for Rockford. I caught a ride with Ken, whose work day began at nine.

Friday night, I was getting a cold and didn't bowl at the Faust. Sunday night when Ken came to see me, I was worse. Monday and Tuesday, I stayed home from work to rest and recover. Wednesday, I returned to the office.

A break in the weather during the last week of January, prompted me to walk slowly and window-shop on my way from the office to Hobson's Drug Store to catch my ride. A white, wedding gown displayed by the Elsie Rogers establishment on the south side of State Street caught my eye. It featured short sleeves, a boat neck and an embroidered, five-tiered, floor-length skirt. I'd already decided I didn't want a train on my dress. I entered the store and inquired about the garment. The clerk asked me to come back the next day to give her time to remove it from the mannequin.

The following afternoon, I returned to the shop and donned the dress. I looked in the mirror and knew it was made for me. My family always paid full price for items, but this time I tried a little 'horse-trading'. I said to the salesgirl, "I see the price tag says eighty-nine-ninety-five. Shouldn't that be reduced because it was displayed in the window?"

"I can let you have it for seventy dollars."

"It's a deal." I was elated. The next day, I bragged to the girls at the office about my bargain.

My co-worker, Lois, said, "Would you like to borrow my headpiece with a fingertip length veil?" Two years earlier, I'd attended her wedding.

"Thank you. That would be great." Her offer would save me some money, which was important in my planning.

Monday, 2 February, was Ken's first day feeding cattle and hogs at Irish Acres. The thermometer read twenty-seven below zero, making it the coldest day of the winter, but it seemed warmer with the sun reflecting on the snow and no wind.

While I was dressing for work that morning, I thought about how drastically my life just changed. Last September, I accepted a proposal from a man who wore a suit, smelled of Old Spice and drove his Lincoln on the job. His work schedule was nine to five with weekends and holidays free. In April, I would wed a guy who wore coveralls, smelled of manure and drove a tractor. His daily hours were unlimited. He would have every other Sunday off, but it might be necessary to work all day on a holiday. At least, I was used to the demands of farming.

In the office, it was a quiet first day of the week. I asked Mary for the afternoon off and she agreed. About ten thirty, I called my mother and asked her to come and see my wedding gown.

When she was ready to drive to Durand, she got into the cold pick-up parked in the corn crib driveway. It wouldn't start until Dad pulled it with the Allis Chalmers. In the village where I'd left our Chevy, she traded vehicles. After picking me up at the office, she parallel-parked along the curb on the south side of State Street in front of the Elsie Rogers shop. We entered and the clerk brought out my dress. It needed a few alterations to fit perfectly.

"It's beautiful," Mom said with a big smile. I was glad she liked it.

We then scurried along the sidewalk to Johnston's luncheonette. The sun was bright but the temperature barely moved above zero. Inside the small restaurant that specialized in ladies' lunches and ice cream, we hung our heavy coats and scarves on the hooks fastened to a post attached to the aisle-end of the booth. We then slid along the turquoise vinyl upholstered benches on opposite sides of the black Formica-topped table. The waitress brought glasses of water, poured cups of coffee and took our order for hamburgers and chips plus hot fudge sundaes.

My parents' twenty-fourth anniversary was coming up Saturday. I asked Mom, "Why were you and Dad married in February? It seems like you would have picked a warmer time."

"A lot of us were married in February to be ready to take over a farm when landlords changed tenants March first. Nobody had a big wedding. Your dad's sister, Marion, and my cousin, 'Spud', who were going together, stood up with us at the Lutheran parsonage on a Thursday afternoon. Maybe you remember Reverend Swenson who performed the ceremony. He was a typical old preacher with white hair and a goatee.

"On Saturday night, we had a wedding dance in the Avon Town Hall just across the line in Wisconsin. The Larisons, shirttail relatives of your dad's, played. Aunt Frannie made a wedding cake and the Tschabolds provided the rest of the lunch. Everyone brought presents. You know that picture of your dad with Buddy and Alfred that hangs on the wall in our bedroom? My cousin, Everett, gave us Alfred that night. He said every farm needs a tomcat."

After Mom and I finished eating and reminiscing, she drove us along Highway 70 to Durand. She then got in the truck and I slid behind the wheel of the sedan to travel the blacktop home.

The following Saturday afternoon, Ken finished work early. Cutting hours was easy when chores consisted of feeding hogs and beef cattle instead of milking dairy cows. Before we went to a movie in Rockford, he showed me through our future home. We entered the empty building through a small rear porch. The back door opened into an unfinished room where our automatic washer would be installed and Ken would leave his stinky, outdoor clothes and work boots. A second door led into the main part of our abode.

In the kitchen, black backing showed through the worn, multi-colored linoleum that covered the wide-board floor. Along the west wall in the north end of the room, wooden cupboards needed a fresh coat of white paint. A shabby, maroon counter-top surrounded a porcelain sink located under a small window. The south end provided a dining area beside a double hung, small-paned window. An archway opened into the living room with the front door on our right. Both rooms were painted a pine green and the seven-foot ceilings were white. The thermostat on the north wall was set for the oil burning furnace in the cellar to provide a minimum amount of heat to keep water pipes from freezing. We walked kitty-cornered across the narrow boards of the hardwood floor coated with sealer and climbed the steps in the opposite corner.

In the bathroom at the head of the stairs, dark green, plastic tile covered the floor.

Wooden cupboards painted a light green were built along the north side of the room between the doorway and the white, porcelain tub. Light gray linoleum protected the walls surrounding the tub and surrounded the area below the west window and behind the pedestal sink and the stool. I needed to choose wallpaper for Joe's mother to hang on the upper portion.

Across the hall, our bedroom was fairly large with a small closet. The slanted, white ceiling met the dusty rose wall on the south side of the room. Two windows to the east and one to the south made the room light and airy. The hallway led to another closet and a tiny nursery. The floors in the hallway and bedrooms were bare, varnished, wide boards.

Back downstairs in the living room, Ken asked, "Well, what do you think?" There was a slight echo each time we spoke in the empty rooms.

I paused before I answered. I didn't want to hurt his feelings. I wasn't impressed with the place, but it would be our home. Joe, an experienced do-it-yourselfer, planned to have Ken help with some remodeling, which would make a big difference. I replied, "I think it will be great when you guys have finished working on it." I measured all of the windows for curtains.

The following week, Joe and Ken began carpenter work on our house. When the rooms were ready for painting in my choice of colors–turquoise for the kitchen, beige for the living room and baby blue for the upstairs bedrooms and hallway–I grabbed a brush and helped during the weekends. After the transformation, I could hardly wait to move in.

By the middle of February, Mom quit wrapping the elastic bandage around her left ankle.

It was finally strong again after her tumble Christmas morning. I was relieved that she would definitely be able to dance at my wedding.

On the following Monday morning, Doris and I were on our way to Rockford to look for her maid of honor dress. All federal offices were closed 23 February, the day after George

Washington's Sunday birthday, but not local businesses. Doris's two bosses at the John Deere and Chevrolet dealership in Durand gave their bookkeeper the day off to shop with me.

City parking close to the retail establishments was limited to one or two hours and violators were ticketed. We left Doris's Chevy on Church Street two blocks north of the stores where all day parking was permitted. We were dressed to walk in the cold. I'd worn jeans and the warm, three-quarter-length, surcoat I'd bought six years ago. The shoe boots I'd purchased when I attended beauty school kept my feet cozy. Doris was similarly bundled up.

We traipsed from 'Monkey Wards' to Sears and turned east on State Street stopping at Block & Kuhl's, Rockford Dry, Elsie Rogers, Penney's, D.J. Stewart's, Wortham's, Owens' and finally Weise's, the last department store before the Rock River ended the shopping area. We followed the same routine in each store. Locate the rack with long dresses in Doris's size and look through them. Prom season provided an ample supply of garments, but nothing appealed to us. While trudging the six blocks back to the sedan, Doris said, "Let's try Castronovo's. We can at least look."

Castronovo's Bridal Shop was located seven blocks north of the downtown business district. Whenever my folks left the city, they usually drove along Main Street past the stately, white house. I always admired the gowns on display in their large, lighted windows, but I couldn't imagine buying anything in the expensive store. Doris parked in their lot and we entered the specialty shop. My cousin quickly found her perfect long dress with a scoop neck and cap sleeves. The pinkish-orchid color flattered her.

With that purchase out of the way, I checked their rack of suits for a going-away outfit. A beige dress with a matching full-length coat caught my eye. The price tag said seventy-nine-ninety-nine but, I couldn't resist trying it on. The outer garment was princess style with push-up sleeves and a pink and orange print, synthetic lining. The belted sheath featured a square neckline and short sleeves. The rough material reminded me of the burlap bags I held for Dad to fill with oats to be ground at the Davis Mill. The combo fit perfectly and I loved it, but. I couldn't see any way to 'horse-trade' the price lower like I did with my gown. I hesitated.

Doris encouraged me, "After you're married, you won't be buying new things very often."

I knew my friends would attest to that, but could I justify the expense? The outfit was a classic I'd wear for years to come. The navy blue, patent-leather, sling back shoes and matching purse I'd gotten last Easter would work well with it, saving me money there. I splurged. Later, I added navy blue accessories—a pair of, elbow-length gloves, a little, bow-shaped, synthetic-straw hat with a small veil and a pair of clip-on earrings.

A week later, I called in sick at work so Mom and I could go to Monroe. I needed a screw replaced in the bow of my gray, plastic-framed glasses I used for reading. I'd acquired specs last June when my first eye check-up at the clinic revealed astigmatism, which was the reason close work was slightly indistinct. After visiting the optical department, we looked at furniture in a couple of stores to get ideas for my new home.

March was a week old but it was snowing hard and drifting Thursday morning. Mom chauffeured me to Durand. Driving on Highway 70 to Rockford, Betty couldn't see much farther than the hood ornament on the front of her Ford. She turned around at the fish hatchery flats about half-way to the city and returned to the village. After dropping off her other riders, she took me to the farm. I spent the rest of the morning giving Mom a permanent.

After dinner, I addressed our fifty wedding invitations. A few weeks earlier, Hazel and I compiled a guest list limited to the hundred people that could be seated in our church. I'd ordered the printing at a small shop in Beloit. The cards, a guest book and a hundred-and-fifty, small napkins embossed in silver with our first names and date cost twenty-five dollars.

By the next morning, the storm was over, the roads were plowed and I could get to work.

Saturday, Wayne accompanied Ken to Rockford. My groom bought a navy-blue suit with a harmonizing tie, a white shirt with French cuffs and black shoes to wear for our wedding. He also purchased shirts, pants, a robe and a pair of pajamas for our New Orleans honeymoon.

Afterward, Wayne told Gloria and his in-laws about the clothes shopping trip.

In the evening, Ken and I went with Tracys to the Mercury Ballroom just north of Freeport on Highway 26. Inside the hall, we walked past the horseshoe-shaped bar to join Gloria's folks. Jack and Ilene sat with several of their friends at one of the long tables adjoining the hardwood dance floor. The middle-aged group followed the popular Jack Busch's band throughout the area because Gloria's dad knew the musicians. After introductions, Gloria's dad announced to the others, "Can you believe it? Ken's got new pajamas for his honeymoon. What guy's going to wear pajamas on his honeymoon?"

Ken's face glowed bright pink. Jack repeated those remarks several times during the evening and each time my fiancé blushed.

I'd shopped alone for my honeymoon clothes. All I bought were two pairs of short, frilly, baby doll pajamas, one white and one blue, and a pair of black, lace panties that caught my eye. I didn't need any more clothes, but I splurged for a bottle of the expensive Chanel #5 cologne.

The following Wednesday night, Aunt Elnora accompanied Mom and me to Mrs. Clark's living room in Durand for the Ladies Aid monthly gathering. During their business meeting, we discussed my reception. The group of eight churchwomen agreed to provide dishes, sandwiches, punch, coffee, cream and sugar and do the work for twenty-five dollars. We would buy a wedding cake, nuts and mints. The three of us then joined their Bible study and enjoyed the chocolate cake and coffee served by the hostess.

Saturday afternoon, Lola Mae and I went to Everson Floor Coverings in Brodhead to select linoleum for the kitchen floor in our future home. She purchased my choice, a spatter pattern that was mostly gray with touches of turquoise, pink and yellow.

At seven that evening, my parents and I left for Rockford to attend Mary's birthday party.

It was the middle of March, but it was snowing. When we stopped in Durand to pick up Ken, Mom asked him to take her place behind the wheel and she joined me in the back seat. She assumed he wouldn't want to ride with her.

Inside the apartment, the group spent the evening playing Five Hundred and eating birthday cake. Outside, the storm turned into a blizzard. Ken drove cautiously along the snow-covered Highway 70 to Durand. Mom continued slowly along the blacktop to the farm. At home, the electricity was off and didn't come back on until noon the next day. Dad hooked up the tractor motor to power the machines for the morning milking.

On the last work day of the following week, I used getting a cold as an excuse to stay home. I felt well enough to go shopping in Rockford with Mom for her mother-of-the-bride dress. She didn't have any better luck than Doris did. We went to the department stores where we usually shopped and found nothing. As a last resort, we entered Owens', one of the expensive establishments we didn't patronize. She purchased a navy blue, crepe dress with three-quarter length sleeves, a square neckline and a pleated collar gathered at the left and right front corners with small rhinestone clips. It cost twenty-three dollars, three times what she usually paid, but it would be her good dress for many years to come. In a nearby shop, she found a matching hat for three dollars.

We stopped to pick up my wedding gown at the Elsie Rogers shop. I added a floor-length, half-slip with a small hoop at the bottom and a merry widow, an undergarment that combined a strapless bra and a short corset with attached garters.

The next morning, Mom and I went to Beloit to our favorite jeweler, Wyman Tracy, no relation to Wayne. His little shop was located on Fourth Street a couple blocks north of the high-rent, business district. I selected a thirty-five-dollar ring for Ken. The thick, white-gold band etched with a deep, S-shaped pattern should hold up on a farmer's hand. For his wedding gift, a pair of gold cufflinks set with onyx and diamonds caught my eye. I didn't care that the price tag said one hundred thirty dollars. They were for my husband. I also bought a yellow gold, Bulova watch for Doris, my maid of honor.

Our next stop was Stanton's. We wanted comfortable shoes to wear for the wedding because we'd be on our feet for most of the evening. Mom found a pair of navy-blue pumps to match her dress and I bought white brocade heels.

Ken called at four o'clock that afternoon. "I'm home and cleaned up. We've got time to look at furniture before Mrs. Chapin closes for the day."

"That's a great idea."

"I'll be right out to pick you up."

At the Durand store, we chose a Kroehler bedroom set that included a mirrored, double dresser, a four-drawer bureau and walnut double bed with the popular, bookcase headboard. We added a foam rubber mattress and a box spring. For our living room, we selected a brown, upholstered davenport and chair set. The slanted arms and four-inch, wooden legs gave the two pieces a modern look. An RCA console TV completed our purchases. We signed an agreement to make monthly payments for our furnishings.

Ken's parents provided a walnut coffee table and two matching end tables as our wedding present. Until we could afford to buy a dinette set, my folks loaned us the card table and chairs I had given them for Christmas.

The old saying was 'April showers bring May flowers' ,but March showers brought many of the things Ken and I would need for our new home. Sis and Doris hosted my side of the family. Lola Mae invited her relatives. My boss, Mary, entertained our co-workers from the ASC office plus her kin. My classmates met at Eva Jean's home in Rockton.

At each of the gatherings, we chatted, played a few silly games such as identifying different kitchen baking ingredients by their looks and smells or unscrambling words pertaining to a wedding. Then the high point of the evening–I carefully opened the wrapped packages. Folk lore decreed each broken ribbon meant a baby. My gifts included scatter rugs, throw pillows, bath towels and kitchen items. There were often duplicates. I could use the three sets of four matching snack trays with small glass cups for future entertaining, but I exchanged a few casserole dishes. Each hostess topped off the night with dessert, coffee and punch. At last I was joining the ranks of married women.

Two weeks before our marriage, Mom placed notices about our public wedding dance in the Durand and Brodhead weeklies. She mailed penny postcards to relatives and friends who wouldn't see the newspapers.

The first Monday in April, I marked off another item on my 'to do' list. Ken and I obtained our marriage license. He picked me up from work promptly at four thirty so we could get to the county clerk's office on the second floor of the stately, old courthouse before everyone went home at five. I brought the results of the required blood tests done by Dr. Hein to prove neither of us had a sexually transmitted disease.

On Friday a week before our marriage, I stayed home from work so I could go to Beloit with my mother. Mary was excited about my wedding, too, so getting time off was easy. In Mortag's Bakery, we ordered a cake that would serve one-hundred-twenty-five people and cost twenty-five dollars. We'd invited a hundred and not all of them would attend, but we didn't want Lola Mae to skimp cutting the pieces. We then walked down the street to McNeany's department store. I bought two sets of beige fiberglass drapes with brown, coral and white floral print for our living room, which was painted beige.

Later in the afternoon, Mrs. Chapin, who had business contacts with florists, helped me order wedding flowers. For Doris and me, we chose cascade bouquets to match our gowns. We then selected corsages—rosebuds for our mothers and mixed flowers for Ella, the church organist, and Mary Ann, the singer who had been my long-time schoolmate. My adviser suggested gardenias for Gloria, who would have charge of the guest book, and servers at the reception, Aunt Elnora, Lola Mae and Mary. The six men would wear white carnation boutonnieres. We added two white arrangements to fill the brass vases that sat on the church altar. The total floral bill was fifty-two dollars.

In the evening, Ken and I stopped by our house to see the three Kenmore appliances Sears had delivered in the afternoon. The previous Monday night, I learned Ken's a committed, one-stop shopper. When we saw the white, top-loading automatic washer, the electric range and the refrigerator with a freezer in the bottom in Beloit, he said, "We've found what we want. Why go anywhere else?"

I'd expected to go from store to store in all of the surrounding towns like Mom did before making a purchase, but I couldn't argue with his logic. My thousand-dollar savings account paid the total invoice. I was glad I followed my mother's advice and banked my money instead of filling a hope chest with expensive china and sterling silver I would rarely use.

The next day, I washed windows at the 'corner house'. Even that mundane chore was fun at our future home.

When young women wed during the fifties, they quit their jobs and became full-time housewives. Many mothers told their daughters, "If he doesn't treat you right, you just come back home to Ma." I watched a few of my friends do that every time they were miffed at their husbands, even when it entailed dragging a clothes basket full of baby food and diapers.

Mom never was like other mothers and she raised me to be different from other daughters. She warned me, "Remember, after you're married, you can't come home again."

That admonition proved to be the best thing she could have said to me. As an only child, I never learned the negotiation, compromise and just plain giving in that became second nature to siblings and was necessary in marriage. Through the years, when I got mad at my husband and felt like stomping out, slamming the door behind me, I never did. With no place to go, I cooled off and worked things out with him.

During the week before our Friday night ceremony, Tuesday was the only day I worked in the office. That evening, we met with Ken's Uncle Bob at Ditzlers' house. Rolland's half-brother worked at Camera Craft in Rockford and photography was his hobby. We discussed the wedding album of eight-by-ten, black and white pictures that would be his gift to us.

The next day, I sorted out the clothes I would need for our ten-day, New Orleans honeymoon and boxed the rest to take to our new home. I laid Ken's navy picture and my musical jewelry box on top of the garments in the carton. What about the yellow paper leis from Davis Days that had hung on my dresser for the past seven years? Time for them to go in the waste basket. Looking around at my bare room brought a feeling of nostalgia. I was no longer the child who belonged there.

Thursday morning immediately after breakfast, I washed my hair, wound it up in fat pin curls, sat under my hair dryer for an hour and combed it out. Mom and I made a quick trip to Beloit to buy bakery buns and Spudnuts, tasty donuts made from potatoes. In the afternoon, my mother made two apple and two pumpkin pies. While they baked, she filled the buns with the roast pork she'd cooked and ground the day before. The food would be served at the wedding rehearsal in the evening.

After chores, we picked up Elnora and her children, Ronnie and Joyce, on our way to the church. In the vestibule, we met Ken, his parents, Doris, the Tracys and Pastor Gene Moen. We all took our places in the nave with our parents and Gloria sitting in the front pews. Ken and I were a little shaky standing with Wayne and Doris in front of the ornate, dark wood altar. The minister led us through the ceremony he would perform the following evening. Then everyone went to the basement where Elnora and Joyce served the lunch Mom prepared.

I gave Doris her watch and Ken his cuff links. He opened the box and said, "Wow! These are really fancy. Thank you."

Ken's gift to me was an aurora borealis necklace, bracelet and earrings in a silver leaf pattern with small, rainbow-reflecting stones. Ignoring our audience, I kissed him and said, "Thank you. They're beautiful."

Ken gave each of the boys a set of cuff links and Wayne a shirt with a harmonizing tie.

Before we all left the church, Ken asked, "Do you want to stay at the dance until the end or leave early?"

"Let me think about it. I'll give you a call tomorrow morning."

My parents and I returned home by ten. After crawling into my bed, I thought about it being the last time I would sleep alone. Ken had made a reservation for our wedding night at Charnocks motel in Rochelle, about an hour's drive away. I didn't know much about making love, but I looked forward to learning together.

The next morning, I was up bright and early, but I waited until about 10 A.M. to call Ken. Tradition said we mustn't see each other before the wedding, but talking on the telephone didn't count. Hazel answered and said in a disgusted tone, "He's still sleeping. I'll tell him to call you."

While I waited for Ken to return my call, I finished packing shorts, skirts and sleeveless blouses for our honeymoon in the South. I expected to bask in warm, spring weather.

It was almost noon when the phone rang. After exchanging hellos, Ken said, "Mom's not happy with me. Last night after rehearsal, Wayne and Gloria wanted to buy me a last beer while I was single, so we stopped downtown at the Farmer's Tap. As usual, Charlie, Joe and Dick were in there. After Wayne and Gloria went home, each of those guys bought me another beer. Then I went with them to a South Beloit bar. I didn't get home until after that tavern closed at 2 A.M. It was the first time in my life I got drunk. I got up today with a hangover. Mom was really mad at those guys. I tried to tell her it was my own fault. I went with them willingly."

I didn't tell him how stupid I thought he was. I said, "I've thought it over and I definitely want to stay at the dance until it ends at midnight. Then you can take me home to change out of my wedding gown and we'll leave for Rochelle." I wanted to savor every minute of the wedding day I'd waited so long for.

"Okay. I'll see you this evening at the church."

After dinner, Mom drove in the rain to Durand to prepare for our reception in the church basement. When we entered the building, a slight odor of lemon furniture polish hung in the air. The women of the congregation took turns doing the weekly cleaning. Ella sat at the organ practicing for our ceremony.

Downstairs, Mom and I set up nearly one-hundred, wooden, folding chairs on the cement floor. We then covered the serving table with a four-yard long, white tablecloth provided by one of the ladies.

When Mrs. Mortag carried in our wedding cake from their panel delivery truck, she protected it from the rain with a large piece of plastic. I was in awe when I saw the cake sitting on the serving table. The white frosting was decorated with pink roses and topped with a bell inside a heart. I didn't want the traditional bride and groom figures that usually stood on a tiered cake.

Before we left, I took a last look around downstairs and upstairs. Seeing everything in place for our wedding ceremony and reception assured me that it was going to happen. When we exited the church and headed back to the farm, it was still raining.

As soon as we arrived home at four o'clock, my parents started milking. I took my bath and put on jeans and a shirt. Mom left the barn at five thirty and drove in the rain to deliver me and the two dresses to the church. On the way she recalled, "My dad always said you don't start anything on Friday." Was the weather a bad omen?

We carried the garments to the back of the building and hung them in the women's restroom where Doris and I would prepare for the ceremony. Mom hurried back home to bathe and dress.

I wouldn't put on my gown until Doris came at six fifteen. With a half-hour to kill, I turned on the fluorescent lights in the nave and sat down in the first, wooden pew on the bride's side. Listening to the building creak and groan like all old-timers was a little scary. Logically, I knew there was nothing to fear. I didn't believe in the boogieman or ghosts. In Durand, there were no worries about intruders.

Marriage didn't frighten me. I was excited, but not apprehensive. I knew I was doing the right thing. I didn't realize that saying yes to a ride on a Ferris wheel when I was fourteen would set the course for the rest of my life. During the past seven years, Ken and I matured separately and together while our love for each other deepened

I looked forward to changing my last name after years of having people mispronounce and misspell Tschabold. I hated the socially correct Mrs. Kenneth Ditzler. I would be Lolita Ditzler.

As I waited, my mind wandered back to the 'what if's' during our seven-year courtship. What if sixteen-year-old Kenny was too shy to ask me to ride on the Ferris wheel while I walked around Davis Days with my boyfriend, Ronnie during the summer of '52? What if I said no?

What if I just said good-bye when he started his four-year enlistment in the Navy instead of promising to wait for him? What if he found someone else during his travels? What if he hadn't let another sailor use his ticket to board that ill-fated plane that crashed in the Grand Canyon in '56? What if he called it quits when he came home on leave in '57 and I was on a date with Ron? What if my mother's worries came true and I succumbed to either the appendicitis infection or TB? I firmly believed we were meant to be together.

The opening of the church's front door brought me back to the present. Doris entered with two tidbits of good news. "It quit raining. Mom's all ready for Sis and Joe to pick her up on their way into town."

I was relieved to hear Aunt Frannie would be well enough to attend. About a month earlier, an ambulance took her to Swedish American Hospital in Rockford. She was diagnosed with an acute attack of arthritis and a kidney infection. Five days later, she returned home, but since then, she spent a lot of time in bed.

Doris and I went to the restroom in the back of the church to don our gowns. The tight quarters wasn't made to be a dressing room. She moved over to the men's and I used the ladies'. I complied with all of the 'something old, something new, something borrowed, something blue' traditions. Aunt Frannie's gold bracelet on my left wrist was old, my dress was new and a blue garter encircled the stocking covering my right thigh. After checking my hair and make-up in the mirror above the sink, I added the veil borrowed from my co-worker, Lois. My watch showed five minutes to seven. Time for us to go to the front of the church. Ella played an organ prelude. Fluorescent lights brighten the nave as the ushers escorted the last of the guests to pews.

Doris and I slipped through the adjoining dark Sunday school room to join the parents standing in the vestibule. Gary seated the Ditzlers in the front pew on the groom's side. Hazel wore a light blue, lace dress, with a matching hat and Rolland, a dark suit. Ronnie escorted Mom to the front pew on the bride's side.

Pastor Moen led Ken and Wayne from his office at the rear of the church to their places in front of the altar rail. That was Doris's cue to begin the customary step, stop, step, stop pace down the carpet runner in the center aisle.

I stood beside Dad, who was wearing a new stripped tie with his two-year-old, dark gray suit. I think he was more nervous than I was. The organist's sharp notes signaled "Here Comes the Bride" and I took his arm. He clenched his jaw so no emotion would leak out as we began the step, stop trip down the aisle. I joined Ken at the altar and Dad stepped back to stand beside Mom in the front pew.

With everyone in place, the ushers turned off the electric lights and the service began in the glow of the candelabra. Ken and I joined hands and knelt at the dark, wooden rail surrounding the matching altar while Mary Ann sang "The Lord's Prayer." We then faced each other and clasped right hands. Pastor Moen led our promises "to have and to hold from this day forward for better, for worse; for richer, for poorer; in sickness and in health; to love and to cherish until death us do part."

Our ceremony went off without a hitch until I tried to slip Ken's ring on the third finger of his left hand. It stuck at his knuckle. To stop the struggle, he left it there and pushed it on later. Ken kissed his bride, the minister introduced us to the congregation, and the joyful "Recessional" accompanied us down the aisle. We stood at the basement doorway to greet our guests as they made their way to the reception. The four of us signed the necessary papers, Uncle Bob took pictures of our wedding party and we all went to the basement.

Downstairs, presents covered with fancy paper and tied with ribbons would remain piled on a long table pushed against the wall out of the way. It was the custom in our community for guests to bring their gifts to the reception where the packages would be opened and displayed. Because we were pressed for time, Mom planned to entertain our wedding party and extended families for an evening of unwrapping after our honeymoon.

Ken and I stood behind the serving table. Tall, white tapers in Mary's silver candle holders glowed on each side of the wedding cake. The two of us cut and shared the first piece. I then passed the knife to Lola Mae to serve our guests. Mary sat at one end of the serving table and poured coffee using Doris's refinished silver service. Aunt Elnora stood at the other end of the table and dipped punch from the glass bowl borrowed from Mrs. Chapin. I had used an aluminum Jell-O mold to make the heart-shaped block of ice that floated in the liquid.

Doris, Wayne and Gloria followed Ken and me filling our plates with sandwiches, cake, nuts and mints plus cups of punch. We all sat down at the round oak table prepared for us. Our guests helped themselves.

When Ken and I exited the church through the front door, everyone showered us with rice symbolizing abundance and fertility. It was a cool night and we scurried to climb into the back seat of his Lincoln with Wayne and Doris in front. Someone already started the sedan and the heater warmed the interior, which felt good on my bare arms. Friends stuck a hand-printed, "Just Married" cardboard sign on the trunk. Our best man drove around town honking the horn. Tin cans tied to the back bumper rattled along behind.

Wayne parked in front of the Grange Hall and we climbed the steep, concrete, front steps. Our friends and relatives crowding the large room applauded as we entered. The Bel Air Ranch Boys began to play and John Pela crooned *I Love You Truly* into the microphone. Ken took me in his arms and we never missed a step during our first solo dance as a married couple.

Ken was my first date, my last date and my husband for the rest of my life.

Epilogue

To celebrate our Golden Anniversary in April 2009, Ken and I stood before Pastor Lee to exchange wide, yellow gold, wedding bands while repeating the traditional vows, "to have and to hold from this day forward: for better, for worse; for richer, for poorer; in sickness and in health; to love and to cherish until death us do part." A lot had changed during the fifty years we'd lived those simple words. The carved oak altar had been moved from the Trinity Lutheran Church on Main Street in Durand to a new brick building at the west edge of the village. Our daughter, Lisa, and our son, Kurt, were beside us in place of my cousin, Doris, and Ken's buddy Wayne, who had both passed away. Sitting in the front pew were daughter-in-law, Sandy, who had her camera in her hands to record this momentous occasion. With her were our grandchildren, Katelyn, fifteen, and Jacob, thirteen, plus Wayne's widow, Gloria.

Also missing from the day was our oldest child, Linda, who had died of breast cancer eight months earlier. Outliving a child is considered a parent's worst nightmare, but Linda was forty-eight years old with no expectation of becoming an independent adult. It was a blessing to care for her all of her life.

After the Saturday afternoon ceremony, we all drove to the opposite end of town to greet friends and relatives during an open house at the American Legion Hall. To begin the festivities, Kurt gave the following tribute: "I believe it is customary for the best man to toast the couple. I cannot fill the shoes of the original best man, but I am honored to be able to offer my comments, just the same. Today, we celebrate a fiftieth wedding anniversary, and we should take time to remember those who are not here. We remember our dear sister, Linda; best man Wayne Tracy; and maid of honor Doris Rowley Strampe. Also, each of your parents, Alex and Edith

Tschabold, and Rolland and Hazel Ditzler, and all the other friends and relatives who have gone before us.

Now, let's remember, we are here to celebrate with those who are here, all of us, who have come together to honor a couple who have reached a real milestone in their relationship. To Mom (Lolita) and Dad (Ken) who have taught me, and probably all of us here today, the true meanings of devotion, commitment, and love. Thank you for the example you have given me and to each one of us about how to raise a family and make a marriage last. We raise our glass to you as you celebrate a lifetime together. May your love carry you for another 50 years!"

Our favorite guitar player, Roger, provided classic country music beginning with Anne Murray's "Could I Have This Dance?" Ken took me in his arms and we moved together perfectly like we did fifty years ago during our solo dance.

Later, Roger performed "our song," Johnny Horton's "The Battle of New Orleans." Those lyrics about the War of 1812 aren't romantic, but they always made us smile. That recording saturated the air waves while we were on our honeymoon in the Big Easy. It also reminded us of our conflicts through the years that seemed important at the time.

Our milestone was a time for looking back beginning with the seven years Ken worked at Irish Acres as hired man for his brother-in-law, Joe.

As soon as the Fourth of July fireworks faded away that first summer, I had my own explosive news—we were going to have a baby. Like most young women, I quit my office job to be a fulltime wife and mother. Linda was born 18 February 1960. Lisa followed fourteen months later, 29 April 1961.

Our first tragedy happened on a rainy, Friday night, 19 October 1962. Ken's parents, Rolland, 55, and Hazel, 51, were killed in a two-car crash on their way home from their office jobs in Rockford. The community mourned with us.

Kurt was born 24 May 1963. We squeezed bunk beds and a crib into the tiny, upstairs nursery.

During the first week of December 1964, I was preparing to host a card party on Saturday night to celebrate Dad's fifty-second birthday. It was mid-morning on Friday when my sister-in-law, Lola Mae, called. I chatted on the phone while our kids played upstairs. Lisa, 3 1/2, spotted a book of matches that her smoker father had left lying on top of a tall, chest of drawers in our bedroom. She pulled a chair close to the bureau, climbed up and grabbed the matchbook. Her brother and sister watched as she knelt on the floor and struck a match. Her fringe-trimmed, cowgirl shirt accidently caught fire. She ran screaming down the stairs, through the living room and across the kitchen to me. I grabbed a rug from the floor in front of the sink and wrapped it around her to smother the flames. Ken and I took her to our family physician, Dr. Hein, in Brodhead. Second and third degree burns on the left side of her chest and the inside of her left arm covered twenty percent of her body. The injuries weren't causing her a lot of pain because the nerves had been destroyed. He sent us to St. Clare Hospital in Monroe.

During eighteen months of recovery, Lisa underwent three grafting operations. Thin layers of skin were peeled from the tops of her thighs and applied to her wounds. After each surgery, the brave, little girl was a pathetic sight. A plaster cast held her left arm up away from her body in an L-shape for two weeks to allow the grafts to heal. Bandages above her knees forced her to walk with her legs bent like a crippled, old lady. Thursday, 26 May 1966, was a day of celebration when Dr. Hein said it was her last weekly appointment for a bandage change. He helped us cope with the expenses by writing "no charge" on most of his bills. The Boy Scouts and our church conducted fund raisers for us.

Ken's being called for jury duty in Rockford during the summer turned out to be life-changing. While serving, he spent some of their breaks talking to the bailiff, who urged him to join the sheriff's police. The county department recently replaced their politically appointed staff with a merit system. The sheriff continued to be elected every four years, but the deputies had job security and the promise of a pension after twenty-five years of service. My husband loved farming, but he had no future as a hired man. He applied and it took several months for him to pass the required tests and background check.

I was elated Ken was changing jobs. The morning he started at Irish acres, Monday, 2 February 1959, the thermometer read twenty-seven degrees below zero making it the coldest day of the winter. I began thinking of it as "that cold day in hell." Ken was satisfied with his situation, but I chafed at having our lives controlled by his boss. Joe decided the hours my husband worked, how much money we had to spend and where we lived because the house went with the job.

Different employment meant moving. We thought Durand was a good place to buy a home and raise our family, but we saw no "for sale" signs. Through the grapevine, we learned that Ernie and Audrey, friends of my parents, were remodeling to resell one of the oldest houses in the village. We met with the couple, talked to the local banker about a mortgage and agreed on a price of $8,500 for the story and a half, three-bedroom residence at the corner of West Howard and Freemont Streets. Six years later, we hired Ernie to add a family room and a two-car garage.

Sunday, 23 October 1966, was moving day. The next morning, Ken arose at five, donned a blue uniform, pinned a badge over his heart and wrapped a gun belt around his waist. He drove our Corvair to Rockford to begin the seven to three shift with the Winnebago County Sheriff's Police. While ascending the steps to enter the courthouse, he met another deputy who asked, "Are you Ditzler?"

"Yes."

"I'm Wilcox, your new partner. We've got a call." The two men climbed into a midnight blue Buick parked at the Elm Street curb and roared off with red lights flashing and siren blaring.

The following summer, Ken and three others were the first members of the department to attend a six-week, basic police training course at the Southern Illinois University in Carbondale. Later, he used his navy ordnance training to take charge of the bomb squad formed to disarm explosive devices.

Two months after Linda had started first grade, school officials suggested she be psychologically tested and we agreed. We were stunned when the psychologist referred her to an educable mentally handicapped class. She had crawled, walked, talked and completed all of the usual milestones up to the time she started school. With Lisa just fourteen months younger and all of our friends having babies at the same time, we thought any lag in her development would have been obvious to us.

The following February, Linda had a seizure at school and we were called to take her to the hospital. An electroencephalogram at St. Clare in Monroe confirmed she had brain damage from an undetermined origin. Medication controlled her epilepsy.

A county co-operative including all of the school districts outside of Rockford provided special education classes, which were housed wherever space was available. Each day Linda and three others were driven to Winnebago, a small town about fifteen miles southeast of Durand.

I joined the parents' group's efforts to create a sheltered workshop for our children when they became adults. The not-for-profit Illinois Growth Enterprises opened in 1970 with ten employees.

A couple years after we moved to town, Ernie, the elderly Durand Township Supervisor who lived across the street, asked me to join him and six others running unopposed in the spring election for township officials. I have continued as clerk, which consists of taking minutes at monthly, evening meetings and a few other tasks.

To make extra money, Ken learned to drive a semi and, like many of his co-workers, moonlighted for sixteen years. Every four weeks, he rotated eight-hour shifts at the sheriff's department, but no matter what time of the day or night he was off duty, there was often grain or livestock to haul for Ray Satness's trucking firm located at the east edge of Durand.

After our three children were enrolled in school, I wasn't content to be "just a housewife." I started checking the *Rockford Morning Star* help wanted section for a part-time, office job. The daily newspaper's ad for correspondents in several small towns surrounding the county seat intrigued me. I met with the regional editor and learned the only requirements to be a freelance reporter were a typewriter and a 35mm camera, which I had. I poked my nose into local government meetings where I wasn't always wanted, chased fire trucks and wrote features about people doing interesting things. I'd found my calling. I attended writers' workshops in the area and learned to submit articles to various national magazines for farmers, police officers and women. I joined the Illinois Woman's Press Association, which was affiliated with the National Federation of Press Women., and received many awards in their annual contests for published articles.

My parents left a lifetime of farming on New Year's Day 1971. The Anderson acreage, where they'd spent the past twenty-four years, had been sold to become part of a private, man-made, lake development. Dad and Mom moved into their new, two-bedroom, ranch located six blocks east of us. He worked as a janitor at the school complex and she was a housewife.

When Linda turned sixteen, we agreed with school officials that she should stay at home.

She was our conundrum that was never solved. Special education classes weren't helping her and she was being disruptive to the other students.

In the evening of 10 July 1976, I was shocked when Mom phoned from Branson, Missouri., to tell me Dad, sixty-three, died of a heart attack. The funeral home in Branson and McCorkle's here in Durand met in southern Illinois, to drive my parents home from the tour bus trip. We were a close family and the loss was devastating.

After high school graduation. Lisa and Kurt each worked part-time and commuted to Rock Valley Community College in Rockford to earn a two-year, police science degree. Lisa became an Illinois State Trooper and bought a home in a Rockford subdivision. Kurt served as a Rockford Police officer for two years and then joined his father as a deputy.

Kurt and Sandy McLamarrah, a cute, friendly, blonde, from Elizabeth, were married 11 May 1991 and settled in the house Kurt owned in Durand. Katelyn and Jacob made us attentive grandparents and Lisa a devoted aunt.

At the same time, Ken retired from the sheriff's police after twenty-five years. He'd risen to the rank of lieutenant and served as commander, similar to chief, in Machesney Park, a recently formed village that contracted with the county department for police protection. He joined three retired city cops to work part-time for the U.S. Marshals Service as a court security officer in the Rockford Federal Building for the next twelve years.

Mom turned ninety years old on 18 May 2003 and died sixteen days later.

In January 2008, I was drying Linda off after a shower when I discovered a lump in her right breast. We had no history of breast cancer in our family and she was the picture of health–slender, active and ate whatever I put on her plate. Tests confirmed that she had a malignant tumor and she underwent a mastectomy. Following her operation, the surgeon said, "I couldn't remove all of the cancer because it's a fast-growing type that has spread to her lymph nodes."

In consultation with the doctors, Ken and I decided not to put her through the rigors of chemo or radiation, which would only prolong her life for a short time—not cure the disease. An oncologist prescribed a tablet, which we hoped would slow the growth of the cancer cells in our daughter's body. She recovered quickly from the surgery, but five months later, I found a lump in her left breast. Again, she recovered quickly from the second mastectomy. A few weeks later, she appeared to have pain when rising from a chair. She no longer communicated with us, but only spoke a few words at random.

We watched her actions to determine how she felt. We took her to the hospital emergency room and she was admitted. After several days of tests, it was confirmed that the cancer had spread to her pelvic bones. We brought her home and engaged hospice. Linda died in her sleep 9 August 2008, six months after her first mastectomy. We laid her beside her grandparents in Laona Township Cemetery.

With time on my hands, I read the diaries Mom had left behind. Her daily jottings took me back to that first ride with Kenny on the Ferris wheel in 1952. I began writing a memoir about our seven-year courtship in the fifties. Life on a family dairy farm during the Eisenhower Era was so different from today.

On April 17, 2009, we felt blessed to reach our fiftieth anniversary. Each of us had survived a serious health problem. In 1980, histoplasmosis, a fungus often found in bird droppings, caused my left lung to collapse and it was surgically removed. Ken's prostate cancer was cured with surgery followed by six weeks of radiation in 1996. Together, we've celebrated the happy times, consoled one another through the sad times and look forward to the future with our family. We thank God for that first Ferris wheel ride.

Acknowledgements

Thank you to my husband, Ken, who is half of this story. Through the years, he stepped up to take care of things on the home front when I wanted to spend several days attending a writers' conference. I appreciate the many ways the rest of my family has supported me.

Thank you to old friends Gloria Tracy, Esther Dixon, Willabea Francis, Jan Bosman and Joyce Waldorf, who brighten my life and were first readers of this story about our coming of age.

A list of the presenters at workshops and conferences that have taught me how to make a career of writing is too long for me to remember or include. I appreciate the editors at the various publications that gave my work their seal of approval. Thank you to the Illinois Woman's Press Association and the National Federation of Press Women for their camaraderie and awards, which proved I was learning the craft. I want to thank the In-Print Writers Organization, affiliated with the Chicago Writers Association, for the opportunity to do radio interviews with authors and learn from their successes. A special mention of the Janesville Area Writers, who listened to my reading excerpts from this memoir and made helpful suggestions. The Continuing Education Department of the

University of Wisconsin-Madison instructed me in writing creative nonfiction and crafting a book proposal, which was accepted by Adelaide Books.

Table of Contents

Chapter 1 - The Love Story Began - Kenny and I were locked in each other's arms wishing our last Saturday night date didn't have to end. Monday he would begin his four-year-hitch in the navy. His murmured, "I love you, Honey," shocked me. He'd never said that before.

It took me a few moments to respond, "I love you, too, and I'll wait for you." He was eighteen and I was sixteen in July of 1954.

The Cold War, a state of political and military tension between the United States and Russia, threatened the Eisenhower Era of peace and prosperity. Boys were required to register for the draft when they turned eighteen. They either waited for 'Greetings' from Uncle Sam and served two years in the Army or enlisted in their preferred branch of the service for a longer period. Men in uniform were trained and ready to do whatever might become necessary.

The following weekend I accompanied my parents to Davis Days, a summer festival in the village where our post office was located. Afterward, I sat on the bed in my room and my thoughts drifted back to the same event two years ago when Kenny asked me to ride the Ferris wheel. Dad and Mom considered me too young to go out with boys, but I hoped my fifteenth birthday, which was only seven weeks away, would be the magic dating age.

My parents, who were pushing forty, were typical Midwest dairy farmers with one exception—Mom donned slacks and worked outdoors with Dad instead of wearing a housedress covered by an apron and staying inside. They provided the labor and machinery to rent the average-sized, two-hundred-forty-acre-farm located in the northwest corner of Winnebago County, Illinois, a mile south of the Wisconsin state line. Milking our herd of twenty-four cows.at 5:00 A.M. and 5:00 P.M. punctuated our days and provided a monthly paycheck. Raising butcher hogs to ship to the Chicago markets each fall added to our annual income. The cows and pigs belonged jointly to the landlord and tenant with income and expenses split fifty/fifty.

On Thursday evenings during the summer, my family drove into Durand, the village where I attended high school. Adults and children gathered in the Center Street Park to view the free shows sponsored by the businessmen. Kenny and I were among a group of teenagers who sat on the grass in front of the bedsheet screen tied between two large trees. The two of us snuggled while watching the movies.

Every Saturday night, my parents and I joined three generations of dancers at the Wigwam, a hall seven miles west of Beloit, Wisconsin. Teens like me, middle-agers like my parents and oldsters including Kenny's great uncle and aunt, Harry and Pearl, who had been married about fifty years, waltzed and fox trotted to old time music. Circle two-steps mixed us all together. I spent the evenings with my close friends, Willabea, Janice and Joyce, who attended the nearby Orfordville High School.

On the last Wednesday in August, the three girls and I met at the Trask Bridge Picnic sponsored by the Burritt Grange and held in a cow pasture along Highway 70 between Durand and

Rockford, the county seat. Rural families from miles around attended the largest farm picnic in the world. The day was similar to a county fair with exhibits, free entertainment, food and a traveling carnival. I introduced my girlfriends to Kenny and his buddy, Wayne. Willabea and Wayne fell for each other, but she wasn't allowed to date either.

When school started in September, Kenny was a senior and I was a sophomore. Every morning before classes, the two of us chatted in study hall where desks for the one-hundred-plus students were located. At noon, we were among couples who gathered on wooden, balcony benches to eat our sack lunches together.

September fourth was my birthday. My mother's parents had died before she was married. Mom's eldest sister, Aunt Frannie, and her husband, Uncle Hookie, loved me like a grandchild. Their grown daughters, Doris and Sis, seemed more like aunts than cousins. The four of them added gifts to my celebration.

My turning fifteen didn't make any difference to my mother. She still said no when Kenny asked me to go to Durand High's Homecoming to be held the night before Thanksgiving. Wayne was still interested in seeing Willabea so I asked her to stay overnight with me and the two of us attended together. Kenny and Wayne played in the evening's basketball game and afterward escorted us to the dance across the street. When the evening ended at 1:00 A.M., the boys walked us to the car where my parents waited in front of the high school.

Chapter 2 -1953 – The year began with a reminder that death wasn't reserved for the old. All high school students mourned our young, English teacher, Miss Cullinan, who was killed in an auto accident.

In early March, Kenny asked me to go to the Future Homemakers of America dance in the school gym. I could hardly believe it when Mom said, "I guess you can go." We finally had our first date.

The month ended with a mumps epidemic sweeping our community. One of the rites of passage for those of us growing up in the forties and fifties was suffering through the communicable childhood diseases—mumps, measles, chicken pox and whooping cough.

From the time I started school, my parents had ingrained in my brain, 'Don't get the mumps'. Somehow, they had missed the childhood malady and feared I would bring the disease home. Two or three weeks later, both of them would be sick and unable to milk our cows twice a day.

Being a dutiful child, I went to great lengths to avoid the illness. The Easter Bunny brought me appendicitis, which required surgery. An infection followed. I missed five weeks of school and the mumps epidemic.

I returned to classes in time to participate in the joint chorus and band concert at Orangeville, another small high school about twenty-five miles west of Durand. A day of rehearsals preceded the Friday evening performance. Kenny and I spent the morning singing with the mixed chorus. In the afternoon, the band practiced and we had nothing to do until the bus left at 2:30 P.M. Another couple accompanied us strolling downtown in search of ice cream cones.

In the evening, while riding the bus back to Durand after the concert, Kenny gave me his class ring to signify we were going steady. The next morning, I wrapped the yellow gold band with gobs of adhesive tape, painted it with pink fingernail polish to keep the material dry and slipped the man-sized ring on the slim, third finger of my left hand.

The following Monday morning, our bald-headed, school superintendent stood before the students sitting at their desks in the study hall. 'PG' congratulated the Friday concert performance. He then referred to the "four juvenile delinquents" who spoiled our school's reputation when they went down town during the afternoon. Names weren't mentioned but our faces burned with embarrassment and anger. Nobody had told us to stay on the school grounds that day. We assumed we were free to leave at any time the same as we were at our home school.

On Friday night, Kenny escorted me to his senior prom. I donned my long blue, dress, pinned his corsage of red rose buds on my left shoulder and danced the night away with my handsome boyfriend who wore a suit and tie. The next morning my mother yelled at me for getting home fifteen minutes after my 2:00 A.M. curfew. Our trip to Rockford for cheeseburgers to top off the evening had taken longer than we expected.

Two weeks later, Kenny and twenty of his classmates graduated. The following Monday, he turned into a working man earning about sixty dollars a week running a machine at Barber Colman, a Rockford factory. Like most adults, he smoked cigarettes.

With his own paycheck, Kenny traded in his first car, a '40 Chevy coupe, for a Harley-Davidson motorcycle. He rode down our gravel driveway to show off his new wheels and asked me to go for a ride. Mom surprised both of us by saying, "I guess it's alright." We took several rides that summer, but none was as memorable as the night in mid-August when he brought me home from a free show. He walked me to the house and kissed me goodnight for the first time. I floated like a balloon climbing the wooden steps to enter the house.

School started on Tuesday after Labor Day. During fifth period every afternoon, nine of us junior and senior girls gathered around a table in the home economics room and learned to manage our future homes. Questions about the relationship between a husband and wife that we were too modest to ask aloud could be written on slips of paper and dropped into a box sitting in front of us. The teacher's answers were the closest we came to sex education.

During the fifties, sex wasn't talked about much, especially at our house. Before I started dating, Mom basically told me nice girls don't and you're a nice girl. Society expected young women to remain virgins until they married and became housewives caring for children while husbands supported the family.

In the fall, Kenny bought a '47, medium-blue Plymouth convertible with a white canvass top. Every afternoon, he drove me home from school before he left for his second-shift factory job.

During Christmas vacation, three months after my sixteenth birthday, I passed the state driver's test to receive my license. It didn't provide the freedom I'd expected. My parents had done a good job teaching me to drive, but they rarely let me take our '52 Chevy by myself.

Chapter 3 -1954 – Early New Year's afternoon, Kenny took me ice skating on a Pecatonica River backwater behind Derwent's farm south of Durand on Highway 70. We met friends and skated until the sun and the temperature started sinking.

A couple weeks later, my parents finally let me stay home alone at night while they attended a neighborhood card club. I often felt over-protected.

One of the biggest influences in my life was something that didn't happen—I didn't have siblings like everyone else in my junior class. When I was six and seven years old, my parents lost two baby boys at birth. I was an only child, by chance not choice.

In May, the class play and the prom highlighted my school year. Dancing with Kenny at the prom, I felt like a fashion model wearing the dress I'd bought shopping in Chicago with my cousin, Doris.

At the end of the school year, the Girls Athletic Association served a farewell cake for our sponsor and P.E. teacher, Miss Elsner, who was leaving us after two years. The club's twice-a-week meetings after school to play games provided the only sports offered to females.

On weekends, Kenny and I saw most of the movies shown in our community until he enlisted in the navy in July. At the end of our last date, before he left for boot camp at Great Lakes Naval Base north of Chicago, we declared our love for each other and I promised to wait for him.

Labor Day weekend Mom helped me make fudge to send to Ken. It reminded me of her mailing candy to our friend, Bob Weaver, a soldier during World War II. Everyone on the home front, including kids, participated in the war effort.

In October, Ken finished boot camp and came home on a fourteen-day leave. He was a full-fledged sailor, indoctrinated and tattooed. Saturday night on our way home from seeing the musical, *Brigadoon*, Ken turned from Highway 75 onto Weber Road just east of Durand. After passing the only farmhouse located on the mile-long, single-lane blacktop, he pulled two wheels of his parents' Ambassador off on the grass alongside and parked. He slid the seat back and we cuddled together while the radio played pop music in the background. We avoided Mom's turning the spotlight on us if she thought we necked too long when he parked in our driveway after a

date. When his furlough ended, he flew to Norman, Oklahoma, to train for duty aboard an aircraft carrier.

Attending the high school Homecoming basketball game
and dance alone the night before Thanksgiving emphasized
my loneliness.

Ken came home on a fourteen-day leave for the holidays
in December. He gave me a black, short-sleeved, cashmere
cardigan for Christmas. When I opened it, I wondered if it was
too intimate a gift for me to accept when we weren't engaged.
A glance at the pride in my boyfriend's face convinced me I
couldn't refuse it. Besides, I'd never had an expensive cashmere
sweater. We celebrated New Year's Eve by going out with our
friends, Wayne and Gloria, to a movie and dancing till 3:00
A.M. His good-bye kiss would have to last me for months.

Chapter 4 - 1955 – Ken wrote to me from ordnance school in
warm, sunny Jacksonville, Florida. He was learning to handle
the ammunition and bombs carried by planes based on an
aircraft carrier. He didn't seem worried about his dangerous
job, so I tried not to fret either.

In May, my sailor's two-week leave occurred at the wrong
time and the right time. Ken and his buddy, Paul, hitchhiked
from their navy base in Florida and arrived home the day
before my senior class trip to Washington, D.C. I felt guilty
leaving, but I enjoyed the five days of sightseeing.

Having my boyfriend escort me to my senior prom made
the evening complete. When he left five days later to board
the aircraft carrier, U.S.S. Bennington, he kissed me and said,
"Bye. See you next year." For the remaining three years of his
enlistment, he would have an annual, thirty-day leave.

The Big Benn sailed half-a-world away to join the Seventh
Fleet. Ken visited Japan, Hong Kong and other Asian countries.

I couldn't imagine what it was going to be like having him gone for twelve months.

My senior year culminated with graduation. Nine days later I began a hair styling course at The Rockford School of Beauty Culture. Mom wanted me to try working in an office using the business skills I'd learned in high school, but I knew what I wanted. It took only a month for me to admit I'd made a mistake. I didn't feel the satisfaction I thought I would. I wanted to quit, but my mother insisted that I finish the six-month session because tuition had been paid. It was a long, hot summer in the second-floor salon above the Woolworth dime store. The open south windows and large, floor fans did little to relieve the heat.

When I turned eighteen in September, the State of Illinois considered me an adult female who could drink alcohol or get married. Neither would happen while I resided with my teetotaling parents and my boyfriend lived aboard a navy aircraft carrier.

Chapter 5 - 1956 – During the first month of the new year, I finished beauty school. Two of my classmates and I spent two days in Chicago to take our state tests and receive our cosmetology licenses.

I was spared the ordeal of job-hunting when our longtime, family friend, Mary, who managed the Winnebago County Agricultural Stabilization and Conservation office in Rockford, offered me a position paying $1.25 an hour. I enjoyed guiding farmers to take advantage of the U.S. Department of Agriculture programs.

My mother demanded that I pay fifty dollars a month for room and board. I'd never heard of any child having to pay a quarter of her salary to live at home.

Some of my friends spent their extra cash to fill 'hope chests' with expensive china and sterling purchased one place setting at a time. Mom urged me to open a savings account at the Brodhead bank. She said, "After you're married, a vacuum cleaner and a washing machine are needed a whole lot more than fancy dishes and silverware." I agreed.

On an April Saturday night at the Wigwam dancehall, Dick, a young farmer I'd met there several years ago, asked me to go to a movie. I agreed. I wasn't looking for a new boy-friend—I just wanted to have a little fun. With Ken gone for a whole year, I missed dating.

During the month of June, I needed a ride home from the office in Rockford three times and my boss asked her friend, Clarence, to provide it. My parents and I had met him at Mary's birthday party the previous March. Dad and Mom threw a hissy fit because he was divorced and ten years older than I was.

It infuriated me that my parents controlled my life when I was nineteen years old. Still, I wasn't ready to live on my own like my best friend, Esther. She checked out customers at the Bonnie Bee grocery store in Beloit, Wisconsin, and rented a room with kitchen privileges from an elderly lady who lived in the city.

I was surprised when Ken arrived home on a thirty-day leave during the Durand Centennial celebration in July. He told me about originally having a seat on the United flight from California to Chicago that had crashed in the Grand Canyon. Before Ken boarded, another sailor had asked to trade tickets so he could get home as soon as possible to see his mother who was dying. My boyfriend took a later flight. I offered a quick, silent prayer of thanksgiving. Our month together reminded me how much I loved Ken. It would be another long year before I saw him again.

In August, chores increased but so did the milk check. Our landlord remodeled the barn to hold forty cows instead of twenty-four. A modern, pipeline system carried the milk from the cows to a bulk cooler sitting in a new, small building. No more lifting full pails and cans.

Late in the summer, I enjoyed a five-day vacation touring the state of Michigan with my cousin, Doris. I had always tagged after her like a baby sister, but after I graduated from high school, the fourteen years difference in our ages melted away. She treated me like a contemporary capable of making my own decisions and paying my own way.

In the fall, to fill some of my lonely hours, I started bowling on Tuesday nights with the women's league in Durand. I didn't do very well until I purchased my own ball that had been drilled with holes to fit my grip.

In November, the nagging cough that interrupted my sleep drove me to see Dr. Hein, who had replaced Dr. Stovall in Brodhead. The young, family man prescribed a bottle of wild cherry flavored syrup, but it didn't help. Coughing wore me out during my first office Christmas party and my first holiday with Ken's family.

Chapter 6 - 1957 – I kept getting sicker and sicker. Our family physician referred me to the nearby Monroe Clinic. After a chest x-ray, Dr. Davis, a specialist, diagnosed me with tuberculosis, which needed to be treated in a sanitarium. I remembered an old movie showing people in robes and pajamas spending years in a TB sanitarium. They coughed and dragged themselves from their beds to a dining room, to lounge chairs on a veranda and back to their beds. Was that my future?

The doctor sent me to St. Clare Hospital for tests to confirm his diagnosis. I was placed in isolation. Only the staff and my parents, who wore masks and gowns, could enter my room and nothing including letters to my boyfriend could leave it.

A few days later, I was admitted to the Rockford Municipal Sanitarium. I was surprised to see no one wore masks and gowns, visitors were unlimited and I could mail letters to Ken.

I felt like a prisoner sentenced to cruel and unusual punishment when I was confined to my bed in a private room on the women's third floor. Instead of walking down the hall to use the communal restroom and shower I used a bed pan and a nurse gave me sponge baths. Twice a day, I took my temperature with a rectal thermometer. Uncle Buck convinced my parents I needed a portable TV in my room although they remained in the world of radio at home.

Treatment with the antibiotic, streptomycin, developed in 1946, had shortened a patient's stay in a sanitarium from years to months. Every Monday and Thursday morning before the night attendant went off duty at 7:00 A.M., she administered a painful shot of 'strep' in my butt.

A few days after I was admitted, three young women stopped by to introduce themselves.

I decided it wasn't such a bad place after all.

Visiting hours were Monday, Wednesday and Saturday evenings from seven to eight thirty and Sunday afternoons from two to four. My parents, my cousin, Doris, Uncle Buck, Aunt Elnora, my boss, Mary, and my best friend, Esther, with her boyfriend, Donnie, came regularly.

I wrote to Ken daily but I had not heard from him since Christmas. Each time Dad and Mom visited without bringing a letter from him, I worried a little more. I wondered if my steady was busy working, had nothing to write about or, worst of all, if he didn't want a sick girlfriend, but hesitated to tell me. January was almost over, when Mom finally handed me a letter. I tore open the envelope and scanned both sides of the sheet of paper. When I read that he wished me well and closed with his usual, *All my love, Ken,* I sighed with relief and laid his letter aside to savor later.

Patients received a chest x-ray and a gastric test the first of each month. Dr. Bryan, an older man with thinning, dark hair and jowls that reminded me of my English bulldog, used these results to determine how much exercise each patient could have. It took six weeks before the director released me from my bed to use the toilet and shower in the communal bathroom down the hall. After another month, the physician said I could be the resident hair stylist giving patients cuts and permanents. For the first time, I was glad I'd attended beauty school.

In April, I discovered Dr. Bryan had a soft spot for his patients. He approved my request to attend a wedding reception for Esther and Donnie at her parents' farm.

After five months, I returned home, but my treatment continued. Twice a week I drove to the san for a shot of strep. Once a month, I continued to have a chest x-ray and a gastric. TB made me appreciate little things such as going to the bathroom, sleeping in my own bed and living a boring life with my parents.

Ken's plan to surprise me when he came home on a thirty-day furlough in mid-August backfired. I was on a date with a soldier on leave. Two nights later, when I went to a movie with my boyfriend, neither of us mentioned the incident.

The following weekend, I joined Ken's family to watch the slides he'd taken while aboard the aircraft carrier. His commentary helped me understand his dangerous work. I would be more patient when a lot of time elapsed between his letters.

A few days later, my parents and I heard on the radio noon news that our neighbors, Keron and Anne, lost a second teenage son to polio. After finishing our dinner, Mom and I were doing dishes and discussing the family who had been hard hit with the scourge of the age. I said "It must be hard to lose a child, even when you have fourteen of them. Each one has to be special."

Mom responded, "Anne is still a mother. If your only child dies, you are no longer a mother." After a pause, Mom added, "You know, you almost died twice."

I was dumbfounded. I'd never thought about dying when I had infection following appendicitis or TB. Had doctors told my mother more than they told me?

Mom went outside to help make hay. I pondered what she'd said and the stories she'd told about her early life. She was only seven years old when her mother died at home. When she was twenty-one, her father who raised her passed away after surgery in a hospital. She lost two infant sons at birth when I was six and seven. I realized she'd lived in death's shadow for as long as she could remember. I understood why she worried that I would die.

The fourth of September was my twentieth birthday. To celebrate, Dad and Mom splurged for supper and the play at the world-famous Wagon Wheel resort near Rockton. While we ate, Ken told us about the people he'd met in Sydney, Australia. A couple who ran a restaurant there had lived in Peoria, Illinois, and played vaudeville at the Palace Theater in Rockford. He might have seen them when he was growing up and his parents took their family to see a movie and stage show.

A few days later, Ken kissed me good-bye and said, "The next time I see you, I'll be home for good."

Dr. Bryan said I could return to my office job part-time, which would make the next nine months pass a little faster.

THE VIEW FROM A MIDWEST FERRIS WHEEL

On October 4, 1957, people around the world trembled with fear when Russia launched Sputnik, the first artificial satellite to circle the earth. Rockets used for space travel could also be used as guided missiles in warfare. The Russians had an important military advantage. Success in the new Space Race within the Cold War became the measure of a nation's leadership in science, engineering and national defense.

The month also brought a personal milestone. Dr. Bryan replaced my twice-a-week shots of strep with twelve pills a day. I would soon be plopping down in a chair instead of sitting carefully on one butt cheek or the other.

Chapter 7 -1958 – The new year began with the jangle of the telephone startling us awake from a sound sleep—a long and a short, our ring on the party line. Good news did not arrive at 2:00 A.M.

Mom got out of bed, scuffled to the kitchen, picked up the phone and said a tentative, "Hello." After a pause, "Happy New Year." She loudly said, "Lolita, it's for you." Her tone dripped with exasperation.

Ken was celebrating in a San Diego bar and called to wish me a 'Happy New Year'.

In the spring, Dad paid two hundred and fifty dollars for his first pick-up truck, a twelve-year-old Chevy. I painted his name and address on the dark-blue doors as required by state law to prevent rustling of farm animals. When I was little, I secretly hoped that when Dad could afford a pick-up, he would include '& Daughter' with his name like other men included '& Son'. At twenty, I was still Daddy's girl, but I no longer wanted it proclaimed on the side of a vehicle.

During a thunderstorm at the end of May, lightning killed our horse, Mickey. I wiped tears and remembered the fall of 1941 when Dad bought the Morgan/Tennessee Walker cross at an auction. After the animal was in our pasture, we learned he could stand beside a fence and leap frog over it.

The following spring, my parents purchased a two-year-old sorrel pony for me. When Dad and I rode our steeds, he held a lead rope snapped to my pony's bridle because my four-year-old arms weren't strong enough to control her. We were galloping along a makeshift road behind the farm buildings when I slipped out of the saddle, landed in a bed of sand and started to cry. I wasn't hurt, just scared.

Dad immediately stopped, jumped down from Mickey and checked that I was okay. I didn't want to ride any more but he lifted me into the saddle and planted my feet firmly in the stirrups. I clung to the horn with both hands. Dad mounted Mickey and we slowly walked the animals the rest of the way to the barn.

After I turned twelve, I felt I was too big for Millie. We placed an ad in the daily newspaper and sold my pony to another family. I couldn't hold back the tears when Millie rode up our driveway in the back of a horse trailer pulled by a pick-up truck.

I began mounting Mickey to bring the bovines in from the pasture for evening milking. Afterward, I left the cow yard through the wooden gate beside the barn. One summer day, I tried jumping Mickey over the barrier that was about four feet high. With only a hundred and fifteen pounds on his back, the horse didn't need much urging. My lower body slammed against the pommel of our Western-style saddle and it hurt, but that didn't stop me. Jumping was a lot more fun than dismounting, lifting the gate open, leading the horse through, lifting the gate closed and climbing back into the saddle.

After chores and supper, Dad and I went to Durand to call the rendering works because the storm had put our phone out. It felt like contacting the undertaker to retrieve a dead relative.

The end of June, Ken was discharged and we could spend unlimited time together. He purchased his dream car, a '56 Lincoln, and drove it for his new job collecting money from people who were behind in repaying their small loans from Public Finance Co. in Rockford. Those who didn't have the collateral necessary to borrow money from a bank did business with a finance company and paid higher interest rates.

In August, my parents, my cousin, Doris, and I took what I thought of as our farewell tour. I expected the nine-day trip to South Dakota to be the last vacation I spent with my family. It was the ideal time to take our longest time-off ever. The hay was baled, the oats were combined and it would be a month or two before the corn was ready to pick. Our neighbor, Ed, agreed to do our chores for fifty dollars. His family could handle their milking while we were away.

September fourth, I turned twenty-one. Ken proposed and gave me a diamond engagement ring. We set a wedding date for April 17, 1959. Girls of my generation, even tomboys like me, dreamed of that life-changing occasion.

Not all events in September were happy. My parents, who rarely visited doctors, both had medical problems. Dad learned that he had an eye disease. He could no longer see well enough to pass the test to drive the car, a blow to his manhood. Mom fell and pulled a ligament in her left ankle. Before the month ended, my beloved Uncle Hookie, who was like my grandfather, died of a heart attack

December began with the in-laws-to-be getting together for the first time. Mom invited Ken and his parents, Rolland and Hazel, for s Saturday night supper to celebrate birthdays– Dad would turn forty-six on the fifth and Hazel would be forty-seven on the eighth. Our mothers were old friends from high school but, as often happens, they lost touch after marriage. Our fathers were strangers.

Chapter 8 – 1959 -Time to plan our church wedding and life together. My cousin, Doris, loaned me her *Emily Post's Etiquette* book so I would do things properly. She was my logical choice for maid of honor. Ken's brother, Tom, had joined the army, so Ken asked his long-time, buddy, Wayne, to be best man.

My husband-to-be was happy about our upcoming nuptials, but unhappy with his employment. After five months of trying to collect money from people who obviously didn't have it, he hated working for Public Finance Company.

Ken's brother-in-law offered him a job as hired man on the five-hundred-acre hog and feeder cattle enterprise he and his father operated. Joe laid out the following particulars, "We'll pay you a hundred dollars twice a month on the first and fifteenth. You'll have every other Sunday off. When it comes to holidays, we'll have to wait and see what we're doing. At the end of the year, you'll receive a bonus based on the farm's profit. That should be about a thousand dollars going by the last couple years." A house plus beef and pork for our table would also be provided.

Ken jumped at the chance. He'd enjoyed working on the farm during the summers when he was in high school. He gave his boss, Jack, at Public Finance two weeks' notice and started at Irish Acres February second. Joe, an experienced do-it-yourselfer, and Ken would have time during the days before our wedding to remodel the house where we would live.

While window shopping in Rockford after work, I saw my wedding gown on a mannequin in the Elsie Rogers Shop and made a deal for a bargain price of seventy dollars. Finding the perfect garments for my attendant and my mother wasn't so easy. It took a full day of shopping for each one and the invasion of expensive stores that we didn't usually enter.

Our wedding took a lot of planning. There were meetings with the minister about our evening candlelight ceremony and the Ladies Aid to discuss their help with the reception to follow in the church basement. We engaged a band and hired a hall for our public dance.

Ken and I selected furniture and appliances for our future farm home. I quickly learned, he was a one-stop shopper, but that was alright because we had similar tastes. When we bought a white, top-loading automatic washer, an electric range and a refrigerator with a freezer in the bottom at the Beloit Sears store, my savings account paid the invoice. I was glad I'd saved my money instead of filling a hope chest with expensive china and silver I would rarely use.

During the month of March, our female friends and relatives showered me with gifts including bed sheets, towels, cookware and decorator items to enhance our new home.

During the fifties, young women quit their jobs and became fulltime housewives when they married. Many mothers told their daughters, "If he doesn't treat you right, you just come back home to Ma." I watched a few of my friends do that every time they were miffed at their husbands, even after it entailed dragging a clothes basket full of baby food and diapers.

Mom never was like other mothers and she raised me to be different from other daughters. She warned me, "Remember, after you're married, you can't come home again."

It was the best thing she could have said to me. As an only child, I'd never learned the negotiation, compromise and just plain giving in that became second nature to siblings and was necessary in marriage. Through the years, when I got mad at my husband and felt like stomping out, slamming the door behind me, I never did. With no place to go, I cooled off and worked things out with him.

Early in the evening of our wedding, Mom dropped me and the two dresses at the church and hurried back home. While I sat alone waiting for Doris so we could prepare for the ceremony, my thoughts drifted back to all of the 'what ifs' during our seven-year courtship.

What if sixteen-year-old Kenny had been too shy to ask me to ride on the Ferris wheel while I walked around Davis Days with my boyfriend, Ronnie, during the summer of '52? What if I'd said no? What if I'd just said good-bye when he started his four-year enlistment in the navy instead of promising to wait for him? What if he'd found someone else during his travels? What if he'd been aboard that ill-fated plane that crashed in the Grand Canyon in '56 instead of trading tickets with another sailor and taking a later flight? What if he'd called it quits when he came home on leave in '57 and I was on a date with another guy? What if my mother's worries came true and I'd succumbed to either the appendicitis infection when I was fifteen or TB when I was nineteen? I firmly believed we were meant to be together.

When Dad walked me down the aisle, everything followed according to my plan. Ken was my first date, my last date and my husband for the rest of my life.

Epilogue – We celebrated our golden anniversary in April 2009 by exchanging wide, yellow gold bands while repeating the old vows in the new Trinity Lutheran Church. Our children, Lisa and Kurt, stood beside us in place of our best man and maid of honor who had passed away. Also missing, our oldest child, Linda, who had died of breast cancer eight months earlier. After the ceremony, we all drove to the American Legion Hall on the other side of Durand to greet friends and relatives at an open house.

Our milestone was a time for looking back. After seven years on the farm, Ken joined the Winnebago County Sheriff's police and continued for twenty-five years. We moved to Durand where our children attended school. Linda was psychologically tested and referred to special education classes for students with special needs. She would never leave our care.

I found two part-time jobs. I was elected Durand Township clerk and became a community correspondent for the *Rockford Morning Star* on a freelance basis. I went on to write articles for various police, farm and women's national magazines. I joined the Illinois Woman's Press Association, which was affiliated with the National Federation of Press Women. I've won many awards in their contests for published work.

After Kurt and Lisa each completed a two-year degree in police science at Rock Valley Community College, they followed their father into law enforcement. Lisa became an Illinois State Trooper and Kurt joined his dad with the sheriff's department.

Looking at our family and our accomplishments together, we thank God for that first Ferris wheel ride.

About the Author

Lolita Ditzler slipped into the writing world through the side door of learn by doing. When her three children were enrolled in school, she began checking the Rockford Morning Star help wanted section looking for an office job like she'd had before her marriage. The area daily's ad seeking community correspondents to report news from small towns surrounding the county seat intrigued her. An editor told her all she needed to be a part-time stringer was a typewriter and a 35mm camera–no training, no experience. Her parents had given her a Royal portable for Christmas when she was a sophomore in high school learning to type. She and her husband purchased the camera as a gift for their first Christmas together.

Using the newspaper as a guide for submitting articles, Lolita wrote features about Durand people doing interesting things, chased firetrucks and attended civic meetings. She enjoyed sticking her nose in where it wasn't always wanted and seeing her byline. She'd found her calling.

She took advantage of being only an hour or two's drive from area cities to join writers' organizations. Although she was happy doing newspaper work, she took notes when presenters at workshops included information about freelancing for magazines.

After thirteen years, the Star abruptly dropped all part-timers. Lolita was devastated. After she dried her tears, she could see that she had two options—quit writing or find other markets. She sent query letters to various national publications for women, farmers and police officers. Some of them accepted the articles she proposed. She entered her published work in the annual Illinois Woman's Press Association contests and won numerous awards. A few received firsts and were submitted to the National Federation of Press Women competition where she also earned recognition.

When Lolita's ninety-year-old mother passed away, she left behind her diaries. Reading those barebones, daily jottings of who, what, when and where stirred memories of coming of age on the family dairy farm during the fifties. She wrote a memoir of her seven-year courtship.

Lolita and Ken continue to live in Durand, Illinois, surrounded by their children and grandchildren.

Prom 53

Engaged

Sailor Ken

Office Christmas '57

Farewell party

Joyce, Lolita, Janice

Willabea & Lolita

Donnie & Esther reception

Parents

1st piece of cake

Wedding party

San Gang

Steeds

Made in the USA
Middletown, DE
10 June 2021